CHILD ABUSE

BETRAYING A TRUST

CHILD ABUSE
BETRAYING A TRUST

Mei Ling Rein

INFORMATION PLUS® REFERENCE SERIES
Formerly published by Information Plus, Wylie, Texas

GALE GROUP

Detroit
New York
San Francisco
London
Boston
Woodbridge, CT

CHILD ABUSE: BETRAYING A TRUST

Mei Ling Rein, *Author*

The Gale Group Staff:

Editorial: John F. McCoy, *Project Manager and Series Editor*; Andrew Claps, *Series Associate Editor*; Jason M. Everett, *Series Associate Editor*; Michael T. Reade, *Series Associate Editor*; Rita Runchock, *Managing Editor*; Luann Brennan, *Editor*

Image and Multimedia Content: Barbara J. Yarrow, *Manager, Imaging and Multimedia Content*; Robyn Young, *Project Manager, Imaging and Multimedia Content*

Indexing: Lynne Maday, *Indexing Specialist*; Amy Suchowski, *Indexing Specialist*

Permissions: Julie Juengling, *Permissions Specialist*; Maria Franklin, *Permissions Manager*

Product Design: Michelle DiMercurio, *Senior Art Director*; Kenn Zorn, *Product Design Manager*

Production: Evi Seoud, *Assistant Manager, Composition Purchasing and Electronic Prepress*; NeKita McKee, *Buyer*; Dorothy Maki, *Manufacturing Manager*

ISBN 0-7876-5103-6 (set)
ISBN 0-7876-5398-5 (this volume)
ISSN 1534-1607 (this volume)
Printed in the United States of America
10 9 8 7 6 5 4 3 2 1

TABLE OF CONTENTS

This chapter describes historical opinions on children and abuse, especially the shift in attitudes that occurred around the beginning of the twentieth century which led to current opinions on what constitutes abuse. Special attention is given to the history of child abuse protection legislation in America, and to international child labor and child abuse issues.

In order to identify and prevent child abuse, one must define it. However it is difficult to draw a line between harsh discipline and outright abuse. Some general methods of determining if a child has been or is at risk of being abused are explored here.

This chapter examines the effectiveness of the child abuse reporting and investigation systems. Statistics on child abuse reporting and investigation are presented. The many controversies and criticisms surrounding these systems are also discussed.

The prevalence of child abuse in the United States is explored in this chapter. Statistics are provided on child abuse rates for people of different race, family structure, income, and other characteristics. The characteristics of abusers are also examined.

There is no definitive reason or reasons why people abuse children. The vast majority of adults never commit child abuse no matter what the circumstances. Similarly, the long-term consequences of being abused vary greatly from person to person. Patterns do exist, however, and some of the most pronounced are discussed here.

The sexual abuse of children is the most troubling of all forms of child abuse. It often has severe long-term consequences for the children who endure it. As described here, however, detecting, preventing, and treating child sexual abuse is unfortunately even more difficult than dealing with other forms of abuse.

CHAPTER 7

Child abuse cases present many problems to the legal system, leading to a number of innovations and special procedures, which are outlined here. Also discussed are the legal issues surrounding false accusations of child abuse, laws against child pornography, and the registration of sex offenders.

Repressed memories of childhood abuse are an issue of great controversy. This chapter details the complex psychological and legal debates surrounding the reliability of repressed memories.

PREFACE

Child Abuse: Betraying a Trust is the latest volume in the ever-growing *Information Plus Reference Series*. Previously published by the Information Plus company of Wylie, Texas, the *Information Plus Reference Series* (and its companion set, the *Information Plus Compact Series*) became a Gale Group product when Gale and Information Plus merged in early 2000. Those of you familiar with the series as published by Information Plus will notice a few changes from the 1999 edition. Gale has adopted a new layout and style that we hope you will find easy to use. Other improvements include greatly expanded indexes in each book, and more descriptive tables of contents.

While some changes have been made to the design, the purpose of the *Information Plus Reference Series* remains the same. Each volume of the series presents the latest facts on a topic of pressing concern in modern American life. These topics include today's most controversial and most studied social issues: abortion, capital punishment, care for the elderly, crime, health care, the environment, immigration, minorities, social welfare, women, youth, and many more. Although written especially for the high school and undergraduate student, this series is an excellent resource for anyone in need of factual information on current affairs.

By presenting the facts, it is Gale's intention to provide its readers with everything they need to reach an informed opinion on current issues. To that end, there is a particular emphasis in this series on the presentation of scientific studies, surveys, and statistics. This data is generally presented in the form of tables, charts, and other graphics placed within the text of each book. Every graphic is directly referred to and carefully explained in the text. The source of each graphic is presented within the graphic itself. The data used in these graphics is drawn from the most reputable and reliable sources, in particular from the various branches of the U.S. government and from major independent polling organizations. Every effort was made

to secure the most recent information available. The reader should bear in mind that many major studies take years to conduct, and that additional years often pass before the data from these studies is made available to the public. Therefore, in many cases the most recent information available in 2001 dated from 1998 or 1999. Older statistics are sometimes presented as well, if they are of particular interest and no more-recent information exists.

Although statistics are a major focus of the *Information Plus Reference Series* they are by no means its only content. Each book also presents the widely held positions and important ideas that shape how the book's subject is discussed in the United States. These positions are explained in detail and, where possible, in the words of those who support them. Some of the other material to be found in these books includes: historical background; descriptions of major events related to the subject; relevant laws and court cases; and examples of how these issues play out in American life. Some books also feature primary documents, or have pro and con debate sections giving the words and opinions of prominent Americans on both sides of a controversial topic. All material is presented in an even-handed and unbiased manner; the reader will never be encouraged to accept one view of an issue over another.

HOW TO USE THIS BOOK

The abuse of children is one of America's most tragic social problems. The effects of abuse on a child, be it verbal, physical, sexual, or neglect, can be profound. Thousands of children die each year as a direct result of abuse, and countless others develop psychological and emotional problems that may well last a lifetime. The causes of abusive behavior in adults and their effects on children are therefore a matter of much scientific interest. The latest studies and theories on these issues are covered in this book. Dealing with child abuse also raises complicated and controversial legal questions, which this book presents and addresses.

Child Abuse: Betraying a Trust consists of eight chapters and three appendices. Each chapter is devoted to a particular aspect of the problem of child abuse in the United States. For a summary of the information covered in each chapter, please see the synopses provided in the Table of Contents at the front of the book. Chapters generally begin with an overview of the basic facts and background information on the chapter's topic, then proceed to examine sub-topics of particular interest. For example, Chapter 5: Causes and Effects of Child Abuse begins with a discussion of how the normal pressures of caring for children can sometimes overwhelm people and lead to abuse. It then examines the factors which have been linked to an increased likelihood of abuse, such as living in a single parent family, young first-time parents, a history of drug abuse by the parents, and other characteristics. Later, the chapter addresses the effects of child abuse on a child's intelligence and behavior over the short and long term. Readers can find their way through a chapter by looking for the section and sub-section headings, which are clearly set off from the text. Or, they can refer to the book's extensive index, if they already know what they are looking for.

Statistical Information

The tables and figures featured throughout *Child Abuse: Betraying a Trust* will be of particular use to the reader in learning about this issue. These tables and figures represent an extensive collection of the most recent and important statistics on child abuse and related issues; for example: its overall prevalence in the United States, the impact of socio-economic factors on the likelihood of abuse, and comparisons of the intelligence and achievement of abused children with their non-abused peers. Gale believes that making this information available to the reader is the most important way in which we fulfill the goal of this book: To help readers understand the issues and controversies surrounding child abuse in the United States and reach their own conclusions about them.

Each table or figure has a unique identifier appearing above it, for ease of identification and reference. Titles for the tables and figures explain their purpose. At the end of each table or figure, the original source of the data is provided.

In order to help readers understand these often complicated statistics, all tables and figures are explained in the text. References in the text direct the reader to the relevant statistics. Furthermore, the contents of all tables and figures are fully indexed. Please see the opening section of the index at the back of this volume for a description of how to find tables and figures within it.

In addition to the main body text and images, *Child Abuse: Betraying a Trust* has three appendices. The first is the Important Names and Addresses directory. Here the reader will find contact information for a number of organizations that study child abuse, fight child abuse, or that advocate influential opinions and policies on child abuse. The second appendix is the Resources section, which is provided to assist the reader in conducting his or her own research. In this section, the author and editors of *Child Abuse: Betraying a Trust* describe some of the sources that were most useful during the compilation of this book. The final appendix is this book's index. It has been greatly expanded from previous editions, and should make it even easier to find specific topics in this book.

COMMENTS AND SUGGESTIONS

The editor of the *Information Plus Reference Series* welcomes your feedback on *Child Abuse: Betraying a Trust*. Please direct all correspondence to:

Editor
Information Plus Reference Series
27500 Drake Rd.
Farmington Hills, MI, 48331-3535

ACKNOWLEDGEMENTS

The editors wish to thank the copyright holders of the excerpted graphics included in this volume and the permissions managers of many book and magazine publishing companies for assisting us in securing reproduction rights. We are also grateful to the staffs of the Detroit Public Library, the Library of Congress, the University of Detroit Mercy Library, Wayne State University Purdy/Kresge Library Complex, and the University of Michigan Libraries for making their resources available to us. Following is a list of the copyright holders who have granted us permission to reproduce material in Child Abuse. *Every effort has been made to trace copyright, but if omissions have been made, please let us know.*

ILLUSTRATIONS APPEARING IN INFORMATION PLUS-CHILD ABUSE, WERE RECEIVED FROM THE FOLLOWING SOURCES:

From a study "Child-Labour Battle Split over Where to Draw Line" in *Child Newsline,* June, 1997; February 1998. Copyright © 1997, 1998 by UNICEF. Reproduced by permission.

From a study in "The Effects of Sociodemographic Variables, Training, and Attitudes on the Lifetime Reporting Practices of Mandated Reporters," in *Child Maltreatment,* November, 1997; August 1998. Sage Publications, Inc. November 1997, August, 1998. Copyright © 1997, 1998 by Sage Publications, Inc. Reproduced by permission.

From a study "In the Wake of Childhood Maltreatment," in *OJJDP Juvenile Justice Bulletin,* August 1997. Office of Juvenile Justice and Delinquency Prevention, 1997. Reproduced by permission of the NCJRS.

From a study in *FMS: False Memory Syndrome Foundation Newsletter,* v. 6, February 1997. Copyright © 1997 by FMS Foundation. Reproduced by permission.

The Gallup Poll Monthly, tables, December, 1995; March, 1997. The Gallup Organization, 1995, 1997. Reproduced by permission of the Gallup Organization.

Kendall-Tackett, Kathleen A. and Linda Meyer Williams, and David Finkelhor. From a study in *Impact of Sexual Abuse on Children: A Review and Synthesis of Recent Empirical Studies,* v. 113, 1993. Copyright © 1993 by the American Psychological Association. Reproduced by permission.

Schene, Patricia A., illustration. From a study *The Future of Children.* David and Lucile Packard Foundation. Copyright © 1998 by the David and Lucile Packard Foundation. Adapted by the permission of the David and Lucile Packard Foundation.

Straus, Murray A., illustration. From a study in *Corporal Punishment by American Parents: National Data on Prevalence, Chronicity, Severity, and Duration, in Relation to Child and Family Characteristics.* Copyright © 1998 by Family Research Laboratory,

University of New Hampshire. Reproduced by permission.

Straus, Murray A., illustration. From a study *The Neglect Scale.* Copyright © 1995 by Family Research Laboratory, University of New Hampshire. Reproduced by permission.

Straus, Murray A., illustration. From a study in *Spanking and the Making of a Violent Society.* Copyright © 1996 by Family Research Laboratory, University of New Hampshire. Reproduced by permission.

Straus Murray A. and Mallie J. Paschall, illustration. From a study in *Corporal Punishment by Mothers and Child's Cognitive Development: A Longitudinal Study, 1998.* Copyright © 1998 by Family Research Laboratory, University of New Hampshire. Reproduced by permission.

From a study in *The Third National Incidence Study of Child Abuse and Neglect, 1996.* National Clearinghouse on Child Abuse and Neglect, 1996. Reproduced by the permission of the National Clearinghouse on Child Abuse and Neglect.

William, Lynda Meyer, illustration. From a study in *The Characteristics of Incestuous Fathers.* Copyright © 1992 by Family Research Laboratory, University of New Hampshire. Reproduced by permission.

CHAPTER 1

CHILD ABUSE—A HISTORY

OVERVIEW

Recognizing child abuse in its several forms (physical abuse, sexual abuse, emotional abuse, and neglect) is a 20th century phenomenon. Child abuse is also more likely to be recognized in economically developed countries than in developing countries. Children have been beaten and abandoned for many thousands of years, based primarily on the belief that children are the property of their parents.

Early civilizations regularly abandoned deformed or unwanted children, and the ritual sacrifice of children to appease the gods took place in the Egyptian, Carthaginian, Roman, Greek, and Aztec societies. In Roman society the father had complete control over the family, even to the extent that he could kill his children for disobedience. Sexual abuse of children was common in both Greek and Roman societies. Children were also sold as prostitutes. Women often participated in abuse. Petronius (c. 27–c. 66 C.E. [Common Era]), a Roman writer, recorded the rape of a seven-year-old girl witnessed by a line of clapping women.

During the Middle Ages in Europe healthy but unwanted children were apprenticed to work or offered to convents and monasteries. Infanticide (the murdering of unwanted babies) was also common. The Roman Catholic Church contributed to infanticide when it declared that deformed infants were omens of evil and the product of relations between women and demons or animals. In another example of religious support for what would now be considered child abuse, in the seventh century the Archbishop of Canterbury ruled that a man could sell his son into slavery until he reached the age of seven.

In 13th century England the law read, "If one beats a child until it bleeds, it will remember, but if one beats it to death, the law applies." By the child's fourth year, harsh discipline played a major role in his or her socialization. Children and parents were taught that beatings were in the child's best interests. A mother taught her daughter to take a "smart rod" and beat her children until they cried for mercy: "Dear child by this lore/they will love thee ever more."

Children were beaten not only by their parents but also by their teachers. In a poem written in about the year 1500, a schoolboy wrote that he would gladly become a clerk, but learning was such strange work because the birch twigs used for beating were so sharp. The children at an Oxford school must have felt justice was served when their schoolmaster, out early one morning to cut willow twigs for a switch to beat them, slipped, fell into the river, and drowned.

The late Middle Ages and the Renaissance saw changes in how society viewed children, but abuse was still common. Neil Postman, in *The Disappearance of Childhood* (Delacorte Press, New York, 1982), noted that the earlier idea that children were small adults had by that time started to change. Among the upper classes children began to receive a long, formal education, increasingly separated from adults and kept with their peers. It was becoming apparent that children were not really that similar to adults after all, becoming instead like mounds of clay to be molded.

In 16th and 17th century Europe, fathers commonly placed their children in apprenticeships to provide inexpensive labor. The apprentice system was the major job training method of pre-industrial Western society. The apprentice who trained with a master frequently worked under conditions that, by today's standards, would be considered severely abusive.

The practice of paternal control was brought to the American colonies, and the father ruled his wife and children. A child was little more than the property of the parents. At the same time, the child was an asset that could be used to perform work on the farm.

Parental discipline was typically severe, and parents, teachers, and ministers found support for stern discipline in the Bible. "Spare the rod and spoil the child" was cited as justification for beating children. It should be noted that the biblical "rod" referred to was a shepherd's rod used to guide the sheep in the right direction, not to beat the sheep. Church elders taught that children were born corrupted by original sin, and the only path to salvation was "to beat the Devil out of the child." Some colonial legislatures even passed "stubborn children laws," giving parents the legal right to actually kill unruly children.

By their teens, many children were living with other families, bound out as indentured servants or apprentices. It was common for heads of households and masters to brutalize these children without fear of reprisal except in cases involving excessive beatings, massive injury, or death.

Holding a Child Abuser Accountable

The earliest recorded trial for child abuse involved a master and his apprentice. In 1639, in Salem, Massachusetts, Marmaduke Perry was charged in the death of his apprentice. The evidence showed the boy had been ill-treated and subjected to "unreasonable correction." However, the boy's allegation that the master had been responsible for his fractured skull (which ultimately killed him) was called into question by testimony which claimed that he had told someone else his injury had resulted from falling from a tree. Perry was acquitted.

In 1643 a master was executed for killing his servant boy. In 1655, in Plymouth, Massachusetts, a master found guilty of slaying a servant boy was punished by having his hand burned and all his property taken away. Other early records show brutal masters being warned for abusing young servants, and in some cases the children were freed because of the harsh treatment. Virginia passed laws protecting servants against mistreatment in 1700.

Most of the early recorded cases of child abuse were specifically related to offenses committed by masters against servants and did not involve protecting children from abusive parents. Society generally tolerated the abuse of family members as a personal matter while condemning abuse by strangers.

The few recorded cases involving family matters were limited to the removal of children from "unsuitable" home environments, which usually meant that parents were not giving their children a good religious upbringing or were refusing to instill the proper work ethic. In two Massachusetts cases, in 1675 and 1678, children were removed from such "unsuitable" homes. In the first case, the children were taken from the home because the father refused to send them out to apprentice or work. In the second case, the same offense was compounded by the father's

refusal to attend church services. Physical abuse was not an issue in either case.

ABUSE DURING THE INDUSTRIAL REVOLUTION

With the coming of industrialization in Europe and America, the implied right of abuse was transferred to the factory, where orphaned or abandoned children as young as five worked 16 hours a day. In many cases irons riveted around their ankles bound the children to the machines, while overseers with whips ensured productivity. In England the Factory Act of 1802 stopped this pauper-apprentice work system, but the law did not apply to children who had parents. Those youngsters worked in the mills for 12 hours a day at the mercy of often tyrannical supervisors.

Non-working hours offered little relief to poor orphaned or abandoned children. Dependent children such as these were put into deplorable public poorhouses with adult beggars, thieves, and paupers. Not until the beginning of the 19th century did the public recognize the terrible abuses that occurred in these almshouses, and major efforts were begun to provide separate housing for children.

During the 19th century, middle-class families began to see their children as representative of the family's status. For many of these families education for the child, rather than labor, became the goal. With this attitude, many of the labor abuses gradually came to an end. Eventually, child labor laws were passed in most industrialized countries to limit the kinds of jobs children could do and the number of hours they could work.

Private Organizations Take Action Against Abuse

It was during the 19th century that the American legal system began to change in favor of protecting children even against their own parents. In 1840 a Tennessee parent was prosecuted for excessive punishment of a child. According to the testimony, a mother had hit her daughter with her fists, pushed her head against the wall, whipped her, and tied her to a bedpost. A lower court convicted the abusive parent, but a higher court reversed the conviction.

The first case of child abuse that caught public attention in the United States occurred in 1874. Neighbors of Mary Ellen Connolly, a nine-year-old child in New York City, contacted a church social worker, Etta Angell Wheeler, when they heard disturbances from the little girl's apartment.

Upon investigating the child's home, the social worker found her suffering from malnutrition, serious physical abuse, and neglect. Mary Ellen was living with Mary and Francis Connolly. The girl, who was the out-of-wedlock daughter of Mrs. Connolly's first husband, was apprenticed to the couple.

At that time there were laws protecting animals, but no local, state, or federal laws protected children. Consequently, Wheeler turned to the American Society for the Prevention of Cruelty to Animals (ASPCA) for help. The case was presented to the court on the theory that the child was a member of the animal kingdom and therefore entitled to the same protection from abuse that the law gave to animals. The court agreed, and the child, because she was considered an animal, was taken from her brutal foster mother.

In court Mary Ellen related how her foster mother beat her daily with a leather whip and cut her face with scissors. She was not allowed to play with other children and was locked in the bedroom whenever her "mamma" left the house. The court placed the child in an orphanage. She was later adopted by the social worker's family.

The court found Mary Connolly guilty of assault and battery for felonious assault with scissors and for beatings that took place during 1873 and 1874. She was sentenced to one year of hard labor in a penitentiary.

Mary Ellen's case led to the founding of the New York Society for the Prevention of Cruelty to Children. Similar societies were soon organized in other American cities. By 1922, 57 societies for the prevention of cruelty to children and 307 other humane societies had been established to tend to the welfare of children. After the federal government began intervening in child welfare, the number of these societies declined.

The Beginnings of Federal Protection for Children

The first White House Conference on Children took place in 1909. It recommended the creation of the Children's Bureau (under the U.S. Department of Health, Education, and Welfare) to research and provide information about children, a recommendation President William Howard Taft signed into law in 1912. The Children's Bureau promoted the passage of the Keating-Owen Act (39 Stat 675) in 1916, which limited the exploitation of children in factories and mines. The law, however, did not cover youngsters employed in agriculture, domestic work, and sweatshops (small manufacturing plants with long hours, low wages, and poor working conditions). The Bureau also advocated improved prenatal care, especially among the poor, and was a major supporter of the Sheppard-Towner Act of 1921 (42 Stat 224), which promoted prenatal care for mothers.

MODERN AMERICA

The federal government first provided child welfare services with the passage of the Social Security Act of 1935 (49 Stat 620). Under the Title IV-B (Child Welfare Services) program of the act, the Children's Bureau received funding for grants to states for "the protection and care of homeless, dependent, and neglected children and children in danger of becoming delinquent." Prior to 1961, Title IV-B was the only source of federal funding for child welfare services.

The 1962 Social Security Amendments (PL 87-543) required each state to make child welfare services available to all children. It further required states to provide coordination between child welfare services (under Title IV-B) and social services (under Title IV-A, or the Social Services program), which served families on welfare. The law also revised the definition of "child welfare services" to include the prevention and remedy of child abuse. In 1980 Congress created a separate Foster Care program under Title IV-E.

Title IV-A became Title XX (Social Services Block Grant) in 1981, giving states more options as to the types of social services to fund. Today child abuse prevention and treatment services have remained an eligible category of service.

State Programs that Help Children at Risk

Currently, under Title IV-B Child Welfare Services (Subpart 1) and Promoting Safe and Stable Families (Subpart 2) programs, families in crisis receive preventive intervention so that children will not have to be removed from their homes. If this cannot be achieved, children are placed in foster care temporarily until they can be reunited with their families. If reunification is not possible, the children are put up for adoption.

States use the Foster Care (Title IV-E) program funds for the care of foster children and for the training of foster parents, program personnel, and private-agency staff. Title XX funds provide such services as child day care, child protective services, information and referral, counseling, and employment.

The "Battered Child Syndrome" and the Development of a Child Abuse Reporting Network

In 1961 Dr. C. Henry Kempe, a pediatric radiologist, and his associates proposed the term "Battered Child Syndrome" at a symposium on the problem of child abuse held under the auspices of the American Academy of Pediatrics. The term refers to the collection of injuries sustained by a child as a result of repeated mistreatment or beatings. The following year, *The Journal of the American Medical Association* published the landmark article, "The Battered Child Syndrome" (C. Henry Kempe et al., Vol. 181, July 7, 1962). The term "Battered Child Syndrome" developed into "maltreatment," encompassing not only physical assault but other forms of abuse, such as malnourishment, failure to thrive, medical neglect, and sexual and emotional abuse.

Dr. Kempe had also proposed that physicians be required to report child abuse. By 1967, after his findings had gained general acceptance among health and welfare workers and the public, all 50 states had passed legislation that required the reporting of child abuse to official agencies. This was one of the most rapidly accepted pieces of legislation in American history. Initially only doctors were required to report and only in cases of "serious physical injury" or "non-accidental injury." Today all the states have laws that require most professionals who serve children to report all forms of suspected abuse (see Chapter 3) and either require or permit any citizen to report child abuse.

One of the reasons for the lack of prosecution into early child abuse cases was the difficulty in determining whether a physical injury was a case of deliberate assault or an accident. In recent years, however, doctors of pediatric radiology have been able to determine the incidence of repeated child abuse through sophisticated developments in X-ray technology. These advances have allowed radiologists to see more clearly such things as subdural hematomas (blood clots around the brain resulting from blows to the head) and abnormal fractures. This brought about more recognition in the medical community of the widespread incidence of child abuse, along with growing public condemnation of abuse.

Federal Legislation Against Child Abuse

In 1974 Congress passed the Child Abuse Prevention and Treatment Act (CAPTA; PL 93-247). The law stated,

> [Child abuse and neglect refer to] the physical or mental injury, negligent treatment, or maltreatment of a child under the age of 18, or the age specified by the child protection law of the state in question, by a person who is responsible for the child's welfare under circumstances which indicate that the child's health or welfare is harmed or threatened thereby as determined in accordance with regulations prescribed by the Secretary of Health, Education, and Welfare.

This law created the National Center on Child Abuse and Neglect (NCCAN), which developed standards for handling reports of child maltreatment. NCCAN also established a nationwide network of child protective services and served as a clearinghouse for information and research on child abuse and neglect.

Since 1974 CAPTA has been amended a number of times. (See Figure 1.1.) The Child Abuse Prevention, Adoption, and Family Services Act of 1988 (PL 100-294) was enacted mainly to guarantee funding through 1991. It also broadened the definition of abuse, adding a specific reference to sexual abuse and exploitation to the basic definition.

The Children's Justice Act (CJA) offers grants to states to improve the investigation and prosecution of cases of child abuse and neglect, especially sexual abuse and exploitation. The program aims to reduce additional trauma to the child by training persons who are involved in child maltreatment cases, such as law enforcement, mental health personnel, prosecutors, and judges. CJA also supports legislation that would allow indirect testimony from children, shorten the time spent in court, and make their courtroom experience less intimidating.

Until 1995 none of the federal child abuse legislation dealt specifically with punishing sex offenders. In December of that year, with growing acknowledgment of and concern about sex crimes against minors, Congress passed the Sex Crimes against Children Prevention Act of 1995 (PL 104-71). The act increased penalties for those who sexually exploit children by engaging in illegal conduct, or for exploitation conducted via the Internet, as well as for those who transport children with the intent to engage in criminal sexual activity.

Three years later Congress enacted the Protection of Children from Sexual Predators Act of 1998 (PL 105-314) which, among other things, established the Morgan P. Hardiman Child Abduction and Serial Murder Investigative Resource Center (CASMIRC). The purpose of CASMIRC is "to provide investigative support through the coordination and provision of federal law enforcement resources, training, and application of other multidisciplinary expertise, to assist federal, state, and local authorities in matters involving child abductions, mysterious disappearances of children, child homicide, and serial murder across the country."

Pursuant to the 1996 amendments to the Child Abuse Prevention and Treatment Act (PL 104-235), NCCAN (see above) was abolished. Its functions have subsequently been consolidated within the Children's Bureau of the U.S. Department of Health and Human Services.

THE INTERNATIONAL EXPLOITATION OF CHILDREN
Child Soldiers

As more wars occur in different parts of the world, government armed forces and opposition groups have been forcing children to serve as soldiers. Juan Somavia, in "The Lost Children" (*The Progress of Nations 2000*, United Nations Children's Fund [UNICEF], New York, 2000), reported that an estimated 300,000 children under the age of 18 were involved in armed conflicts in the 1990s. For example, during Liberia's seven-year civil war, about 15,000 children, some as young as six, were used as soldiers.

UNICEF, in *The State of the World's Children 2000* (New York, 2000), further noted that warring factions in more than 30 countries have used child soldiers to lay and clear land mines, resulting in loss of limbs and lives. Girls have served as sexual slaves to military officers. In the past decade more than two million children were killed in armed conflicts, and another six million children were injured or disabled. Many of these children experienced psychological trauma.

FIGURE 1.1

Child Abuse Prevention and Treatment Act

Legislative Authority: Child Abuse Prevention and Treatment Act, as amended
U.S. Code Citation: 42 USC 5101 et seq; 42 USC 5116 et seq
ACF Regulations: 45 CFR 1340

Summary of Legislative History:

The Child Abuse Prevention and Treatment Act (CAPTA) was originally enacted in P.L. 93-247. The law was completely rewritten in the Child Abuse Prevention, Adoption and Family Services Act of 1988 (P.L. 100-294, 4/25/88). It was further amended by the Child Abuse Prevention Challenge Grants Reauthorization Act of 1989 (P.L. 101-126, 10/25/89) and the Drug Free School Amendments of 1989 (P.L. 101-226, 12/12/89).

The Community-Based Child Abuse and Neglect Prevention Grants program was originally authorized by sections 402 through 409 of the Continuing Appropriations Act for FY 1985 (P.L. 98-473, 10/12/84). The Child Abuse Prevention Challenge Grants Reauthorization Act of 1989 (P.L. 101-126) transferred this program to the Child Abuse Prevention and Treatment Act, as amended.

A new title III, Certain Preventive Services Regarding Children of Homeless Families or Families at Risk of Homelessness, was added to the Child Abuse and Neglect Prevention and Treatment Act by the Stewart B. McKinney Homeless Assistance Act Amendments of 1990 (P.L. 101-645, 11/29/90).

The Child Abuse Prevention and Treatment Act was amended and reauthorized by the Child Abuse, Domestic Violence, Adoption, and Family Services Act of 1992 (P.L. 102-295, 5/28/92) and amended by the Juvenile Justice and Delinquency Prevention Act. Amendments of 1992 (P.L. 102-586, 11/4/92).

The Act was amended by the Older American Act Technical Amendments of 1993 (P.L. 103-171, 12/2/93) and the Human Services Amendments of 1994 (P.L. 103-252, 5/19/94).

CAPTA was further amended by the Child Abuse Prevention and Treatment Act Amendments of 1996 (P.L. 104-235, 10/3/96), which amended Title I, replaced the Title II Community-Based Family Resource Centers program with a new Community-Based Family Resource and Support Program and repealed Title III, Certain Preventive Services Regarding Children of Homeless Families or Families at Risk of Homelessness.

SOURCE: *Child Abuse Prevention and Treatment Act,* as Amended, October 3, 1996, National Center on Child Abuse and Neglect, U.S. Department of Health and Human Services, Washington, D.C., not dated

---

Trafficking in Children

Trafficking in women and children is a worldwide problem. The Central Intelligence Agency (CIA) reported in *International Trafficking in Women to the United States: A Contemporary Manifestation of Slavery and Organized Crime* (Amy O'Neill Richard, Washington, D.C, November 1999) that between 700,000 and two million women and children are trafficked globally each year. This number does not include trafficking within countries. The President's Interagency Council on Women (U.S. Department of State, Washington, D.C.) defines trafficking in women and children as follows:

Trafficking is all acts involved in the recruitment, abduction, transport, harboring, transfer, sale or receipt of persons; within national or across international borders; through force, coercion, fraud or deception; to place persons in situations of slavery or slavery-like conditions, forced labor or services, such as forced prostitution or sexual services, domestic servitude, bonded sweatshop labor or other debt bondage.

Organized criminal groups in many countries work with one another in procuring or abducting young girls for the prostitution business that makes millions of dollars. Very young children are forced into prostitution because clients mistakenly believe that a nine- or ten-year-old will not be infected with AIDS. Armed conflicts in many parts of the world have also resulted in increased trafficking of children. In refugee camps, criminals prey on minors who are separated from their families, kidnapping and selling them for adoption or prostitution.

Child Labor

In 1989 the United Nations General Assembly adopted the *Convention on the Rights of the Child* as an international human rights treaty. Article 32 of the *Convention* defines child labor as any economic exploitation or work that is likely to be hazardous or interferes with the child's education, or is harmful to the child's health or physical, mental, spiritual, moral, or social development.

Elaine Eliah, in "Child-Labour Battle Split Over Where to Draw Line" (*Child Newsline,* UNICEF, London, England, 1998), noted that Africa has the largest proportion of child laborers in the world. If the trend continues, the 80 million African child laborers will increase to 100 million by the year 2015. It is estimated that, worldwide, child laborers ages 5–14 number more than 250 million. (See Figure 1.2.)

The International Labor Organization (ILO) estimates that 2 out of 5 (41 percent) African children ages 5–14 are in the workplace. In comparison, 21 percent of Asian children and 17 percent of Latin American children are being used as laborers. (See Figure 1.2.) More than a third (37 percent) of African girls are workers, the highest percentage of female child workers in the world. Asia has slightly over half of this proportion (20 percent) of female child laborers. Approximately 120 million children are working full-time and the other 130 million, part-time.

While some developing countries agree that children should not be forced to work, they argue that the parents are so destitute that they are forced to indenture their children. This way they have one less mouth to feed, as well as obtaining some income from their children. On the other hand, in addition to the physical hazards of many jobs (for example, exposure to pesticides and dangerous machines), child workers miss school, lack proper care, have poor health, and suffer all forms of abuse.

CHILD LABORERS IN THE UNITED STATES. The U.S. Department of Labor estimates that in 1998 there were about 3.5 million older children working legally in the United States. Child advocacy groups believe another 1.5 million young children are working illegally on farms and in sweatshops. Amy Printz Winterfeld pointed out that young children working illegally earn an average of $1.38 less per hour than their older counterparts working legally in the same jobs ("Freedom from Economic Exploitation—A Basic Children's Right," *Protecting Children: The Rights of Children,* Children's Services, American Humane Association, September 2000).

CHILDREN AS DOMESTIC WORKERS. Recent public attention has focused on the problem of illegal child labor in such industries as the production of clothing. However, the largest group of child laborers in the world—domestic workers—has not received any attention at all. UNICEF refers to these children as the "invisible workforce" because they usually work by

FIGURE 1.2

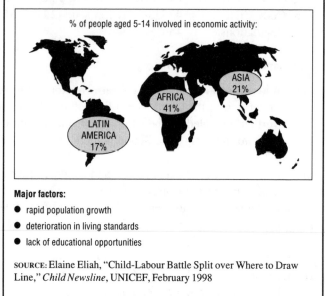

No time for play

More than 250 million children aged between 5 and 14 are at work worldwide.

% of people aged 5-14 involved in economic activity:

ASIA 21%

AFRICA 41%

LATIN AMERICA 17%

Major factors:
- rapid population growth
- deterioration in living standards
- lack of educational opportunities

SOURCE: Elaine Eliah, "Child-Labour Battle Split over Where to Draw Line," *Child Newsline,* UNICEF, February 1998

themselves in private homes. The majority (approximately 90 percent) are girls ages 12–17, but they can be as young as five years old. These children receive very low or no salaries and put in long hours, sometimes seven days a week. In many cases the children's parents or other guardians collect the salaries. Most child domestic workers do not attend school. Those who live with their employers may not have contact with their families and peers.

The CIA has found that children as young as 10 are being smuggled into the United States to work as domestics (*International Trafficking in Women to the United States: A Contemporary Manifestation of Slavery and Organized Crime;* see above). Parents actually pay the smugglers thousands of dollars to bring their children into the United States, in the hope that they will have a better life. The children may be moved from location to location. Due to language barriers, these children cannot even ask for help to save themselves.

AMERICAN INITIATIVES. Child labor in the international setting continues to be a concern for the U.S. government. In 1997 President Clinton signed the Treasury, Postal Service, and General Government Appropriations Act (PL 105-61), which limits importation into the United States of goods produced by "forced or indentured child labor." In 1998 Congress approved the Higher Education Amendments of 1998 (PL 105-244), which include a provision "urging colleges and universities to adopt 'anti-sweatshop' policies when licensing their logos." In December 1998, on the fiftieth anniversary of the Universal Declaration of Human Rights, President Clinton announced new immigration regulations which will let children acquire political asylum more easily. The federal government has also appropriated $30 million per year, up from $3 million, for ILO efforts to eradicate child labor.

Child Mutilation

Actions considered abusive in some cultures are often celebrated as rites of passage by others. In "Female Circumcision: Rite of Passage or Violation of Rights?" (*International Family Planning Perspectives,* The Alan Guttmacher Institute, Vol. 23, No. 3, September 1997), Frances A. Althaus reported that female circumcision is not solely practiced by Muslims, as some people mistakenly believe. Christians, animists, and one Jewish sect also practice it. In patriarchal societies, where females' sexuality and fertility are controlled by men, female circumcision is a rite of passage that ushers young girls into womanhood and marriage.

Female circumcision was first called "female genital mutilation" in the international document *Programme of Action,* from the International Conference on Population and Development in 1994 in Cairo, Egypt. Female circumcision may be performed as early as infancy, although the procedure is usually done between the ages of 4 and 12. It involves the partial or complete removal of the female genitalia. In its most severe form, called infibulation, after the major mutilation of the external genitalia, the vagina is reduced to a small opening "that may be as small as a matchstick" for urination and menstruation. Because of the small vaginal opening, sexual intercourse is quite painful, and the infibulation scar may have to be recut to relieve penetration problems.

According to UNICEF, an estimated two million girls are circumcised each year. About 100 million women worldwide have undergone the procedure. Figure 1.3 shows the countries in which female genital mutilation is most prevalent.

In some countries the practice is almost universal—it is done to virtually every female in Djibouti and Somalia and 9 of 10 women in Eritrea, Ethiopia, Sierra Leone, and northern Sudan. In *Female Genital Cutting: Findings from the Demographic and Health Surveys Program* (Macro International, Calverton, MD, 1997), Dara Carr reported that female circumcision has been so ingrained in many cultures that women themselves support its continued practice. In Egypt 87 percent of women indicated they had had their daughters circumcised or planned to do so.

Some of the health implications of female circumcision include hemorrhage, shock, and death. Infections may lead to sterility and chronic pelvic pain. If a woman has been infibulated, she may have to undergo a series of cutting and resewing procedures during her childbearing years.

FIGURE 1.3

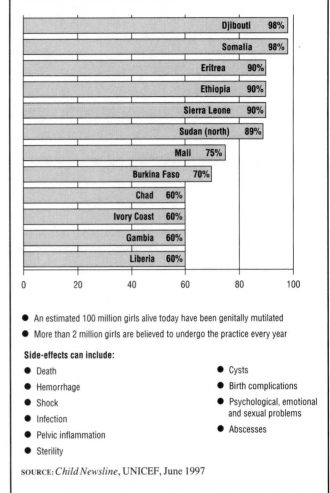

A dangerous tradition

Where female circumcision is most common

- An estimated 100 million girls alive today have been genitally mutilated
- More than 2 million girls are believed to undergo the practice every year

Side-effects can include:

- Death
- Hemorrhage
- Shock
- Infection
- Pelvic inflammation
- Sterility

- Cysts
- Birth complications
- Psychological, emotional and sexual problems
- Abscesses

SOURCE: *Child Newsline*, UNICEF, June 1997

RECENT INTERNATIONAL EFFORTS TO STRENGTHEN CHILDREN'S RIGHTS

In June 1999 the member nations of the International Labor Organization adopted a treaty to prohibit the use of children in such activities as prostitution, slavery, pornography, trafficking, and forced recruitment to the military. In July 2000 governments agreed to add two optional protocols to the *Convention on the Rights of the Child.* The first protocol outlines children's right to education, health care, and freedom from economic and sexual exploitation. The second protocol bans the use of child combatants. However, it allows the recruitment of children under 18 as long as they are not sent to war.

As part of this agreement, the United States agreed for the first time to establish the age of 18 as the minimum for deployment in armed conflicts. The U.S. Department of Defense claims that, in the past, 17-year-olds comprised less than one-half of 1 percent of active U.S. soldiers.

CHAPTER 2
CHILD ABUSE—A PROBLEM OF DEFINITION

WHAT IS ABUSE?

Child abuse is often a secret. Since the 1960s, however, the American people have become increasingly aware of the problems of child abuse and neglect (together referred to as child maltreatment). In 1963 only 150,000 young victims of maltreatment were reported to authorities (*Juvenile Court Statistics,* Children's Bureau, U.S. Department of Health, Education, and Welfare, Washington, D.C., 1966). In 1998 state child protective services (CPS) agencies received more than 2.8 million reports of child maltreatment (*Child Maltreatment 1998: Reports From the States to the National Child Abuse and Neglect Data System,* Children's Bureau, U.S. Department of Health and Human Services, Washington, D.C., 2000). See Chapter 4 for more information on this report.

There is still no agreement on what constitutes child abuse. In September 2000 an Albuquerque, New Mexico, judge granted custody of an overweight three-year-old girl to the state because the parents allegedly committed child neglect. The state claimed the child's life was jeopardized by her parents' failure to follow their doctor's prescribed diet. Diagnosed as morbidly obese, the girl weighed three times as much as the average three-year-old. However, in November 2000 the child was returned home after a court-approved agreement that could not be disclosed by the family.

While extreme cases are easy to label, less severe cases are viewed differently by different people. Is spanking abuse? Is spanking abuse only if the parent uses a belt and leaves welts on the child's body? Is it abuse if the marks fade in a few hours? Many parents consider it their right and duty to spank a wayward child. If a child runs into the street or is about to touch something hot, a smack on the bottom is commonly accepted as an appropriate way to teach the child not to do something dangerous.

Federal Definition

Official definitions of child abuse and neglect differ among institutions, government bodies, and experts. According to the Child Abuse Prevention and Treatment Act (CAPTA; PL 104-235), as amended in October 1996,

> The term "child abuse and neglect" means, at a minimum, any recent act or failure to act, on the part of a parent or caretaker [including any employee of a residential facility or any staff person providing out-of-home care who is responsible for the child's welfare], which results in death, serious physical or emotional harm, sexual abuse or exploitation, or an act or failure to act which presents an imminent risk of serious harm. [The term "child" means a person under the age of 18, unless the child protection law of the state in which the child resides specifies a younger age for cases not involving sexual abuse.]

It should be noted that this definition of child abuse and neglect specifies that only parents and caregivers can be considered perpetrators of child maltreatment. Abusive or negligent behavior by other persons—strangers or persons known to the child—is considered child assault. Nonetheless, both forms of abusive behavior are crimes against children.

Based on a concern that severely disabled newborns may be denied medical care, CAPTA also considers as child abuse and neglect the "withholding of medically indicated treatment," including appropriate nutrition, hydration, and medication, which in the treating physician's medical judgment would most likely help, improve, or correct an infant's life-threatening conditions. This definition, however, does not refer to situations where treatment of an infant, in the physician's medical judgment, would prolong dying, be ineffective in improving or correcting all the infant's life-threatening conditions, or would be futile in helping the infant to survive. In addition, this definition does not include circumstances where the infant is chronically or irreversibly comatose.

State Definitions

CAPTA provides a foundation for states by identifying a minimum set of acts or behaviors that characterize child abuse and neglect. Each state, based on CAPTA guidelines, has formulated its own definitions of the different types of child maltreatment. For purposes of reporting abuse, the state statutes also describe the kind of behaviors requiring intervention. Most state laws also include exceptions, such as religious exemptions, corporal punishment, cultural practices, and poverty.

CAPTA DEFINES FOUR MAIN TYPES OF CHILD MALTREATMENT

Physical Abuse

Physical abuse is the infliction of physical injury through punching, beating, kicking, biting, burning, shaking, or otherwise harming a child. Physical abuse is generally a willful act. However, there are cases in which the parent or caretaker may not have intended to hurt the child. In such cases, the injury may have resulted from over-discipline or corporal punishment. Nonetheless, if the child is injured, the act is considered abusive.

Sexual Abuse

Sexual abuse includes fondling a child's genitals, intercourse, incest, rape, sodomy, exhibitionism, and commercial exploitation through prostitution or the production of pornographic materials. (For more on sexual abuse, see Chapter 6.)

Emotional Abuse (Psychological Abuse, Verbal Abuse, or Mental Injury)

Emotional abuse includes acts or omissions by the parents or by other caregivers that have caused, or could cause, serious behavioral, cognitive, emotional, or mental disorders. In some cases of emotional abuse, the abuser's act alone, without any harm evident in the child's behavior or condition, is enough cause for intervention by CPS. For example, the parent/caregiver may use extreme or bizarre forms of punishment, such as locking a child in a dark room.

Other forms of emotional abuse may involve more subtle acts, such as habitual scapegoating, belittling, or rejecting treatment. For CPS to intervene, demonstrable harm to the child is often required. Although any of the types of child maltreatment may be found separately, different types of abuse often occur in combination with one another. Nonetheless, emotional abuse is almost always present when other types are identified.

Child Neglect

Child neglect is an act of omission characterized by failure to provide for the child's basic needs. Neglect can be physical, educational, or emotional. Physical neglect includes failure to provide food, clothing, and shelter; refusal of or delay in seeking health care (medical neglect); abandonment; inadequate supervision; and expulsion from the home or refusal to allow a runaway to return home. Educational neglect includes permitting chronic truancy, failure to enroll a child of mandatory school age in school, and failure to take care of a child's special educational needs. Emotional neglect includes substantial inattention to the child's needs for affection, failure to provide needed psychological care, spousal abuse in the child's presence, and allowing drug or alcohol use by the child. It is very important to distinguish between willful neglect and a parent's or a caretaker's failure to provide the necessities of life because of poverty or cultural factors.

A DESCRIPTION OF MALTREATED CHILDREN

Perhaps better than a definition of child abuse is a description of the characteristics likely to be exhibited by abused and/or neglected children. The U.S. Department of Health and Human Services indicates that, in general, abused or neglected children are likely to have at least several of the following characteristics:

- They appear to be different from other children in physical or emotional makeup, or their parents inappropriately describe them as being "different" or "bad."

- They seem unduly afraid of their parents.

- They may often bear welts, bruises, untreated sores, or other skin injuries.

- Their injuries seem to be inadequately treated.

- They show evidence of overall poor care.

- They are given inappropriate food, drink, or medication.

- They exhibit behavioral extremes—for example, crying often or crying very little and showing no real expectation of being comforted; being excessively fearful or seemingly fearless of adult authority; being unusually aggressive and destructive or extremely passive and withdrawn.

- Some are wary of physical contact, especially when initiated by an adult. They become fearful when an adult approaches another child, particularly one who is crying. Others are inappropriately hungry for affection, yet may have difficulty relating to children and adults. Based on their past experiences, these children cannot risk getting too close to others.

- They may exhibit a sudden change in behavior—for example, displaying regressive behavior, such as pants-wetting, thumb-sucking, frequent whining, becoming disruptive, or becoming uncommonly shy and passive.

- They take over the role of the parent, being protective or otherwise attempting to take care of the parent's needs.

- They have learning problems that cannot be diagnosed. If a child's academic IQ is average or better and medical tests indicate no abnormalities, but the child still cannot meet normal expectations, the answer may well be problems in the home—one of which may be abuse or neglect. Particular attention should be given to the child whose attention wanders and who easily becomes self-absorbed.

- They are habitually truant or late for school. Frequent or prolonged absences sometimes result when a parent keeps an injured child at home until the evidence of abuse disappears. In other cases, truancy indicates lack of parental concern or inability to regulate the child's schedule.

- In some cases, they arrive at school too early and remain after classes have ended, rather than go home.

- They are always tired and often sleep in class.

- They are inappropriately dressed for the weather. Children who never have coats or shoes in cold weather are receiving less than minimal care. On the other hand, those who regularly wear long sleeves or high necklines on hot days may be dressed to hide bruises, burns, or other marks of abuse.

Many of the psychological symptoms of abuse can be contradictory. One child may be excessively aggressive, while another may be too compliant. One child may be extremely independent, while another may exhibit a clinging behavior. A child may be overly mature, attending to the emotional needs of a parent who is incapable of meeting his or her own needs. These different behaviors are possible symptoms of abuse. No one behavior on the part of a child, however, is conclusive evidence of abuse.

Victims of Physical Abuse

Victims of physical abuse often display bruises, welts, contusions, cuts, burns, fractures, lacerations, strap marks, swellings, and/or lost teeth. While internal injuries are seldom detectable without a hospital examination, anyone in close contact with children should be alert to multiple injuries, a history of repeated injuries, new injuries added to old ones, and untreated injuries, especially in very young children. Older children may attribute an injury to an improbable cause, lying for fear of parental retaliation. Younger children, on the other hand, may be unaware that a severe beating is unacceptable and may admit to having been abused.

Physically abused children frequently have behavior problems. Especially among adolescents, chronic and unexplainable misbehavior should be investigated as possible evidence of abuse. Some children come to expect abusive behavior as the only kind of attention they can receive and so act in a way that invites abuse. Others break the law deliberately in order to come under the jurisdiction of the courts to obtain protection from their parents.

Parents who inflict physical abuse generally provide necessities, such as adequate food and clean clothes. However, they get angry quickly, have unrealistic expectations of their children, and are overly critical and rejecting of their children. While many abusive parents have been mistreated as children and are following a learned behavior, an increasing number who physically abuse their own children do so under the influence of alcohol and drugs.

Victims of Physical Neglect

Physically neglected children are often hungry. They may go without breakfast and have neither food nor money for lunch. Some take the lunch money or food of other children and hoard whatever they obtain. They show signs of malnutrition: paleness, low weight relative to height, lack of body tone, fatigue, inability to participate in physical activities, and lack of normal strength and endurance.

These children are usually irritable. They show evidence of inadequate home management and are unclean and unkempt. Their clothes are often torn and dirty. They may lack proper clothing for different weather conditions, and their school attendance may be irregular. In addition, these children may frequently be ill and may exhibit a generally repressed personality, inattentiveness, and withdrawal. They are in obvious need of medical attention for such correctable conditions as poor eyesight, poor dental care, and lack of immunizations.

A child who suffers physical neglect also generally lacks parental supervision at home. The child, for example, may frequently return from school to an empty house. While the need for adult supervision is, of course, relative to both the situation and the maturity of the child, it is generally held that a child younger than 12 should always be supervised by an adult or at least have immediate access to a concerned adult when necessary.

Parents of neglected children are either unable or unwilling to provide appropriate care. Some neglectful parents are mentally deficient. Most lack knowledge of parenting skills and tend to be discouraged, depressed, and frustrated with their role as parents. Alcohol or drug abuse may also be involved.

Physical neglect can be a result of poverty and/or ignorance and may not be intentional. Dr. Vincent Fontana, who founded the Crisis Nursery for parents in need of support in New York, reported having seen many situations in which young mothers simply did not know what to do with a baby. One mother brought her constantly crying baby to the nursery for help because she could not stand the crying. Workers at the nursery concluded that the child was malnourished. The mother did not know that the baby needed to be fed several times a day every day.

Victims of Emotional Abuse and Neglect

Emotional abuse and neglect are as serious as physical abuse and neglect, although this condition is far more difficult to describe or identify. Emotional maltreatment often involves a parent's lack of love or failure to give direction and encourage the child's development. The parent may either demand far too much from the child in the area of academic, social, or athletic activity or withhold physical or verbal contact, indicating no concern for the child's successes and failures and giving no guidance or praise.

Parents who commit emotional abuse and neglect are often unable to accept their children as fallible human beings. The effects of such abuse can often be far more serious and lasting than those of physical abuse and neglect. Emotionally abused children are often extremely aggressive, disruptive, and demanding in an attempt to gain attention and love. They are rarely able to achieve the success in school that tests indicate they can achieve.

Emotional maltreatment can be hard to determine. Is the child's abnormal behavior the result of maltreatment on the part of the parents, or is it a result of inborn or internal factors? Stuart N: Hart, Marla R. Brassard, and Henry C. Karlson ("Psychological Maltreatment," *The APSAC Handbook on Child Maltreatment,* Sage Publications, Thousand Oaks, CA, 1996) list possible behaviors associated with emotional abuse and neglect, including poor appetite, lying, low self-esteem, aggressive and antisocial behavior, insecure attachment relationships, failure to thrive, inability to be independent, and withdrawal that sometimes leads to suicide.

Victims of Medical Neglect and Abuse

Medical neglect refers to the parents' failure to provide medical treatment for their children, including immunizations, prescribed medications, recommended surgery, and other intervention in cases of serious disease or injury. Some situations involve a parent's inability to care for a child or lack of access to health care. Other situations involve a parent's refusal to seek professional medical care, particularly due to a belief in spiritual healing.

Thorny legal issues have been raised by cases in which parents' freedom of religion clashes with the recommendations of medical professionals. Medical abuse may involve the Munchausen Syndrome by Proxy (MSBP; see below), in which psychologically disturbed parents create illnesses or injuries in children in order to gain sympathy for themselves.

RELIGIOUS BELIEFS. Religious beliefs sometimes prevent children from getting needed medical care. For example, Christian Scientists believe that God heals the sick and that prayer and perfect faith are the proper responses to illness. Other religions, most notably Jehovah's Witnesses, forbid blood transfusions. Religious exemption laws make it difficult to prosecute parents who do not seek treatment for a sick child because their religion forbids it, although courts generally order the emergency treatment of the children.

Rita Swan, a former Christian Scientist who lost her 16-month-old child to untreated meningitis, is the president of Children's Healthcare Is a Legal Duty, Inc. (CHILD, Inc.), an organization that seeks to protect children from abusive cultural and religious practices, especially religion-based medical neglect. CHILD, Inc., reports that as of December 2000, 41 states had religious exemptions from child abuse and neglect charges, and 31 states had a religious defense to criminal charges. All states, except Mississippi and West Virginia, had religious exemptions from immunizations.

In "Child Fatalities from Religion-Motivated Medical Neglect" (*Pediatrics,* Vol. 101, No. 4, April 1998) pediatrician Seth M. Asser and Rita Swan reviewed the deaths of children in faith-healing religious sects in which the children were denied medical care. The authors found that in 140 of the 172 deaths, the likelihood of survival would have been at least 90 percent had the children received medical care. Another 18 deaths would have had survival rates of more than 50 percent.

CHILD, Inc., notes that a federal law allows parents to withhold medical care from their children based on religious beliefs. The 1996 amendments to the Child Abuse Prevention and Treatment Act (see above) provide in Sec. 113 [42 U.S.C. 5106i] that

Nothing in this Act shall be construed:

1. as establishing a federal requirement that a parent or legal guardian provide a child medical service or treatment against the religious belief of the parent or legal guardian; and

2. to require that a state find, or to prohibit a state from finding, abuse or neglect in cases in which a parent or legal guardian relies solely or partially upon spiritual means rather than medical treatment, in accordance with the religious beliefs of the parent or legal guardian.

MUNCHAUSEN SYNDROME BY PROXY. Munchausen Syndrome is a psychological disorder in which patients fake illness or make themselves sick in order to get medical attention. In cases of Munchausen Syndrome by Proxy (MSBP), parents or caregivers suffering from Munchausen Syndrome call attention to themselves by hurting or inducing illnesses in their children. The perpetrator, usually the mother, may make up a child's medical history, alter a child's laboratory tests, or fabricate or cause an illness or injury. In some cases caregivers sexually abuse their children so that they can claim a crime has been committed. Table 2.1 illustrates some of the medical symptoms or illnesses exhibited by MSBP victims and the methods perpetrators use to cause these conditions.

In MSBP situations, children are usually subjected to endless and often painful diagnostic tests, medications, and even surgery. Some children have had as many as 300 clinic visits and repeated hospitalizations in their first 18 months of life. The abuse is most often perpetrated against infants and toddlers before they can talk. Some older children who have been abused in this way do not reveal the deception, however, because they fear they will be abandoned by their parents if they are no longer sick. Others come to believe that they must truly be ill. Experts claim that in about 10 percent of cases, MSBP has led to children's deaths.

Officially, MSBP represents fewer than 1,000 of the nearly three million alleged cases of abuse referred for investigation each year. This figure, however, is almost certainly underestimated because there are no conclusive tests to diagnose the disorder. Data that exist on MSBP reveal that mothers are the perpetrators in 98 percent of the cases. Although there are no specific numbers, experts believe that many of these mothers themselves have been abused as children. A mother with MSBP may think that by devoting her life to "helping" her sick child, she could be a nurturing parent, unlike her own abusive mother. She not only gets the attention that she craves but also the sympathy of those involved in her child's care.

In June 2000 David E. Hall et al. ("Evaluation of Covert Video Surveillance in the Diagnosis of Munchausen Syndrome by Proxy: Lessons From 41 Cases," *Pediatrics,* Vol. 105, No. 6) reported the diagnosis of MSBP in 23 out of 41 suspected cases at Children's Healthcare of Atlanta at Scottish Rite, Atlanta, Georgia. For four years the researchers, after notifying law enforcement, monitored the children through hidden video cameras to determine the reasons for their inexplicable illnesses. The video surveillance showed the mothers abusing their children, from suffocation to injection with chemicals. Critics charged that the families' right to privacy had been invaded, but the researchers argued that abused children cannot speak up for themselves and need others to protect them.

A FAMILY AT RISK FOR MALTREATMENT

While it is impossible to determine whether or not child maltreatment will occur, generally a family may be

TABLE 2.1

Common presentations of Munchausen Syndrome by Proxy and the usual methods of deception

Presentation	Mechanism
Apnea (breathing stops)	Suffocation, drugs, poisoning, lying
Seizures	Lying, drugs, poisons, asphyxiation
Bleeding	Adding blood to urine, vomit, etc.; opening intravenous line
Fevers, blood infection	Injection of feces, saliva, contaminated water into the child
Vomiting	Poisoning with drugs that cause vomiting; lying
Diarrhea	Poisoning with laxatives, salt, mineral oil

SOURCE: *Child Neglect and Munchausen Syndrome by Proxy*, Office of Juvenile Justice and Delinquency Prevention, U.S. Department of Juctice, Washington, D.C., 1997

at risk if the parent is young, has little education, has had several children born within a few years, and is highly dependent on social welfare. A family may also be at risk if the parent:

- Is a "loner"—feels isolated with no family to depend on, has no real friends, or does not get along well with the neighbors.

- Has no understanding of the stages of child development and does not know what to expect of a child at a given age.

- Has a poor self-image and feels worthless, with a pervading sense of failure.

- Feels unloved, unappreciated, and unwanted, with a great fear of rejection.

- Has severe personal problems, such as ill health, alcoholism, or drug dependency.

- Feels that violence can often be the solution to life's problems or has not learned to "blow off steam" in a socially acceptable manner.

- Is experiencing a time of severe stress—for example, sudden unemployment or painful divorce—without any coping mechanism.

- Was abused or neglected as a child.

A family may also be at risk if the child:

- Is "different"—smaller than average, more sickly, disabled, or considered unattractive or was premature.

- Resembles or reminds the parent of someone the parent hates, or if the child "takes after" a disappointing spouse or former loved one.

- Is more demanding or otherwise has more problems than do other children in the family.

- Is unwanted—seen as a "mistake" or burden, having "ruined things" for the parent.

CHAPTER 3
REPORTING CHILD ABUSE

MANDATORY REPORTING

In 1974 Congress enacted the first Child Abuse Prevention and Treatment Act (CAPTA; PL 93-247) that set guidelines for the reporting, investigation, and treatment of child maltreatment. States had to meet these requirements in order to receive federal funding to assist child victims of abuse and neglect. Among its many provisions, CAPTA required the states to enact mandatory reporting laws and procedures so that child protective services (CPS) agencies can take action to protect children from further abuse. (The term CPS refers to the services provided by an agency authorized to act on behalf of a child when his/her parents are unable or unwilling to do so. CPS is also often used to refer to the agency itself.)

The earliest mandatory reporting laws were directed at medical professionals, particularly physicians, because they were considered the most likely to see abused children. Currently each state designates mandatory reporters, including health care workers, mental health professionals, social workers, school personnel, child care providers, and law enforcement officers. However, any individual, whether or not he or she is a mandatory reporter, may report incidents of abuse or neglect.

Some states also require maltreatment reporting from other individuals, such as firefighters, Christian Science practitioners, animal control officers, veterinarians, commercial film or photograph processors, and even lawyers. As of December 1999, 18 states required all citizens to report suspected child maltreatment. Twenty-six states exempted from mandatory reporting the privileged communication between attorney and client, clergy and penitent, and physician and patient. (See Table 3.1.)

In 1998 more than half (53.1 percent) of all reports of alleged child maltreatment came from professional sources—educators (14.9 percent); legal, law enforcement, and criminal justice personnel (13.3 percent); social

services personnel (11.8 percent); medical personnel (8.5 percent); mental health personnel (2.7 percent); and child care and substitute care providers (1.9 percent). Friends, neighbors, parents, and other relatives comprised 23.8 percent of the reporters, while victims and self-identified perpetrators reported abuse in 1 percent of the cases. About 12 percent of reports came from anonymous or unknown sources. (See Figure 3.1.)

All states offer immunity to individuals who report incidents of child maltreatment "in good faith." Besides physical injury and neglect, most states include mental injury, sexual abuse, and the sexual exploitation of minors as cases to be reported.

PROFESSIONAL REPORTERS

Identifying child maltreatment is not an easy process, since the perpetrators usually commit their acts against children in secrecy. Gary King, Robert Reece, Robert Bendel, and Vrunda Patel, in "The Effects of Sociodemographic Variables, Training, and Attitudes on the Lifetime Reporting Practices of Mandated Reporters" (*Child Maltreatment,* Vol. 3, No. 3, August 1998), noted that mandated reporters have to diligently determine whether abuse has actually occurred. Factors that come into play may include the reporter's own experience of abuse, training and experience, attitudes regarding child discipline, and beliefs regarding what official intervention would accomplish and what adverse consequences may result from the reporting.

Physicians

Many physicians fail to report suspected abuse, often because of disagreements about what constitutes appropriate parental discipline. Many do not consider discipline as abusive unless the consequences are serious. Some experts believe that private doctors, because of their poor record of recognizing and reporting child abuse, are part of the problem, not the solution.

FIGURE 3.1

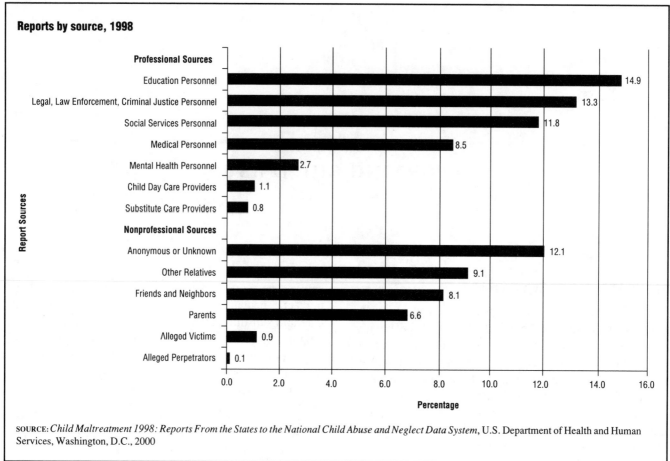

Reports by source, 1998

Professional Sources
- Education Personnel — 14.9
- Legal, Law Enforcement, Criminal Justice Personnel — 13.3
- Social Services Personnal — 11.8
- Medical Personnel — 8.5
- Mental Health Personnel — 2.7
- Child Day Care Providers — 1.1
- Substitute Care Providers — 0.8

Nonprofessional Sources
- Anonymous or Unknown — 12.1
- Other Relatives — 9.1
- Friends and Neighbors — 8.1
- Parents — 6.6
- Alleged Victims — 0.9
- Alleged Perpetrators — 0.1

SOURCE: *Child Maltreatment 1998: Reports From the States to the National Child Abuse and Neglect Data System*, U.S. Department of Health and Human Services, Washington, D.C., 2000

Some physicians are afraid of offending the parents who pay the bills and who may spread rumors about their competence, potentially damaging their practice. Others think that the problem can best be resolved privately with the parents. Many doctors fear the time lost in reporting abuse, the possibility of being sued by an outraged parent, or having to testify in court.

Gary King et al. (see above) examined the attitudes of some mandated professionals (pediatricians, master's level social workers, and physician assistants) as they related to lifetime reporting proportion (LRP; the percentage of ever-suspected cases reported). Some professionals felt that CPS might not be able to adequately protect the abused child after the report of abuse, or that CPS might remove the child from his or her home. Some did not want any publicity; others believed they should respect the family's cultural differences in raising the child. Overall the respondents reported a lifetime mean (average) of about 24 suspected cases of child maltreatment and an LRP of approximately 69 percent. (See Table 3.2.) The table lists these and other factors that influenced the professionals' decisions whether or not to report their suspicions of child maltreatment.

Some physicians believed that CPS workers were not very effective in doing their jobs. The study showed that those professionals who had never received feedback from CPS after they had reported suspected maltreatment indicated a smaller proportion of LRP (58.4 percent) than those who sometimes (76.3 percent) or always/almost always (74 percent) received feedback from CPS.

Mandated professionals who considered as very or extremely important the harm their report would cause the child had a lower LRP (about 57 percent), compared to those who felt this possible consequence of their report was not important (77 percent). Professionals who felt it was very or extremely important that reporting suspected child abuse may result in the child's removal from his/her family had a lower LRP (46 percent) than those who believed this factor was moderately important (64 percent) or not important (74 percent).

PEDIATRIC PRACTITIONERS FAIL TO ADDRESS CHILD SEXUAL ABUSE. A study of pediatricians and other pediatric practitioners revealed their lack of training in addressing child sexual abuse. Mary Ranee Leder, S. Jean Emans, Janet Palmer Hafler, and Leonard Alan Rappaport, in "Addressing Sexual Abuse in the Primary Care Setting" (*Pediatrics*, Vol. 104, No. 2, August 1999), interviewed six focus groups of 65 pediatric practitioners. The researchers found that these health care workers, while

TABLE 3.1

Mandatory reporters of child abuse and neglect

STATE	PROFESSIONS THAT MUST REPORT					OTHERS WHO MUST REPORT		STANDARD FOR REPORTING	PRIVILEGED COMMUNI-CATIONS
	Health Care	Mental Health	Social Work	Education/ Child Care	Law Enforcement	All Persons	Other		
ALABAMA §§ 26-14-3(a) 26-14-10	✓	✓	✓	✓	✓		• Any other person called upon to give aid or assistance to any child	• Known or suspected	• Attorney/client
ALASKA §§ 47.17.020(a) 47.17.023 47.17.060	✓	✓	✓	✓	✓		• Paid employees of domestic violence and sexual assault programs and drug and alcohol treatment facilities • Members of a child fatality review team or multidisciplinary child protection team • Commercial or private film or photograph processors	• Have reasonable cause to suspect	
ARIZONA §§ 13-3620(A) 8-805(B)-(C)	✓	✓	✓	✓	✓		• Parents • Anyone responsible for care or treatment of children • Clergy	• Have reasonable grounds to believe	• Clergy/penitent • Attorney/client
ARKANSAS § 12-12-507(b)-(c)	✓	✓	✓	✓	✓		• Prosecutors • Judges • Have observed conditions which would reasonably result	• Have reasonable cause to suspect	
CALIFORNIA §§ 11166(a), (c), (e) 11165.7(a) 11165.8	✓	✓	✓	✓	✓		• Firefighters • Animal control officers • Commercial film and photographic print processors • Clergy	• Have knowledge of or observe • Know or reasonably suspect	• Clergy/penitent
COLORADO §§ 19-3-304(1), (2), (2.5) 19-3-311	✓	✓	✓	✓	✓		• Christian Science practitioners • Veterinarians • Firefighters • Victim advocates • Commercial film and photographic print processors	• Have reasonable cause to know or suspect • Have observed conditions which would reasonably result	
CONNECTICUT §§ 17a-101(b) 17a-103(a)	✓	✓	✓	✓	✓		• Substance abuse counselors • Sexual assault counselors • Battered women's counselors • Clergy	• Have reasonable cause to suspect or believe	
DELAWARE tit. 16, § 903 tit. 16, § 909	✓	✓	✓	✓	✓	✓		• Know or in good faith suspect	• Attorney/client • Clergy/penitent
DISTRICT OF COLUMBIA §§ 2-1352(a), (b), (d) 2-1355	✓	✓	✓	✓	✓			• Know or have reasonable cause to suspect	
FLORIDA §§ 39.201(1) 39.204	✓	✓	✓	✓	✓	✓		• Know or have reasonable cause to suspect	• Attorney/client
GEORGIA §§ 19-7-5(c)(1), (g) 16-12-100(c)	✓	✓	✓	✓	✓		• Persons who produce visual or printed matter	• Have reasonable cause to believe	
HAWAII §§ 350-1.1(a) 350-5	✓	✓	✓	✓	✓		• Employees of recreational or sports activities	• Have reason to believe	

TABLE 3.1

Mandatory reporters of child abuse and neglect [CONTINUED]

STATE	PROFESSIONS THAT MUST REPORT					OTHERS WHO MUST REPORT		STANDARD FOR REPORTING	PRIVILEGED COMMUNI-CATIONS
	Health Care	Mental Health	Social Work	Education/ Child Care	Law Enforcement	All Persons	Other		
IDAHO §§ 16-1619(a), (c) 16-1620	✓	✓	✓	✓	✓	✓		• Have reason to believe • Have observed conditions which would reasonably result	• Clergy/penitent • Attorney/client
ILLINOIS 325 ILCS 5/4 720 ILCS 5/11-20.2	✓	✓	✓	✓	✓		• Homemakers, substance abuse treatment personnel • Christian Science practitioners • Funeral home directors • Commercial film and photographic print processors	• Have reasonable cause to believe	
INDIANA §§ 31-33-5-1 31-33-5-2 31-32-11-1	✓	✓	✓	✓	✓	✓	• Staff member of any public or private institution, school, facility, or agency	• Have reason to believe	
IOWA §§ 232.69(1)(a)-(b) 728.14(1)	✓	✓	✓	✓	✓		• Commercial film and photographic print processors • Employees of sub-stance abuse programs	• Reasonably believe	
KANSAS § 38-1522(a), (b)	✓	✓	✓	✓	✓		• Firefighters • Juvenile intake and assessment workers	• Have reason to suspect	
KENTUCKY §§ 620.030(1), (2) 620.050(2)	✓	✓	✓	✓	✓	✓		• Know or have reasonable cause to believe	• Attorney/client • Clergy/penitent
LOUISIANA Ch. Code art. 603(13) Ch. Code art. 609(A)(1) Ch. Code art. 610(F)	✓	✓	✓	✓	✓		• Commercial film or photographic print processors	• Have cause to believe	• Clergy/penitent • Christian Science practitioners
MAINE tit. 22, §§ 4011(1) 4015	✓	✓	✓	✓	✓		• Guardian *ad litems* and CASA • Fire inspectors	• Know or have reasonable cause to suspect	• Clergy/penitent
MARYLAND §§ 5-704(a) 5-705(a)(2), (a)(3)	✓	✓	✓	✓	✓	✓		• Have reason to believe	• Attorney/client • Clergy/penitent
MASSACHUSETTS ch. 119, § 51A ch. 119, § 51B	✓	✓	✓	✓	✓		• Drug and alcoholism counselors • Probation and parole officers • Clerks/magistrates of district courts • Firefighters	• Have reasonable cause to believe	
MICHIGAN § 722.623 Sec. 3(1), (8) 722.631	✓	✓	✓	✓	✓			• Have reasonable cause to suspect	• Attorney/client
MINNESOTA §§ 626.556 Subd. (3)(a) 626.556 Subd. 8	✓	✓	✓	✓	✓			• Know or have reason to believe	• Clergy/penitent
MISSISSIPPI § 43-21-353(1)	✓	✓	✓	✓	✓	✓	• Attorneys • Ministers	• Have reasonable cause to suspect	
MISSOURI §§ 210.115(1) 568.110 210.140	✓	✓	✓	✓	✓		• Persons with responsibility for care of children • Christian Science practitioners • Probation/parole officers • Commercial film processors	• Have reasonable cause to suspect • Have observed conditions which would reasonably result	• Attorney/client

TABLE 3.1

Mandatory reporters of child abuse and neglect [CONTINUED]

STATE	PROFESSIONS THAT MUST REPORT					OTHERS WHO MUST REPORT		STANDARD FOR REPORTING	PRIVILEGED COMMUNI-CATIONS
	Health Care	Mental Health	Social Work	Education/ Child Care	Law Enforcement	All Persons	Other		
MONTANA § 41-3-201(1)-(2), (4)	✓	✓	✓	✓	✓		• Guardian *ad litems* • Clergy • Religious healers • Christian Science practitioners	• Know or have reasonable cause to suspect	• Clergy/penitent
NEBRASKA §§ 28-711(1) 28-714	✓	✓	✓	✓	✓	✓		• Have reasonable cause to believe • Have observed conditions which would reasonably result	
NEVADA §§ 432B.220(3), (5) 432B.250	✓	✓	✓	✓	✓		• Clergy • Religious healers • Alcohol/drug abuse counselors • Christian Science practitioners • Probation officers Attorneys	• Know or have reason to believe	• Clergy/penitent • Attorney/client
NEW HAMPSHIRE § 169-C:29 169-C:32	✓	✓	✓	✓	✓	✓	• Christian Science practitioners	• Have reason to suspect	• Attorney/client
NEW JERSEY § 9:6-8.10	✓	✓	✓	✓	✓	✓		• Have reasonable cause to believe	
NEW MEXICO §§ 32A-4-3(A) 32A-4-5(A)	✓	✓	✓	✓	✓	✓	• Judges	• Know or have reasonable suspicion	
NEW YORK Soc. Serv. § 413(1)	✓	✓	✓	✓	✓		• Alcoholism/substance abuse counselors • District Attorneys	• Have reasonable cause to suspect	
NORTH CAROLINA §§ 7B-301 7B-310	✓	✓	✓	✓	✓	✓		• Have cause to suspect	• Attorney/client
NORTH DAKOTA §§ 50-25.1-03 50-25.1-10	✓	✓	✓	✓	✓		• Clergy • Religious healers • Addiction counselors	• Have knowledge of or reasonable cause to suspect	• Clergy/penitent • Attorney/client
OHIO § 2151.421(A)(1)(a) (b), (G)(1)(b), (A)(2)	✓	✓	✓	✓	✓		• Attorney	• Know or suspect	• Attorney/client
OKLAHOMA Tit. 10 §§ 7103(A)(1) 7104 7113 Tit. 21 § 1021.4	✓	✓	✓	✓	✓	✓	• Commercial film and photographic print processors	• Have reason to believe	
OREGON §§ 419B.005(3) 419B.010(1)	✓	✓	✓	✓	✓		• Attorney • Clergy • Firefighter • Court appointed special advocates	• Have reasonable cause to believe	• Mental health/ patient • Clergy/penitent • Attorney/client
PENNSYLVANIA § 23-6311(a),(b)	✓	✓	✓	✓	✓		• Funeral directors • Christian Science practitioners • Clergy	• Have reasonable cause to suspect	• Clergy/penitent
RHODE ISLAND § 40-11-3(a)-(c) 40-11-6(a) 40-11-11	✓	✓	✓	✓	✓	✓		• Have reasonable cause to know or suspect	• Attorney/client

TABLE 3.1

Mandatory reporters of child abuse and neglect [CONTINUED]

STATE	PROFESSIONS THAT MUST REPORT					OTHERS WHO MUST REPORT		STANDARD FOR REPORTING	PRIVILEGED COMMUNICATIONS
	Health Care	Mental Health	Social Work	Education/ Child Care	Law Enforcement	All Persons	Other		
SOUTH CAROLINA §§ 20-7-510(A) 20-7-550	✓	✓	✓	✓	✓		• Judges • Funeral home directors and employees • Christian Science practitioners • Film processors	• Have reason to believe	• Attorney/client • Priest/penitent
SOUTH DAKOTA §§ 26-8A-3 26-8A-15	✓	✓	✓	✓	✓		• Chemical dependency counselors • Religious healers • Parole or court services officers	• Have reasonable cause to suspect	
TENNESSEE §§ 37-1-403(a) 37-1-605(a) 37-1-411	✓	✓	✓	✓	✓	✓	• Judges • Neighbors • Relatives • Friends • Religious healers	• Knowledge of/reasonably • Know or have reasonable cause to suspect	
TEXAS §§ 261.101(a)-(c) 261.102	✓	✓	✓	✓	✓	✓	• Juvenile probation or detention officers • Employees or clinics that provide reproductive services	• Have cause to believe	
UTAH §§ 62A-4a-403(1)-(3) 62A-4a-412(5)	✓	✓	✓	✓	✓	✓		• Have reason to believe • Have observed conditions which would reasonably result	• Clergy/penitent
VERMONT Tit. 33 § 4913(a)	✓	✓	✓	✓	✓		• Camp administrators and counselors	• Have reasonable cause to believe	
VIRGINIA § 63.1-248.3(A)	✓	✓	✓	✓	✓		• Mediators • Christian Science practitioners	• Have reason to suspect	
WASHINGTON §§ 26.44.030 (1), (2), (3) 26.44.060(3)	✓	✓	✓	✓	✓		• Any adult with whom a child resides • Responsible living skills program staff	• Have reasonable cause to believe	
WEST VIRGINIA §§ 49-6A-2 49-6A-7	✓	✓	✓	✓	✓		• Clergy • Religious healers • Judges, family law masters or magistrates • Christian Science practitioners	• Reasonable cause to suspect • When believe • Have observed	• Attorney/client
WISCONSIN § 48.981(2), (2m)(c), (2m)(d)	✓	✓	✓	✓	✓		• Alcohol or drug abuse counselors • Mediators • Financial and employment planners	• Have reasonable cause to suspect • Have reason to believe	
WYOMING §§ 14-3-205(a) 14-3-210	✓	✓	✓	✓	✓	✓		• Know or have reasonable cause to believe or suspect • Have observed conditions which would reasonably result	• Attorney/client • Physician/patient • Clergy/penitent
TOTALS, ALL STATES	51	51	51	51	51	18	N/A	N/A	26

SOURCE: *Statutes at-a-Glance,* National Clearinghouse on Child Abuse and Neglect Information, Washington, D.C., and National Center for Prosecution of Child Abuse, Alexandria, Virginia, May 2000

knowing the signs of sexual abuse, lacked training in identifying these signs in their patients. When they suspected possible sexual abuse, the practitioners did not know what questions to ask the patients and how to handle the cases. Two-thirds of the study participants indicated that, although they realized it was their responsibility to address the possible abuse, they did not feel comfortable in doing so.

TABLE 3.2

Professional opinion and the mean number of ever-suspected cases and lifetime reporting proportion[a]

Independent Variable	Mean of Ever-Suspected Cases	Lifetime Reporting Proportion (LRP)
Overall mean	23.95	68.51
CPS adequately protects children	25.16	69.25
Receive feedback from Child Protective Services (CPS)	29.40**[b]	72.27**
Lack of sufficient evidence	24.21	68.52**
Unwilling to jeopardize relationship with family	24.17	68.76*[b]
Respect for cultural differences	24.19	68.89**
Concern about maintaining anonymity	24.26	68.89**
Reporting process is too time-consuming	24.19	68.89
Reluctance to get involved with courts	24.19	68.89*[b]
CPS interventions not effective	24.36	68.77**
Reporting may harm child	24.11	69.13***
Reporting may result in removal of child	24.38	69.11***
Child already known to CPS	24.19	68.89

[a] Levels within categories were compared by an ANOVA. Sample sizes ranged from 237 to 274 for all variables.
[b] Not significant with a Bonferonni adjustment.
* $p \leq .05$, ** $p \leq .01$, *** $p \leq .001$.

SOURCE: Gary King et al., *The Effects of Sociodemographic Variables, Training, and Attitudes On the Lifetime Reporting Practices of Mandated Reporters,* Child Maltreatment, vol. 3, no. 3, August 1998, pp. 276–283, copyright 1998 by Sage Publications, Inc. Reprinted by permission of Sage Publications, Inc.

Nonphysician Health Care Providers

Traditionally, physicians perform the physical evaluation and treatment of child abuse and neglect. However, registered nurses (RNs), nurse practitioners (NPs), and physician assistants (PAs) trained in child maltreatment are increasingly performing the physical evaluation of suspected cases. Susan J. Kelley and Beatrice Crofts Yorker, in "The Role of Nonphysician Health Care Providers in the Physical Assessment and Diagnosis of Suspected Child Maltreatment: Results of a National Survey" (*Child Maltreatment,* Vol. 2, No. 4, November 1997), found that among a national sample of 104 RNs, NPs, and PAs from 44 states and the District of Columbia, more than 9 in 10 (95.2 percent) had performed physical evaluations in suspected sexual abuse, 7 in 10 (70 percent) diagnosed suspected physical abuse, and more than half (54 percent) evaluated suspected child neglect. (See Table 3.3.)

These nonphysician health care providers also collected evidence for cases of suspected sexual abuse (92.3 percent), with three-quarters (76.9 percent) performing colposcope examinations, and 70.2 percent interpreting the results of these examinations. (A colposcope examination involves visual inspection of the cervix and vagina under magnification.) The health care providers were most likely to practice their child maltreatment specialty in clinics (70 percent), followed by emergency departments (41.4 percent), child abuse programs (27.9 percent), child advocacy centers (23.4 percent), inpatient units (16.4 percent), and public health agencies (14.4 percent). More than two-thirds (68 percent) of RNs, NPs, and PAs were members of a child abuse prevention team. These professionals reported they had practiced their specialty an average of six years. (See Table 3.3.)

A NEED FOR CHILD MALTREATMENT SPECIALISTS

Although child abuse is a well-documented social and public health problem in the United States, few medical schools and residency training programs include child abuse education and other family violence education in their curricula. The Centers for Disease Control and Prevention (CDC) reported an effort by the Virginia Commission on Family Violence to identify the presence of family violence education in the curricula of medical school-based residency programs in the state. The commission created the Task Force on Violence Education and Awareness to survey these residency programs.

The CDC, in "Family Violence Education in Medical School-Based Residency Programs—Virginia, 1995" (*Morbidity and Mortality Weekly Report,* Vol. 45, No. 31, August 9, 1996), reported on the task force survey of 69 residency programs within Virginia's three medical schools (Eastern Virginia Medical School, the Medical College of Virginia, and the University of Virginia). Of the 48 residency programs that responded, 20 programs (42 percent) covered child abuse in their curricula. Sixteen of the 20 programs offered required courses. In some cases, child abuse education programs were offered as electives (not required courses).

This study illustrates the need for integrating family violence education into the nation's medical school and internship/residency programs. However, there is a shortage of medical specialists to provide such education. Dr. Carole Jenny, director of the Child Protection Program, Hasbro Children's Hospital, Providence, Rhode Island, noted that, when medical school and academic teaching hospitals advertised faculty positions for specialists in

TABLE 3.3

Role in cases of suspected child maltreatment (in percentages)

Role	Nurse Practitioners (n = 65)	Registered Nurses (n = 34)	Physician Assistants (n = 5)	Total Sample (N = 104)
Perform physical evaluations in suspected child maltreatment				
Sexual abuse	96.9	91.2	100.0	95.2
Physical abuse	74.4	58.8	80.0	70.0
Neglect	55.4	50.0	60.0	54.0
Collection of evidence for cases of suspected child sexual abuse	92.3	91.2	100.0	92.3
Colposcope examinations	83.1	67.6	60.0	76.9
Interpretation of colposcopic findings	81.5	50.0	60.0	70.2
Use of telemedicine for consultation	0.0	9.1	0.0	2.9
Prescription writing privileges	81.3	0.0	80.0	54.9
Practice settings in CM[a]				
Clinic	78.0	47.0	80.0	70.0
Emergency department	35.4	55.9	20.0	41.4
Child abuse program	20.0	41.2	40.0	27.9
Child advocacy center	29.2	11.8	20.0	23.4
Inpatient unit	15.4	14.7	40.0	16.4
Public health	9.2	23.5	20.0	14.4
Member of a child abuse protection team	73.0	60.0	60.0	68.0
Member of a child fatality review team	10.9	11.8	00.0	10.7
Number of years experience in child maltreatment				
M	6.0	6.1	4.7	6.0
SD	5.1	5.2	3.5	5.0

[a] Total is greater than 100% because of multiple practice settings.

SOURCE: Susan J. Kelley and Beatrice Crofts Yorker, *The Role on Nonphysician Health Care Providers in the Physical Assessment and Diagnosis of Suspected Child Maltreatment: Results of a National Survey,* Child Maltreatment, vol. 2, no. 4, November 1997, pp. 331–340, copyright 1998 by Sage Publications, Inc. Reprinted by permission of Sage Publications, Inc.

child abuse, many positions could not be filled ("Pediatric Fellowships in Child Abuse and Neglect: The Development of a New Subspecialty," *Child Maltreatment,* Vol. 2, No. 4, November 1997).

Dr. Jenny cited four advantages of developing formal fellowship training for physicians who primarily care for child abuse victims. Fellowship programs would help establish the next generation of medical school faculty. More physicians conducting research on child abuse would advance the field. Physicians who have gained expertise in the field could serve as credible expert witnesses in court proceedings. Finally, physicians who have become clinically experienced are able to provide better evaluation, care, and treatment of abused children.

In February 2000 Drs. Suzanne P. Starling, Andrew P. Sirotnak, and Carole Jenny ("Child Abuse and Forensic Pediatric Medicine Fellowship Curriculum Statement," *Child Maltreatment,* Vol. 5, No. 1) reported that the American Academy of Pediatrics Section on Child Abuse and Neglect and the Forensic Pediatrics Physician Leadership Group had developed a model curriculum for fellowship programs in child abuse and forensic pediatrics (CAFP). The authors described the CAFP-trained physician as one who diagnoses and treats child abuse victims, and teaches, conducts research, and directs a multidisciplinary team with involvement in the community, in the court, and in organizations concerned with child abuse issues.

THE HOSPITAL'S ROLE

The injuries a child suffers as a result of accidental trauma differ from those resulting from intentional trauma. These differences allow doctors to determine whether the child was abused, regardless of the parent's report of the cause of injury. Figure 3.2 shows the different locations on a child's body of typical accidental injuries as compared to abuse-related injuries.

The emergency room is often where serious abuse first comes to the attention of the authorities. The American Academy of Pediatrics (AAP) believes that the hospital inpatient unit is the right place for the initial assessment of suspected victims of child maltreatment. The Committee on Hospital Care and the Committee on Child Abuse and Neglect of the AAP recommend that, in communities where no crisis intervention centers exist, hospitals have the obligation to admit children suspected of being abused ("Medical Necessity for the Hospitalization of the Abused and Neglected Child [RE9737]," *Pediatrics,* Vol. 101, No. 4, April 1998).

The AAP observes that, while managed care and peer review organizations may deny reimbursement of the child's hospital stay or limit the length of stay, their actions in no way minimize the treating physician's medical judgment. (A peer review group consists of physicians who review the work and clinical decisions of other physicians.) According to the AAP, peer-review personnel may feel that hospital admission of the alleged child victim may not have been medically necessary, since child maltreatment is a social and not a medical problem.

The AAP, however, believes that the hospital setting affords the medical team and the authorities a first-person observation of parent–child interaction. Moreover, at the time of the child's visit to the emergency room, the hospital may provide the only safe place until child protective services has the chance to decide whether to return the child to a potentially dangerous home situation.

FAILURE TO REPORT MALTREATMENT

Many states impose penalties, either a fine and/or imprisonment, for failure to report child maltreatment. A mandated reporter, such as a physician, may also be sued for negligence for failing to protect a child from harm. The landmark California case *Landeros v. Flood* (551 P.2d 389, 1976) illustrates such a case. Eleven-month-old Gita Landeros was brought by her mother to the San Jose Hospital in California for treatment of injuries. Besides a fractured lower leg, the girl had bruises on her back and abrasions on other parts of her body. She also appeared scared when anyone approached her. At the time, Landeros was also suffering from a fractured skull, but this was never diagnosed by the attending physician, A. J. Flood.

Gita returned home with her mother and subsequently suffered further serious abuse at the hands of her mother and the mother's boyfriend. Three months later Landeros was brought to another hospital for medical treatment, where the doctor diagnosed "Battered Child Syndrome" and reported the abuse to the proper authorities. After surgery the child was placed with foster parents. The mother and boyfriend were eventually convicted of the crime of child abuse. The guardian *ad litem* (a court-appointed special advocate) for Gita Landeros filed a malpractice suit against Dr. Flood and the hospital, citing painful permanent physical injury to the plaintiff, as a result of the defendants' negligence.

The California Supreme Court agreed, stating that "Battered Child Syndrome" (see Chapter 1) was a recognized medical condition that Dr. Flood should have been aware of and diagnosed. The court ruled that the doctor's failure to do so contributed to the child's continued suffering, and Dr. Flood and the hospital were liable for this. While this case applied specifically to a medical doctor, the principles reached by the court are applicable to other professionals. Most professionals are familiar with the court's decision in *Landeros*.

CHILD PROTECTIVE SERVICES

Partly funded by the federal government, Child Protective Services (CPS) agencies were first established in response to the 1974 Child Abuse and Prevention Act

FIGURE 3.2

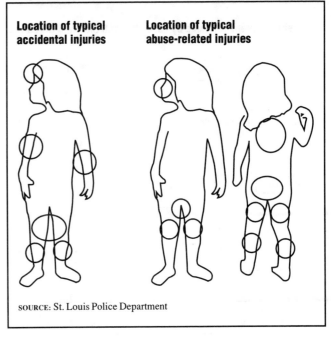

Location of typical accidental injuries

Location of typical abuse-related injuries

SOURCE: St. Louis Police Department

(CAPTA; PL 93-247), which mandated that all states establish procedures to investigate suspected incidents of child maltreatment. Upon receipt of a report of suspected child maltreatment, CPS screens the case to determine its proper jurisdiction. For example, if it has been determined that the alleged perpetrator of sexual abuse is the victim's parent or caretaker, CPS conducts further investigation. On the other hand, if the alleged perpetrator is a stranger or someone who is not the parent or caregiver of the victim, the case is referred to the police because it does not fall within CPS jurisdiction as outlined under federal law. Cases of reported child abuse or neglect typically undergo a series of steps through CPS and child welfare systems. (See Figure 3.3.)

Court Involvement

The civil or juvenile court hears allegations of maltreatment and decides if a child has been abused and/or neglected. The court then determines what should be done to protect the child. The child may be left in the parents' home under the supervision of the CPS agency, or the child may be placed in foster care. If the child is removed from the home and it is later determined that the child should never be returned to the parents, the court can begin proceedings to terminate parental rights so that the child can be put up for adoption. The state may also prosecute the abusive parent or caretaker when a crime has allegedly been committed.

Family Preservation

The Adoption Assistance and Child Welfare Act of 1980 (PL 96-272) mandated, "In each case, reasonable efforts will be made (A) prior to the placement of a child

FIGURE 3.3

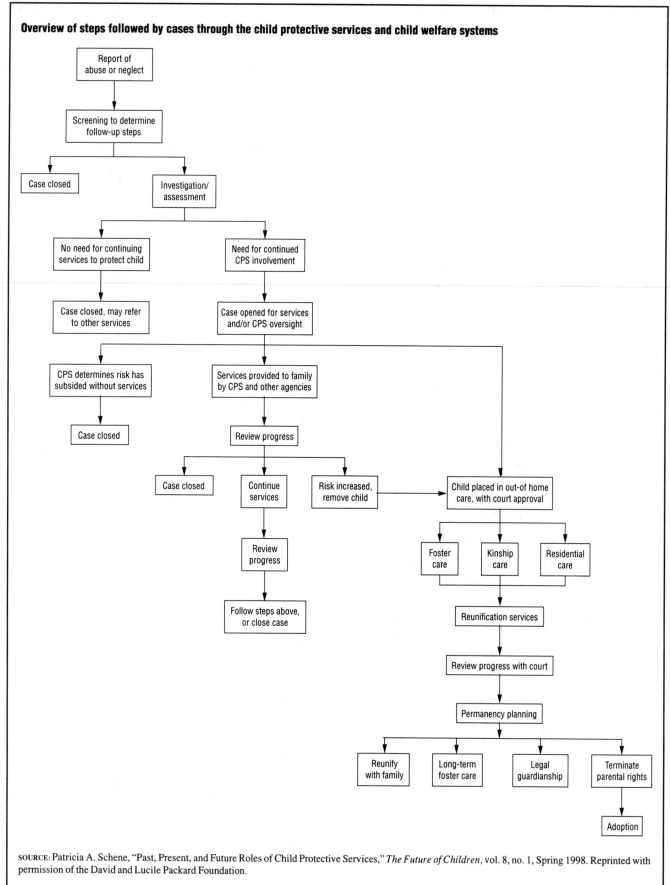

Overview of steps followed by cases through the child protective services and child welfare systems

SOURCE: Patricia A. Schene, "Past, Present, and Future Roles of Child Protective Services," *The Future of Children,* vol. 8, no. 1, Spring 1998. Reprinted with permission of the David and Lucile Packard Foundation.

in foster care, to prevent or eliminate the need for removal of the child from his home, and (B) to make it possible for the child to return to his home." However, because the law did not define the term "reasonable efforts," states and courts interpreted the term in different ways. In many cases, child welfare personnel took the "reasonable efforts" of providing family counseling, respite care, and substance abuse treatment, thus preventing the victim from being removed from abusive parents.

The law was a reaction to what was seen as overzealousness in the 1960s and 1970s, when children, especially black children, were taken from their homes because their parents were poor. Today, however, many agree that circumstances have changed. They feel that problems of drug or substance abuse can mean that returning the child to the home is likely a guarantee of further abuse. In addition, some situations exist where a parent's live-in partner, who has no emotional attachment to the child, may also present risks to the child.

Richard J. Gelles, co-director of the Family Research Laboratory of the University of New Hampshire, Durham, believes some professionals may think that a mother who hurts her child is similar to one who cannot keep house, and that with enough supervision, both types can be turned into good parents. Once a vocal advocate of family preservation, Dr. Gelles had a change of heart after studying the case of 15-month-old David Edwards, who was suffocated by his mother after the child welfare system failed to come to his rescue. Although David's parents had lost custody of their first child because of abuse, and despite reports of David's abuse, CPS made "reasonable efforts" to let the parents keep the child. In *The Book of David: How Preserving Families Can Cost Children's Lives* (BasicBooks, New York, 1996), Dr. Gelles points out that CPS needs to abandon its blanket solution to child abuse in its attempt to use reasonable efforts to reunite the victims and their perpetrators. Dr. Gelles feels that those parents who seriously abuse their children are incapable of changing their behaviors.

The Child Protective Services System Under Siege

INCREASED CASELOADS. The U.S. Government Accounting Office (GAO), the investigative arm of Congress, in *Child Protective Services: Complex Challenges Require New Strategies* (Washington, D.C., July 1997), concluded that the CPS system is in crisis. Reports of child maltreatment have continued to rise, resulting in heavier caseloads for CPS workers. The increasing number of maltreatment reports is due in part to child abuse by drug-dependent parents and caretakers, the mandatory reporting by certain professionals, and the stresses of poverty among families.

The GAO cited a U.S. Advisory Board on Child Abuse and Neglect finding, which revealed that for several years CPS caseworkers have experienced severe problems dealing with the increasing number of reports of child maltreatment. According to the Advisory Board,

> In many jurisdictions, caseloads are so high that CPS response is limited to taking the complaint call, making a single visit to the home, and deciding whether or not the complaint is valid, often without any subsequent monitoring of the family.

WEAKNESSES IN THE SYSTEM. CPS agencies are continually plagued by weaknesses in the system. The work of protecting children from maltreatment can be quite complex. CPS agencies often have difficulty attracting and retaining experienced caseworkers. The low pay not only makes it difficult to attract qualified workers but also contributes to CPS employees leaving for better-paying jobs. In some jurisdictions, due to deficient hiring policies, employees have college degrees that may not necessarily be related to social work. In addition, limited funds preclude sufficient in-service training needed to help workers keep abreast of the changing environments in which child maltreatment occurs.

Some jurisdictions maintain automated data for federal and state reporting purposes. Unfortunately caseworkers find that these data do not help in the day-to-day management of cases. Many workers rely on paper files, which may be filed incorrectly or lost. Retrieving previous information on repeat cases can be time-consuming and is sometimes impossible. Currently some state programs are undergoing computerization designed to provide more systematic case management.

The increasing number of reported child maltreatment cases has also strained the court system. The overcrowded court schedules, judges who may be ignorant of child welfare laws, and overworked lawyers, among other factors, have made the CPS workers' job even harder. The inefficient system of scheduling cases may result in caseworkers spending long hours in court when they could be performing other tasks.

Problem of Substance Abuse

Child welfare workers are faced with the growing problem of substance abuse among families involved with the child welfare system. According to *Blending Perspectives and Building Common Ground: A Report to Congress on Substance Abuse and Child Protection* (U.S. Department of Health and Human Services [HHS], Washington, D.C., 1999), the latest *National Household Survey on Drug Abuse* found that about 8.3 million children under age 18 in the United States—comprising 11 percent of all children in the nation—lived with substance-abusing parents. Among these children, 3.8 million lived with an alcoholic parent, 2.1 million lived with a parent having

FIGURE 3.4

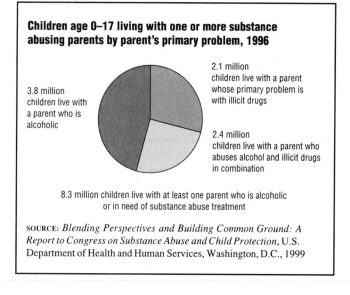

Children age 0–17 living with one or more substance abusing parents by parent's primary problem, 1996

3.8 million children live with a parent who is alcoholic

2.1 million children live with a parent whose primary problem is with illicit drugs

2.4 million children live with a parent who abuses alcohol and illicit drugs in combination

8.3 million children live with at least one parent who is alcoholic or in need of substance abuse treatment

SOURCE: *Blending Perspectives and Building Common Ground: A Report to Congress on Substance Abuse and Child Protection*, U.S. Department of Health and Human Services, Washington, D.C., 1999

FIGURE 3.5

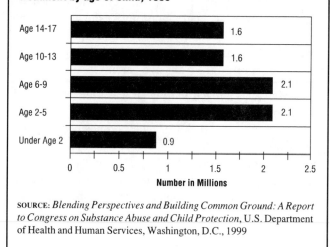

Number of children (in millions) living with one or more parents who are alcoholic or in need of substance abuse treatment by age of child, 1996

Age	Number in Millions
Age 14-17	1.6
Age 10-13	1.6
Age 6-9	2.1
Age 2-5	2.1
Under Age 2	0.9

SOURCE: *Blending Perspectives and Building Common Ground: A Report to Congress on Substance Abuse and Child Protection*, U.S. Department of Health and Human Services, Washington, D.C., 1999

an illicit drug problem, and another 2.4 million lived with parents who abused both alcohol and illicit drugs. (See Figure 3.4.)

The survey found that nearly one million children living with substance-abusing parents were younger than two years old. More than four million were 2–9 years old, and an estimated three million were between the ages of 10 and 17. (See Figure 3.5.)

Women who had children in the home had lower substance abuse rates, compared to those who had no children living with them. Nonetheless, nearly 1 in 10 (9.6 percent) women who had children reported having used illicit drugs in the past month. About 2 in 10 (19.5 percent) reported binge drinking (having five or more drinks on the same occasion for one or more days in the past month). (See Table 3.4.)

PARENTAL SUBSTANCE ABUSE AND CHILD MALTREATMENT. HHS noted (*Blending Perspectives and Building Common Ground* see above) that about one-third to two-thirds of substantiated child maltreatment reports (those having sufficient evidence to support the allegation of maltreatment) involve substance abuse. Younger children, especially infants, are more likely to be victimized by substance-abusing parents, and the maltreatment is more likely to consist of neglect than abuse.

Many children experience neglect when a parent is under the influence of alcohol or is out of the home looking for drugs. Even when the parent is at home, he or she may be psychologically unavailable to the children. (See issues on neglect in Chapters 2 and 5.) The growing number of substance-abusing pregnant women has resulted in many infants being exposed to illegal substances before birth. (See Chapter 7 for the criminal prosecution for drug use during pregnancy.)

A comprehensive study by the National Center on Addiction and Substance Abuse at Columbia University found that substance abuse or addiction is responsible for 7 of 10 cases of child maltreatment (*No Safe Haven: Children of Substance-Abusing Parents,* New York, 1999). A Child Welfare League of America survey of state child welfare agencies (*Alcohol and Other Drug Survey of State Child Welfare Agencies,* Washington, D.C., 1998) found that substance abuse and poverty were the top two main factors contributing to child maltreatment in 40 states.

SUBSTANCE ABUSE AMONG PARENTS ON WELFARE. According to the Legal Action Center of New York City, about 15–20 percent of adults on welfare have substance abuse problems, thus preventing them from working (*Making Welfare Reform Work: Tools for Confronting Alcohol and Drug Problems Among Welfare Recipients,* New York, 1997). In 2000 the Office of National Drug Control Policy, in its report to Congress (*National Drug Control Strategy: 2000 Annual Report,* Washington, D.C.), stressed that without outside intervention, these high-risk families will remain on welfare and get involved in the criminal justice system, jeopardizing their children. To this end, the Center for Substance Abuse Prevention of the U.S. Department of Health and Human Services (HHS) helps teenage parents, who are often on welfare, to prevent or reduce substance use. HHS has also improved its system of providing substance abuse services to personnel involved with welfare programs and child protection.

Holding States Accountable

In August 2000, HHS released the first in a series of annual reports on the states' performance in meeting the needs of at-risk children who have entered the child wel-

TABLE 3.4

Past-month substance abuse by women age 15–44, by pregnancy and child-rearing status, 1996–97

Index	Woman's Pregnancy and Child-Rearing Status (Number in Thousands)							
	Pregnant		Raising Child(ren) <2 Years Old		All Children Are 2+ Years Old		No Children	
	N	%	N	%	N	%	N	%
Population N (thousands)	2,400	100	7,500	100	25,000	100	26,000	100
Any illicit drug	59	2.5	385	5.5	981	4.1	2,579	10.4
Any, excluding marijuana	28	1.2	147	2.1	417	1.7	1,150	4.6
Cocaine	4	0.2	33	0.5	151	0.6	353	1.4
Heroin	4	0.2	5	0.1	19	0.1	41	0.2
Binge drinking[1]	30	1.3	622	9.2	2,395	10.3	4,009	16.7
Heavy drinking[2]	6	0.3	133	2.0	532	2.3	1,100	4.6

[1] Five or more drinks on the same occasion 1 or more days in the past 30 days.
[2] Five or more drinks on the same occasion 5 or more days in the past 30 days.

SOURCE: *Blending Perspectives and Building Common Ground: A Report to Congress on Substance Abuse and Child Protection*, U.S. Department of Health and Human Services, Washington, D.C., 1999

fare system. The report, *Child Welfare Outcomes 1998: Annual Report* (Children's Bureau, Washington, D.C.), was required by the 1997 Adoption and Safe Families Act (ASFA; PL 105-89).

Since the mid-1980s, although most children reported for maltreatment have remained with their parents, a large number have been placed in foster care, many for five years or longer. The number had more than doubled to about 568,000 children as of October 2000. ASFA gives states more flexibility in interpreting the "reasonable efforts" required to reunify a child with the birth family. When victims cannot safely return home, states can start proceedings to terminate parental rights for children who have been in foster care for 15 of the previous 22 months. Children can then be placed in permanent homes.

ASFA now requires that a set of outcome measures must be developed to assess how states are meeting the needs of maltreated children, those in foster care, and those who are waiting for adoption. States will receive bonuses for increasing the number of adoptions and for shortening the time frames for permanent placement decisions for children. However, states that do not protect the children adequately will be penalized.

Lives Saved

Although CPS agencies have had many problems and are often unable to perform as effectively as they should, many thousands of maltreated children have been identified, many lives have been saved, and many more have been taken out of dangerous environments. It is impossible to tally the number of child abuse cases that might have ended in death. These children have been saved by changes in the laws, by awareness and reporting, and by the efforts of the professionals who intervened in their lives.

PUBLIC INVOLVEMENT IN PREVENTING CHILD MALTREATMENT

Prevent Child Abuse America (PCA America; formerly the National Committee to Prevent Child Abuse) asked the American public in 1999 if they had observed certain acts of abuse and/or neglect as adults (*Public Opinion and Behaviors Regarding Child Abuse Prevention: 1999 Survey*, Deborah Daro, Chicago, November 1999). More than half (55 percent) reported having seen a parent neglect a child, and 71 percent reported having seen a parent emotionally abuse a child. (See Table 3.5.) The survey found that respondents with children under age 18 were more likely to report having seen these behaviors.

Overall, 56 percent of all respondents who saw an abusive or neglectful behavior reported responding to this observation. Forty-three percent failed to take action. (See Table 3.5.) The respondents who responded to the situation reported using some combination of strategies, including calming or scolding the abusing parent, giving the abuser a disapproving look, distracting the child or removing him/her from the situation, or alerting an authority to what was happening. Approximately half of those who did not respond to the child maltreatment believed it was "none of their business" or were not sure how to respond.

REFORM OF THE REPORTING AND INVESTIGATING PROCESS

Over the years, child advocates and critics of CPS have called for the reform of child maltreatment reporting and investigation procedures. The Harvard Executive Session, a task force of child welfare administrators, practitioners, policymakers, and experts, suggested a new model for child protection.

TABLE 3.5

Respondents observing an act of abuse and/or neglect, and their response to such observation

Observation	Yes	No	Total
Have you ever seen an adult neglect a child? (e.g. ignore a child's needs, failure to feed, withhold affection, etc.)	55%	42%	47%
Have you ever seen an adult physically abuse a child?	36%	30%	32%
Have you ever seen an adult emotionally abuse a child? (e.g. insult, taunt, harass, etc.)	71%	63%	66%
Total number of respondents	*449*	*799*	*1250*

Response to Observation	Yes	No	Total
Took action	62%	52%	56%
Failure to take action	36%	47%	43%
Total number of respondents	*354*	*574*	*930*

SOURCE: Deborah Daro, *Public Opinion and Behaviors Regarding Child Abuse Prevention:* 1999 Survey, Prevent Child Abuse America, Chicago, IL, November 1999

The Harvard model of child protection calls for a sharing of responsibilities between CPS and the community. CPS would respond to cases involving higher-risk cases of maltreatment, while other public or private agencies in the community would respond to lower-risk cases. These actions would ensure that the system acts aggressively to protect children at higher risk of maltreatment, while not intervening in a coercive manner with families at lower risk.

The Harvard model also stressed the importance of recruiting "informal helpers" to support at-risk families. The task force felt that, since abusive or neglectful parents may have been child maltreatment victims themselves, extended family members may not be ideal protectors for the children. In addition, there may be few social supports within poor neighborhoods for at-risk children. The model suggested that the larger community can provide the support and protection these children need ("Rethinking the Paradigm for Child Protection," *The Future of Children: Protecting Children from Abuse and Neglect,* Vol. 8, No. 1, Spring 1998).

Preventing Inappropriate Reporting

Douglas J. Besharov, the first director of the U.S. National Center on Child Abuse and Neglect of the U.S. Department of Health and Human Services, believes that abused and neglected children are dying, both because neglect and abuse are not being reported to the authorities and because the authorities are being overwhelmed by the need to investigate inappropriate reports. In "Four Commentaries: How We Can Better Protect Children from Abuse and Neglect" (*The Future of Children: Protecting Children from Abuse and Neglect,* Vol. 8, No. 1, Spring 1998), Besharov suggested various steps to overhaul the child protection system:

- Rewrite child maltreatment laws to clarify the reportable parental behaviors that put children at risk of abuse and neglect.

- Provide comprehensive continuing public education and training concerning conditions that warrant reporting as well as those that do not.

- Put in place policies and procedures for screening reports of maltreatment.

- Modify liability laws to address "good-faith" reporters as well as those who have failed to report what may later turn out to be actual child maltreatment.

- Let reporters know the outcome of their personal involvement, which in a later situation may help them assess the presence of maltreatment.

- Set up formal reporting policies for such public and private agencies as schools and child care centers.

IMPROPER ACCUSATION

Although people are outraged by stories about horribly abused and/or neglected children missed by the authorities, there is also a backlash movement against the intrusiveness of CPS and wrongs committed when parents are unjustly accused of abuse. Some parents claim they keep their children home from school if they have a bruise for fear the teacher will report the parents and have them investigated for abuse.

In *Wounded Innocents: The Real Victims of the War Against Child Abuse* (Prometheus Books, Buffalo, NY, 1995), Richard Wexler wrote that after a teacher in Waukeegan, Illinois, was charged with sexual abuse and sued by two parents, the Chicago Teachers' Union provided "self-defense" guidelines to its teachers. Educators were told to use public areas when holding conferences with students and to be discreet in their physical contacts when praising, rewarding, or comforting students.

Wexler, a former newsman who covered child abuse and foster care, also noted that the panic created by unwarranted accusations is driving away the relatively few men who might be willing to work in day care centers. Some day care centers prefer not to hire men at all. According to Wexler, fathers, particularly divorced fathers with visiting children, have become hesitant in showing affection to their own children.

Other critics of the CPS system point out that a large proportion of reports to CPS are not substantiated. For example, the HHS survey, *Child Maltreatment 1998: Reports from the States to the National Child Abuse and Neglect Data System* (Washington, D.C., 2000), reported that 57.2 percent of the reports were not substantiated. (See Figure 4.1 in Chapter 4.)

Hotlines for reporting abuse and neglect accept all calls, even when the reporter cannot give a reason why he or she thinks the child is being maltreated. In addition, CPS is now called upon to handle many cases that previously would have been handled by other agencies. Cutbacks in funding have pushed related problems of poverty, homelessness, truancy, and delinquency on CPS because it is known as a social agency that will at least investigate the reports.

Overreporting Needs to Be Controlled

Richard Wexler, in *Wounded Innocents* (see above), claimed that one reason the number of abuse reports is deceptive is that in the majority of reports, the children have not been maltreated at all. He explained that reports of child maltreatment are sometimes made when a parent is guilty of nothing more than poverty. For example, child abuse was reported in the following cases:

- A woman's home was in disrepair.

- A man could not pay his utility bill.

- A woman could not afford to buy a pair of eyeglasses for her child.

- A woman was evicted from two apartments because of "no children allowed" rules.

The Problem May Be Underreporting

David Finkelhor and Donileen Loseke, in "The Main Problem Is Still Underreporting, Not Overreporting" (*Current Controversies on Family Violence,* Sage Publications, Thousand Oaks, CA, 1993), asserted that the problem is underreporting, not overreporting. One statistic they offered in support of their assertion is that, when adults are asked whether they were abused as children, the percentages are far higher than the number of children who are reported each year. If, for example, 15 percent of women and 5 percent of men were sexually abused in childhood (a low estimate according to some experts), this would translate to yearly rates of child abuse two to three times higher than the rates reported today. (See Chapter 6 for more on rates of sexual abuse.)

Finkelhor and Loseke also rejected claims that many reports of abuse are "minor situations." They offered examples of cases that they said would be dismissed by critics but which they insisted are part of the crucial effort to discover an abusive situation before serious injury occurs. These include cases of emotional abuse, such as when a child is locked in a room or threatened with death; physical neglect, such as when a parent leaves young children alone but who are rescued before they suffer any harm; or physical abuse, such as when a child is shot at but missed.

In defense of CPS investigations of reports that may turn out to be unfounded cases of child maltreatment, the authors compared the investigation process to the criminal justice system in which only about 55 percent of the persons arrested are ever convicted. (A difference Finkelhor and Loseke ignored is that the perpetrator of a crime is often unknown, while the child abuser can nearly always be identified.) They believed that Americans tolerate inefficiencies in the criminal justice system that are remarkably similar to the deficiencies in the child protective system—charges that cannot be proved, technicalities that prevent prosecution, and overworked investigators.

Furthermore, according to the authors, Americans accept the intrusions of tax audits and airline security measures because the overall goals of catching tax evaders and ensuring airline safety outweigh the inconveniences. If Americans can live with these systems, the authors believe they can accept an occasional false accusation for the benefit of saving children.

Gail L. Zellman and Kathleen Coulborn Faller, in "Reporting of Child Maltreatment" (*The APSAC Handbook on Child Maltreatment,* Sage Publications, Thousand Oaks, CA, 1996), discussed the results of a survey of over 1,000 mandated reporters in 15 states. These professionals included physicians, child psychiatrists, clinical psychologists, school principals, and heads of child care centers.

The survey found that nearly 40 percent of mandated reporters had not reported child maltreatment at some time in their career even when they had suspected such practice. About 60 percent failed to report due to lack of sufficient evidence that abuse had taken place. One-third (33.4 percent) felt that the suspected maltreatment was not serious enough to warrant reporting. About one-fifth indicated that they thought they could help the abused child themselves, while 19 percent felt the reporting might disrupt the treatment the child was already receiving. Nearly 16 percent did not report a suspected case of child abuse because they believed that child protective services offered poor quality intervention.

Diana E. H. Russell and Rebecca M. Bolen, experts in child sexual abuse research, also observed the underreporting of child maltreatment cases. In *The Epidemic of Rape and Child Sexual Abuse in the United States* (Sage Publications, Thousand Oaks, CA, 2000), the authors concluded from their studies of child sexual abuse over the past 20 years that just one-half of the cases of incestuous abuse known to professionals are reported. Incestuous abuse involves the use of a child for sexual satisfaction by family members. (See Chapter 6 for more on child sexual abuse and the underreporting of such abuse.)

Harassment

A small proportion of reports are false or ill-considered, either because the reporter has been mistaken or because the reporter has been deliberately lying to get the alleged abuser in trouble. Sexual abuse is the most common form of false accusation because it is such a heinous crime and does not require physical evidence.

False, vindictive reports are sometimes made anonymously to CPS to harass parents. Richard Wexler (*Wounded Innocents;* see above) reported how, in one case, social workers demanded entry to a woman's house more than five times in a two-year period. They ordered her to wake up her sleeping children and strip them naked while social workers examined them for signs of abuse. All of the reports turned out to be false, but the caller, whose anonymity was protected by the law, could start the process again with a simple phone call.

IS THERE BIAS IN REPORTING?

Some critics claim that reporting of child abuse and neglect is biased against parents and caretakers in the lower socioeconomic classes. Brett Drake and Susan Zuravin, in "Bias in Child Maltreatment Reporting: Revisiting the Myth of Classlessness" (*American Journal of Orthopsychiatry,* 68 [2], April 1998), discussed four forms of potential bias that may be responsible for the overrepresentation of child maltreatment among the poor in CPS caseloads.

Visibility bias, also called "exposure bias," is the belief that poor families, who are more likely to use such public services as welfare agencies and public hospitals, tend to be noticed by potential reporters. The researchers claimed that, to date, no scientific studies have ever been done to investigate the visibility bias theory.

Drake and Zuravin surmised that if the visibility bias does exist, it will follow that mandated reporters who have more contact with the poor will file more reports of abuse among poor children. They studied six Missouri sites with the lowest percentage of families living below the poverty line. When they compared the mandated reports about child maltreatment among upper middle-class suburban families (44.4 percent) and among inner-city poor families (49.2 percent), they did not find a large overrepresentation of the poor.

The researchers also noted that mandated reporters (for example, law enforcement, medical, and social services personnel), who are more likely to come into contact with a larger proportion of poor families than non-poor families, accounted for one-third of all referrals. This proportion could not possibly be responsible for the overrepresentation of maltreatment reports of poor families.

Labeling bias refers to the predisposition to look for and find maltreatment among certain groups of individuals. Review of empirical studies showed no such bias exists among mandated reporters. Drake and Zuravin found, in one study, that Head Start personnel were not likely to look for signs of maltreatment among the children in their care just because these children belonged to a lower socioeconomic status.

Reporting bias implies a person's failure to report what he or she suspects to be child maltreatment among certain groups. In the late 1970s and early 1980s, studies found that professionals were very likely not to report child maltreatment among higher-income families. The authors found that mandated professionals are more likely to report maltreatment because of the legal ramifications associated with failure to comply with child maltreatment laws. Hence, the reporting bias theory does not hold true.

Substantiation bias describes any tendency on the part of CPS investigators to base substantiation conclusions on such factors as a family's socioeconomic status. Empirical studies show that this is not the case.

The researchers concluded that, although a large percentage of child abuse and neglect occurs among the poor, empirical studies have shown that this overrepresentation is not a result of reporting biases.

CHAPTER 4

HOW MANY CHILDREN ARE MALTREATED?

Statistics on child abuse are difficult to interpret and compare because there is very little consistency in how information is collected. The definitions of abuse vary from study to study, as do the methods of counting incidents of abuse. Some methods count only reported cases of abuse. Some statistics are based on estimates projected from a small study, while others are based on interviews. In addition, it is virtually impossible to know the extent of child maltreatment that occurs in the privacy of the home.

INCIDENCE AND PREVALENCE OF CHILD MALTREATMENT

Researchers use two terms—incidence and prevalence—to describe the estimates of the number of victims of child abuse and neglect. Andrea J. Sedlak and Diane D. Broadhurst (*Third National Incidence Study of Child Abuse and Neglect* [NIS-3], U.S. Department of Health and Human Services, Washington, D.C., 1996; see below) define incidence as the number of new cases occurring in the population during a given period of time. The incidence of child maltreatment is measured in terms of incidence rate: the number of children, per 1,000 children in the U.S. population, who are maltreated annually. A major source of incidence data are surveys based on official reports by child protective services (CPS) agencies and community professionals. Private national organizations, such as Prevent Child Abuse America (PCA America), also collect and analyze data regarding the incidence of child abuse and neglect.

Prevalence, as defined by NIS-3, refers to the total number of child maltreatment cases in the population at a given point in time. Some researchers use lifetime prevalence to denote the number of people who have had at least one experience of child maltreatment in their lives. To measure the prevalence of child maltreatment, researchers use self-reported surveys of parents and child victims. Examples of self-reported surveys are the land-

mark 1975 and 1985 *National Family Violence* surveys, conducted by Murray A. Straus and Richard J. Gelles. (See Chapter 5.)

Official Reports

Studies based on official reports depend on a number of things happening before an incident of abuse can be recorded. The victim must be seen by people outside the home; these people must recognize that the child has been abused. Once they have recognized this fact, they must then decide whether to report the abuse, and find out where to report it. Once CPS receives and screens the report for appropriateness, action can be taken.

In some cases the initial call to CPS is prompted by a problem that needs to be handled by a different agency. It may be a case of neglect due to poverty rather than abuse, although the initial report is still recorded as abuse.

For the data to become publicly available, CPS must keep records on its cases and then pass them on to a national group that collects those statistics. Consequently, final reported statistics are understated estimates—valuable as indicators but not definitive findings. It is very unlikely that accurate statistics on child abuse will ever be available.

DATA COLLECTION OF CHILD MALTREATMENT

The 1974 Child Abuse Prevention and Treatment Act (CAPTA; PL 93-247) created the National Center on Child Abuse and Neglect (NCCAN) to coordinate nationwide efforts to protect children from maltreatment. As part of the former U.S. Department of Health, Education, and Welfare, NCCAN commissioned the American Humane Association (AHA) to collect data from the states. The first time the AHA collected data, in 1976, it recorded approximately 669,000 reports of child maltreatment. Between 1980 and 1985 the AHA reported a 12 percent annual increase in maltreatment reports to CPS agencies.

In 1985 the federal government stopped funding data collection on child maltreatment. In 1986 the National Committee to Prevent Child Abuse (NCPCA) picked up where the government left off. The NCPCA started collecting detailed information from the states on the number of children abused, the characteristics of child abuse, the number of child abuse deaths, and changes in the funding and extent of child welfare services.

In 1988 the Child Abuse Prevention, Adoption, and Family Services Act (PL 100-294) replaced the 1974 CAPTA. The new law mandated that NCCAN, as part of the U.S. Department of Health and Human Services, establish a national data collection program on child maltreatment. In 1990 the National Child Abuse and Neglect Data System (NCANDS), designed to fulfill this mandate, began collecting and analyzing child maltreatment data from CPS agencies in the 50 states, the District of Columbia, the territories, and the armed services. The first three surveys were known as *Working Paper 1, Working Paper 2,* and *Child Maltreatment 1992. Child Maltreatment 1998* is the latest NCANDS survey (see below).

As part of the 1974 Child Abuse Prevention and Treatment Act, Congress also mandated NCCAN to conduct a periodic *National Incidence Study of Child Abuse and Neglect* (NIS). Data on maltreated children were collected not only from CPS agencies but also from professionals in community agencies, such as law enforcement, public health, juvenile probation, mental health, and voluntary social services, as well as from hospitals, schools, and day care centers. The NIS is the single most comprehensive source of information about the incidence of child maltreatment in the United States, because it analyzes the characteristics of child abuse and neglect that are known to community-based professionals, including those characteristics not reported to CPS. (See below for NIS-3, the most recent federal study of child maltreatment.)

In 1996, pursuant to amendments to the Child Abuse Prevention and Treatment Act (CAPTA; PL 104-235), NCCAN ceased operating as a separate agency. Since then all child maltreatment prevention functions have been consolidated within the Children's Bureau of the U.S. Department of Health and Human Services (HHS).

MALTREATMENT REPORTS TO CHILD PROTECTIVE SERVICES

Collecting child maltreatment data from the states is difficult because each state has its own method of gathering and classifying the information. Most states collect data on an incident basis; that is, they count each time a child is reported for abuse or neglect. If the same child is reported several times in one year, each incident is counted. Consequently, there may be more incidents of child maltreatment than the number of maltreated children.

Reports of Maltreated Children

In 1998 CPS agencies received an estimated two million reports, alleging the maltreatment of about 2.8 million children (*Child Maltreatment 1998: Reports From the States to the National Child Abuse and Neglect Data System,* U.S. Department of Health and Human Services, Washington, D.C., 2000). (As discussed above, some children may have been reported and counted more than once.) States may vary in the rates of child maltreatment reported. There are not only differences in the state definitions of maltreatment but also in the methods of counting reports of abuse. Some states counted reports based on the number of incidents or the number of families involved, rather than on the number of children allegedly abused. Other states counted all reports to CPS, while others counted only investigated reports. Although the states varied in the rate of children reported and referred for investigation, about two-thirds of the states reported a rate between 14 and 67 per 1,000 children under age 18. (See Table 4.1.)

Dispositions of Investigated Reports

Alleged reports of child maltreatment normally receive one of the following dispositions:

- Substantiated—means that sufficient evidence exists to support the allegation of maltreatment or risk of maltreatment.

- Indicated or reason to suspect—means that the abuse and/or neglect cannot be substantiated, but there is reason to suspect that the child has been maltreated or is at risk of maltreatment.

- Unsubstantiated or unfounded—means sufficient evidence does not exist to conclude that the child has been maltreated.

In 1998 CPS investigated 1.8 million out of the two million reports of child maltreatment. In 57.2 percent of the investigations, the allegations of maltreatment were judged to be unsubstantiated. More than a quarter (26.1 percent) were substantiated, and 3.1 percent were indicated. (See Figure 4.1.)

VICTIMS OF MALTREATMENT

Rates of Victimization

In 1998 more than 903,000 children were victims of maltreatment in the United States. The rate of victimization, 12.9 per 1,000, dropped from the 1997 rate of 13.3. The rate of maltreatment has been declining since a high of 15.3 in 1993. (See Figure 4.2.)

Types of Maltreatment

In 1998 more than half (53.5 percent) of victims suffered neglect. Another 2.4 percent experienced medical neglect. About one-quarter (22.7 percent) were physically abused, and 11.5 percent were sexually abused. An addi-

TABLE 4.1

Total referrals, by state

State	Child Population	Screened Out	Rate of Screened-In Reports per 1,000 Children	Screened In	Rate of Screened-Out Reports per 1,000 Children	Total Referrals
Alaska	192,261	4,501	23.4	11,202	58.3	15,703
Arkansas	653,721	7,876	12.0	20,511	31.4	28,387
California	8,911,372	1,553	0.2	122,622	13.8	124,175
Colorado	1,040,580	17,889	17.2	28,573	27.5	46,462
Connecticut	790,715	10,119	12.8	31,221	39.5	41,340
Delaware	179,071	2,215	12.4	6,473	36.1	8,688
Florida	3,539,932	0	0.0	125,359	35.4	125,359
Georgia	2,022,351	23,645	11.7	47,007	23.2	70,652
Idaho	351,158	8,612	24.5	10,100	28.8	18,712
Indiana	1,517,366	8,012	5.3	102,155	67.3	110,167
Kansas	697,452	8,950	12.8	18,480	26.5	27,430
Maine	291,585	9,749	33.4	4,121	14.1	13,870
Massachusetts	1,457,703	23,808	16.3	37,091	25.4	60,899
Michigan	2,551,615	67,295	26.4	62,659	24.6	129,954
Missouri	1,406,616	49,089	34.9	48,119	34.2	97,208
New Hampshire	298,610	6,000	20.1	6,391	21.4	12,391
New Mexico	504,210	8,720	17.3	12,781	25.3	21,501
New York	4,502,611	191,709	42.6	142,174	31.6	333,883
Oklahoma	879,367	17,798	20.2	34,790	39.6	52,588
Oregon	825,170	14,156	17.2	17,300	21.0	31,456
Rhode Island	237,917	3,802	16.0	8,117	34.1	11,919
South Carolina	959,296	5,189	5.4	20,000	20.8	25,189
Texas	5,629,200	29,673	5.3	121,183	21.5	150,856
Utah	701,300	4,811	6.9	16,931	24.1	21,742
Washington	1,472,490	43,778	29.7	32,880	22.3	76,658
West Virginia	404,254	5,728	14.2	16,350	40.4	22,078
Wyoming	129,406	1,498	11.6	1,927	14.9	3,425
Total	**42,147,329**	**576,175**	**13.7**	**1,106,517**	**26.3**	**1,682,692**
National Estimate	**69,872,059**	**Estimated Screened-Out**	**955,186**	**Actual Screened-In**	**1,851,267**	**2,806,453**

The national estimate of 2,806,453 is based on an estimate of screened-out reports and the actual number of screened-in reports from 51 jurisdictions. The number of screened-out reports is based on a rate of 13.7 per 1,000 children in the population.

SOURCE: *Child Maltreatment 1998: Reports From the States to the National Child Abuse and Neglect Data System,* U.S. Department of Health and Human Services, Washington, D.C., 2000

---

tional 6 percent were subjected to emotional maltreatment. One-quarter (25.3 percent) suffered other types of maltreatment, including abandonment, congenital drug addiction, and threats to harm a child. Some children were victims of more than one type of maltreatment.

RATES OF MALTREATMENT BY TYPE. Data from 40 states were used to compare the rates of the different types of maltreatment in 1990 and 1998. Between 1990 and 1998 the rate of neglect increased from 6.3 to 7.2 children per 1,000. The rates for three types of maltreatment declined: physical abuse, from 3.5 to 2.9; sexual abuse, from 2.3 to 1.6; and psychological abuse, from 0.8 to 0.6. (See Figure 4.3.)

Age of Victims

In 1998, as in 1990, younger children accounted for most of the maltreated children. As the children got older, they made up a smaller and smaller proportion of victims. In 1998 the victimization rate was 14.8 per 1,000 for infants and toddlers up to age three. At ages 16–17, the victimization rate was down to 6.6. (See Figure 4.4.)

FIGURE 4.1

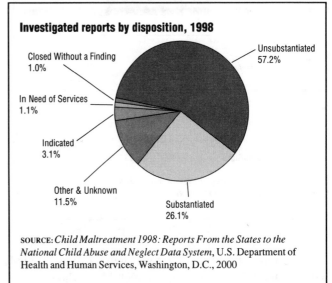

Investigated reports by disposition, 1998

Closed Without a Finding 1.0%
Unsubstantiated 57.2%
In Need of Services 1.1%
Indicated 3.1%
Other & Unknown 11.5%
Substantiated 26.1%

SOURCE: *Child Maltreatment 1998: Reports From the States to the National Child Abuse and Neglect Data System*, U.S. Department of Health and Human Services, Washington, D.C., 2000

FIGURE 4.2

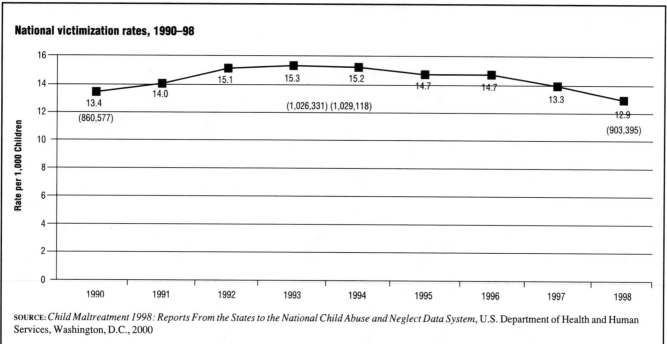

National victimization rates, 1990–98

SOURCE: *Child Maltreatment 1998: Reports From the States to the National Child Abuse and Neglect Data System*, U.S. Department of Health and Human Services, Washington, D.C., 2000

FIGURE 4.3

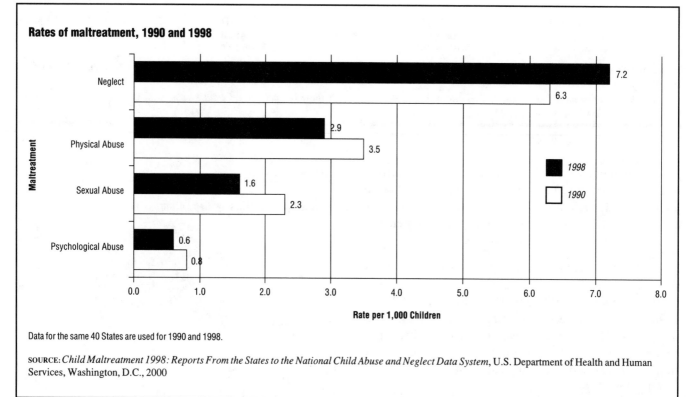

Rates of maltreatment, 1990 and 1998

Data for the same 40 States are used for 1990 and 1998.

SOURCE: *Child Maltreatment 1998: Reports From the States to the National Child Abuse and Neglect Data System*, U.S. Department of Health and Human Services, Washington, D.C., 2000

The type of maltreatment was generally associated with the child's age. The number of children who suffered neglect decreased with age: 9.7 per 1,000 for infants and toddlers up to age three, compared with 2.1 per 1,000 for those 16–17 years old. Medical neglect rates were 0.9 per 1,000 for the youngest children, compared with 0.1 for children ages 16–17. In contrast, the victimization rates for children who were sexually abused increased with age; for example, while 0.5 per 1,000 of those three years old or younger were sexually abused, higher rates of victimization occurred for children over three years of age. (See Table 4.2.)

FIGURE 4.4

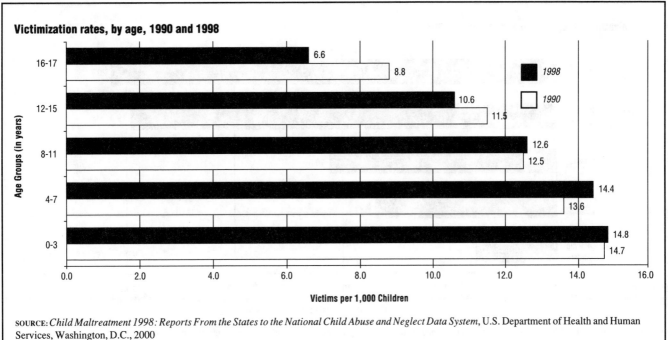

Victimization rates, by age, 1990 and 1998

SOURCE: *Child Maltreatment 1998: Reports From the States to the National Child Abuse and Neglect Data System*, U.S. Department of Health and Human Services, Washington, D.C., 2000

TABLE 4.2

Victimization rates, according to maltreatment type, by age and sex, 1998

Type of Maltreatment	Maltreatment Incidents								
	Age					Sex		Mean Age	
	0-3	4-7	8-11	12-15	16-17	Female	Male	Female	Male
Physical Abuse	2.4	3.1	2.9	3.2	1.9	2.8	2.8	9.2	7.9
Neglect	9.7	8.2	6.5	4.8	2.1	6.8	6.6	7	6.4
Medical Neglect	0.9	0.4	0.3	0.3	0.1	0.4	0.4	5.7	5.4
Sexual Abuse	0.5	1.6	1.7	2.1	1.2	2.3	0.6	10.4	8.6
Psych. or Emotional Abuse	0.7	0.9	0.9	0.8	0.4	0.8	0.7	8.6	7.7
Other	6.1	4.6	4	3.1	1.5	4.3	3.9	7	6.5
Unknown	0.3	0.4	0.3	0.2	0.2	0.3	0.3	7.7	7.5
All	21	19.3	16.6	14.2	7.1	17.6	15.6	7.7	6.8

Maltreatment incidents per 1,000 children ages 0–17 in the estimated U.S. child population.

SOURCE: *Child Maltreatment 1998: Reports From the States to the National Child Abuse and Neglect Data System*, U.S. Department of Health and Human Services, Washington, D.C., 2000

Gender of Victims

Overall in 1998, more female children (17.6 per 1,000) were maltreated than their male counterparts (15.6 per 1,000). Although victimization rates for both genders were about the same for physical abuse, neglect, medical neglect, and psychological or emotional abuse, nearly four times as many females were sexually abused than males (2.3 versus 0.6 per 1,000). (See Table 4.2.)

Race and Ethnicity of Victims

In 1998 black children suffered the highest victimization rate (20.7 per 1,000), followed by American Indians and Alaska Natives (19.8). The victimization rates for Hispanic children (10.6) and whites (8.5) were lower than the national victimization rate of 12.9. Asian and Pacific Island children experienced the lowest rate of victimization: 3.8 per 1,000. (See Figure 4.5.)

PERPETRATORS OF CHILD MALTREATMENT

The law considers as perpetrators those persons who abuse or neglect children under their care. They may be parents, relatives, other household members, or day care providers. In 1998, 16 states reported that nearly 9 of 10 victims (87.1 percent) were maltreated by one or both parents. Relatives of the victims accounted for another 4 percent of perpetrators. (See Figure 4.6.)

FIGURE 4.5

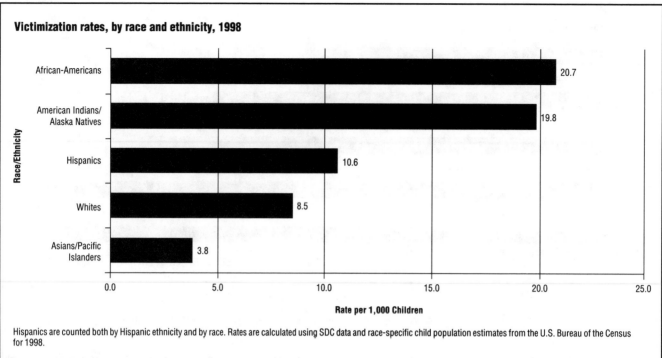

Victimization rates, by race and ethnicity, 1998

Hispanics are counted both by Hispanic ethnicity and by race. Rates are calculated using SDC data and race-specific child population estimates from the U.S. Bureau of the Census for 1998.

SOURCE: *Child Maltreatment 1998: Reports From the States to the National Child Abuse and Neglect Data System*, U.S. Department of Health and Human Services, Washington, D.C., 2000

FIGURE 4.6

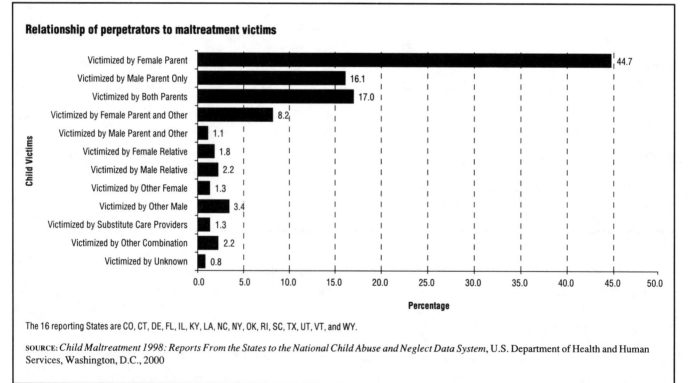

Relationship of perpetrators to maltreatment victims

The 16 reporting States are CO, CT, DE, FL, IL, KY, LA, NC, NY, OK, RI, SC, TX, UT, VT, and WY.

SOURCE: *Child Maltreatment 1998: Reports From the States to the National Child Abuse and Neglect Data System*, U.S. Department of Health and Human Services, Washington, D.C., 2000

Nearly 4 of 5 perpetrators (78.3 percent) were under age 40. Perpetrators were most likely to be female (60.4 percent), and between the ages of 20 and 29 (32 percent) and 30 and 39 (39.6 percent). (See Figure 4.7.)

Female parents acting alone were responsible for more than half of the cases of neglect (52.3 percent) and medical neglect (58.7 percent). On the other hand, 22 percent of sexual abuse was perpetrated by male parents only.

FIGURE 4.7

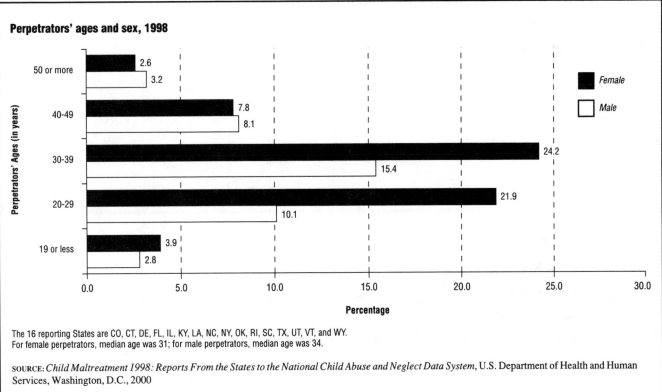

Perpetrators' ages and sex, 1998

The 16 reporting States are CO, CT, DE, FL, IL, KY, LA, NC, NY, OK, RI, SC, TX, UT, VT, and WY.
For female perpetrators, median age was 31; for male perpetrators, median age was 34.

SOURCE: *Child Maltreatment 1998: Reports From the States to the National Child Abuse and Neglect Data System*, U.S. Department of Health and Human Services, Washington, D.C., 2000

Nearly 60 percent of the sexual abuse victims were abused by male parents, male relatives, or other males. Female parents (34.6 percent) were more likely than male parents (26.8 percent) to inflict physical abuse on their children. (See Table 4.3.)

DEATHS FROM CHILD MALTREATMENT

In 1998 an estimated 1,100 deaths from child maltreatment were reported to CPS and other agencies, including coroners' offices and fatality review boards. The national fatality rate was about 1.6 deaths per 100,000 children in the general population.

Experts believe that there were likely more deaths due to child abuse and neglect than were reported to these agencies. The U.S. Advisory Board on Child Abuse and Neglect, in *A Nation's Shame: Fatal Child Abuse and Neglect in the United States* (U.S. Department of Health and Human Services, Washington, D.C., 1995), reported that an estimated 2,000 children (a rate of five children a day) die each year as a result of maltreatment. The National Center for Prosecution of Child Abuse, which provides aid and information to investigators, prosecutors, and professionals working for child maltreatment litigation, believes the number of fatalities to be as high as 5,000.

In 1998 deaths occurred mostly among very young victims of abuse and neglect. Infants younger than a year old comprised 37.9 percent of the fatalities, and children younger than five accounted for three-quarters (77.5 percent) of all deaths. Just 7.3 percent of those who died from child maltreatment were older than 10.

TABLE 4.3

Relationships of perpetrators to child victims by type of maltreatment, 1998

Perpetrators' Relationships to Child Victims	Maltreatment Type			
	Physical Abuse (%)	Neglect (%)	Medical Neglect (%)	Sexual Abuse (%)
Female Parent Only	34.6	52.3	58.7	3.8
Male Parent Only	26.8	12.5	5.9	22.0
Both Parents	14.0	17.1	21.2	12.0
Female Parent and Other	7.6	8.4	8.4	11.2
Male Parent and Other	1.3	1.0	0.9	2.1
Female Relative	2.2	1.9	1.9	1.0
Male Relative	1.8	0.8	0.3	16.8
Other Female	1.7	1.3	0.5	1.2
Other Male	4.6	1.8	0.3	17.1
Substitute Care Provider(s)	1.6	1.1	0.8	2.5
Other Combination	2.8	1.4	0.9	7.6
Unknown	1.0	0.5	0.2	2.6
Total	**100.00**	**100.00**	**100.00**	**100.00**
Count of Victims	**54,649**	**203,986**	**9,789**	**24,598**

The 16 reporting States are CO, CT, DE, FL, IL, KY, LA, NC, NY, OK, RI, SC, TX, UT, VT, and WY.

SOURCE: *Child Maltreatment 1998: Reports From the States to the National Child Abuse and Neglect Data System*, U.S. Department of Health and Human Services, Washington, D.C., 2000

FIGURE 4.8

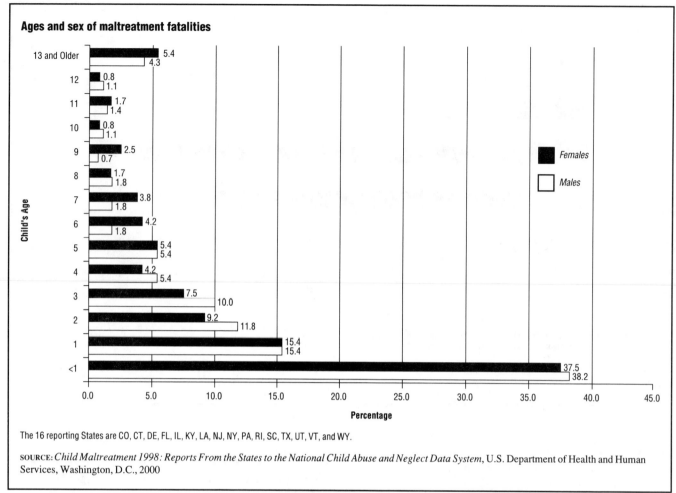

Ages and sex of maltreatment fatalities

The 16 reporting States are CO, CT, DE, FL, IL, KY, LA, NJ, NY, PA, RI, SC, TX, UT, VT, and WY.

SOURCE: *Child Maltreatment 1998: Reports From the States to the National Child Abuse and Neglect Data System*, U.S. Department of Health and Human Services, Washington, D.C., 2000

(See Figure 4.8.) Whereas more male children (53.8 percent) died from maltreatment than did female children (46.2 percent), among those ages 6–9, nearly twice as many females died (63 percent) as did males (37 percent).

More than one-third (36 percent) of child fatalities resulted from a combination of several types of maltreatment. About one-quarter (25.2 percent) of fatalities were related to both physical abuse and neglect. Nearly 3 of 5 deaths were caused by physical abuse (59 percent) and neglect (57.3 percent). (See Table 4.4.) States also provided data on the victims' prior contact with CPS agencies. In 1998 almost one-fifth (18.7 percent) of the victims' families had received family preservation services during the five years before the deaths occurred.

Perpetrators of Fatalities

Child maltreatment researchers have found that persons who commit fatal child abuse are often young adults in their mid-twenties. They have not graduated from high school and live at or below the poverty level. They suffer depression and have difficulty handling stress. In many cases these perpetrators have themselves experienced violence.

In 1998 about 4 of 5 (80.6 percent) maltreatment deaths were inflicted by one or both parents of the victims. Compared with maltreatment perpetrators in general, perpetrators responsible for maltreatment deaths were younger: 62.3 percent were under age 30. The overall proportion of maltreatment perpetrators under age 30 was 38.7 percent. The National Child Abuse and Neglect Data System researchers surmised that fatality victims, who are generally younger than other maltreatment victims, are more likely to have younger parents.

Child Fatality Review Teams

In response to the increasing child maltreatment fatalities, many states have created Child Fatality Review Teams to investigate the deaths and develop solutions to support families in crisis. These teams consist of prosecutors, medical examiners, law enforcement personnel, CPS personnel, health care providers, and others. As of December 1999, 32 states had laws mandating or authorizing the establishment of these teams.

THE THIRD NATIONAL INCIDENCE STUDY (NIS-3)

The *National Incidence Study of Child Abuse and Neglect* (NIS) was a congressionally mandated periodic survey of child maltreatment. The results of the first NIS were published in 1981, and those of NIS-2 in 1988. The most recent NIS, the *Third National Incidence Study of Child Abuse and Neglect* (NIS-3; U.S. Department of Health and Human Services, Washington, D.C.), was published in 1996. NIS-3 differed from the annual *Child Maltreatment* surveys (see above) because NIS-3 findings were based on a nationally representative sample of more than 5,600 professionals in 842 agencies serving 42 counties. NIS-3 included not only child victims investigated by CPS agencies, but also children seen by community institutions (such as day care centers, schools, and hospitals) and other investigating agencies (such as public health departments, police, and courts). In addition, counts were unduplicated, which means that each child was counted only once.

Definition Standards

NIS-3 used two standardized definitions of abuse and neglect:

- Harm Standard—required that an act or omission must have resulted in demonstrable harm in order to be considered as abuse or neglect.

- Endangerment Standard—allowed children who had not yet been harmed by maltreatment to be counted in the estimates of maltreated children if a non-CPS professional considered them to be at risk of harm or if their maltreatment was substantiated or indicated in a CPS investigation.

Incidence of Maltreatment

In 1993, under the Harm Standard, an estimated 1,553,800 children were victims of maltreatment, a 67 percent increase from the NIS-2 estimate (931,000 children) and a 149 percent increase from the NIS-1 estimate (625,100 children). Significant increases occurred for all types of abuse and neglect, as compared with the two earlier NIS surveys. The more than 1.5 million child victims of maltreatment in 1993 reflected a yearly incidence rate of 23.1 per 1,000 children under age 18, or 1 in 43 children. (See Table 4.5.)

TABLE 4.4

Maltreatment fatalities by maltreatment type, 1998

Maltreatment Type	Count of Fatality Victims	Percent of All Victims*
Physical Abuse	307	59.0%
Neglect	298	57.3%
Medical Neglect	46	8.8%
Sexual Abuse	5	1.0%
Psychological Abuse	7	1.3%
Other	48	9.2%
Unknown	23	4.4%
Multiple Types of Maltreatment	187	36.0%
Physical Abuse and Neglect	131	25.2%
Total	**1,052**	

The 16 reporting States are CO, CT, DE, FL, IL, KY, LA, NJ, NY, PA, RI, SC, TX, UT, VT, and WY.

* Sum of percents greater than 100% as victims may be associated with more than one type of maltreatment.

SOURCE: *Child Maltreatment 1998: Reports From the States to the National Child Abuse and Neglect Data System*, U.S. Department of Health and Human Services, Washington, D.C., 2000

TABLE 4.5

National incidence of maltreatment under the Harm Standard in the NIS-3 (1003), and comparison with the NIS-2 (1988) and the NIS-1 (1980) Harm Standard estimates.

Harm Standard Maltreatment Category	NIS-3 Estimates 1993		Comparisons With Earlier Studies					
			NIS-2: 1986			NIS-1: 1980		
	Total No. of Children	Rate per 1,000 Children	Total No. of Children	Rate per 1,000 Children		Total No. of Children	Rate per 1,000 Children	
ALL MALTREATMENT	1,553,800	23.1	931,000	14.8	*	625,100	9.8	*
ABUSE:								
ALL ABUSE	743,200	11.1	507,700	8.1	m	336,600	5.3	*
Physical Abuse	381,700	5.7	269,700	4.3	m	199,100	3.1	*
Sexual Abuse	217,700	3.2	119,200	1.9	*	42,900	0.7	*
Emotional Abuse	204,500	3.0	155,200	2.5	ns	132,700	2.1	m
NEGLECT:								
ALL NEGLECT	879,000	13.1	474,800	7.5	*	315,400	4.9	*
Physical Neglect	338,900	5.0	167,800	2.7	*	103,600	1.6	*
Emotional Neglect	212,800	3.2	49,200	0.8	*	56,900	0.9	*
Educational Neglect	397,300	5.9	284,800	4.5	ns	174,000	2.7	*

* The difference between this and the NIS-3 estimate is significant at or below the p < .05 level.
m The difference between this and the NIS-3 estimate is statistically marginal (i.e., .10 > p > .05).
ns The difference between this and the NIS-3 estimate is neither significant nor marginal (p > .10).
Note: Estimated totals are rounded to the nearest 100.

SOURCE: *The Third National Incidence Study of Child Abuse and Neglect*, National Center on Child Abuse and Neglect, Washington, D.C., 1996

FIGURE 4.9

TABLE 4.6

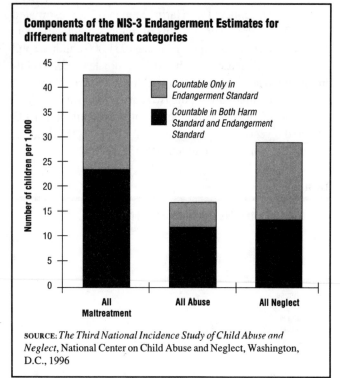

Components of the NIS-3 Endangerment Estimates for different maltreatment categories

Number of children per 1,000

Countable Only in Endangerment Standard

Countable in Both Harm Standard and Endangerment Standard

All Maltreatment — All Abuse — All Neglect

SOURCE: *The Third National Incidence Study of Child Abuse and Neglect*, National Center on Child Abuse and Neglect, Washington, D.C., 1996

National incidence of maltreatment under the Endangerment Standard in the NIS-3 (1993), and comparison with the NIS-2 (1986) Endangerment Standard estimates

Endangerment Standard Maltreatment Category	NIS-3 Estimates 1993		Comparison With NIS-2 1986		
	Total No. of Children	Rate per 1,000 Children	Total No. of Children	Rate per 1,000 Children	
ALL MALTREATMENT	2,815,600	41.9	1,424,400	22.6	*
ABUSE:					
ALL ABUSE	1,221,800	18.2	590,800	9.4	*
Physical Abuse	614,100	9.1	311,500	4.9	*
Sexual Abuse	300,200	4.5	133,600	2.1	*
Emotional Abuse	532,200	7.9	188,100	3.0	*
NEGLECT:					
ALL NEGLECT	1,961,300	29.2	917,200	14.6	*
Physical Neglect	1,335,100	19.9	507,700	8.1	*
Emotional Neglect	584,100	8.7	203,000	3.2	*
Educational Neglect	397,300	5.9	284,800	4.5	ns

* The difference between this estimate and the NIS-3 estimate is significant at or below the p < .05 level.
Note: Estimated totals are rounded to the nearest 100.

SOURCE: *The Third National Incidence Study of Child Abuse and Neglect*, National Center on Child Abuse and Neglect, Washington, D.C., 1996

In 1993, under the Endangerment Standard, an estimated 2,815,600 children experienced some type of maltreatment. This figure nearly doubled the NIS-2 estimate of 1,424,400. As with the Harm Standard, marked increases occurred for all types of abuse and neglect. The incidence rate was 41.9 per 1,000 children under age 18, or 1 in 24 children. (See Table 4.6.)

COMPARISON OF MALTREATMENT ESTIMATES UNDER THE TWO STANDARDS. In 1993 the Endangerment Standard included an additional 1,261,800 children under age 18 (an 81 percent increase) beyond those counted under the stricter Harm Standard. This means that children included under the Harm Standard represented 55 percent of those counted under the Endangerment Standard. Harm Standard children accounted for 61 percent of the Endangerment Standard total of all abused children, and 45 percent of the Endangerment Standard total of all neglected children. (See Figure 4.9.)

Characteristics of Abused Children

GENDER. Under both the Harm and Endangerment Standards, more females were subjected to maltreatment than males. Females were sexually abused about three times more often than males. Males, on the other hand, were more likely to experience physical and emotional neglect under the Endangerment Standard. Under both standards, males suffered more physical and emotional neglect, while females suffered more educational neglect. Males were at a somewhat greater risk of serious injury and death than females. (See Tables 4.7 and 4.8.)

AGE. NIS-3 found a lower incidence of maltreatment among younger children, particularly 0- to 5-year-olds. This may be due to the fact that, prior to reaching school age, children are less observable to community professionals, especially educators—the group most likely to report suspected maltreatment. In addition, NIS-3 noted a disproportionate increase in the incidence of maltreatment among children between the ages of 6 and 14. (See Figures 4.10 and 4.11.) Andrea J. Sedlak and Diane D. Broadhurst, the authors of NIS-3, noted a lower incidence of maltreatment among children older than 14 years. Older children are more likely to escape if the abuse becomes more prevalent or severe. They are also more able to defend themselves and/or fight back.

Under the Harm Standard, only 10 per 1,000 children in the 0–2 age group experienced overall maltreatment. Among those ages six and over, the incidence rate was 22 per 1,000. Under the Endangerment Standard, 26 per 1,000 children ages 0–2 were subjected to overall maltreatment, compared with 44 per 1,000 ages 6–14. Among the oldest age group, ages 15–17, 29.7 per 1,000 children suffered maltreatment of some type. (See Figures 4.10 and 4.11.)

RACE. NIS-3 found no significant differences in race in the incidence of maltreatment. The authors noted that this finding may be somewhat surprising, considering the overrepresentation of black children in the child welfare population and in those served by public agencies. They attributed this lack of race-related difference in maltreatment incidence to the broader

TABLE 4.7

Sex differences in incidence rates per 1,000 children for maltreatment under the Harm Standard in the NIS-3 (1993)

Harm Standard Maltreatment Category	Males	Females	Significance of Difference
ALL MALTREATMENT	21.7	24.5	m
ABUSE:			
All Abuse	9.5	12.6	*
Physical Abuse	5.8	5.6	ns
Sexual Abuse	1.6	4.9	*
Emotional Abuse	2.9	3.1	ns
NEGLECT:			
All Neglect	13.3	12.9	ns
Physical Neglect	5.5	4.5	ns
Emotional Neglect	3.5	2.8	ns
Educational Neglect	5.5	6.4	ns
SEVERITY OF INJURY:			
Fatal	0.04	0.01	ns
Serious	9.3	7.5	m
Moderate	11.3	13.3	ns
Inferred	1.1	3.8	*

* The difference is significant at or below the p < .05 level.
m The difference is statistically marginal (i.e., .10 > p > .05).
ns The difference is neither significant nor marginal (p > .10).

SOURCE: *The Third National Incidence Study of Child Abuse and Neglect*, National Center on Child Abuse and Neglect, Washington, D.C., 1996

TABLE 4.8

Sex differences in incidence rates per 1,000 children for maltreatment under the Endangerment Standard in the NIS-3 (1993)

Endangerment Standard Maltreatment Category	Males	Females	Significance of Difference
ALL MALTREATMENT	40.0	42.3	ns
ABUSE:			
All Abuse	16.1	20.2	*
Physical Abuse	9.3	9.0	ns
Sexual Abuse	2.3	6.8	*
Emotional Abuse	8.0	7.7	ns
NEGLECT:			
All Neglect	29.2	27.6	ns
Physical Neglect	19.7	18.6	ns
Emotional Neglect	9.2	7.8	*
Educational Neglect	5.5	6.4	ns
SEVERITY OF INJURY:			
Fatal	0.04	0.01	ns
Serious	9.4	7.6	m
Moderate	14.1	15.3	ns
Inferred	2.1	4.6	*
Endangered	14.5	14.8	ns

* The difference is significant at or below the p>.05 level.
m The difference is statistically marginal (i.e., .l0>p>.05).
ns The difference is neither significant nor marginal (p>.10).

SOURCE: *The Third National Incidence Study of Child Abuse and Neglect,* National Center on Child Abuse and Neglect, Washington, D.C., 1996

FIGURE 4.10

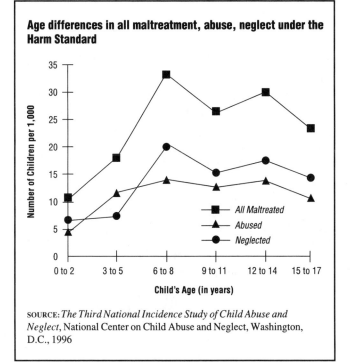

Age differences in all maltreatment, abuse, neglect under the Harm Standard

SOURCE: *The Third National Incidence Study of Child Abuse and Neglect*, National Center on Child Abuse and Neglect, Washington, D.C., 1996

FIGURE 4.11

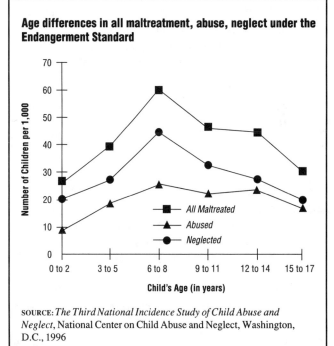

Age differences in all maltreatment, abuse, neglect under the Endangerment Standard

SOURCE: *The Third National Incidence Study of Child Abuse and Neglect*, National Center on Child Abuse and Neglect, Washington, D.C., 1996

range of children identified by NIS-3, compared with the smaller number investigated by public agencies and the even smaller number receiving child protective and other welfare services. NIS-2 also had not found any disproportionate differences in race in relation to maltreatment incidence.

Family Characteristics

FAMILY STRUCTURE. Under the Harm Standard, among children living with single parents, an estimated 27.3 per 1,000 under age 18 suffered some type of maltreatment—almost twice the incidence rate for children

TABLE 4.9

Incidence rates per 1,000 children for maltreatment under the Harm Standard in the NIS-3 (1993) for different family structures

Harm Standard Maltreatment Category	Both Parents	Single Parent Either Mother or Father	Mother only	Father only	Neither Parent	Significance of Differences
ALL MALTREATMENT	15.5	27.3	26.1	36.6	22.9	A, C, D
ABUSE:						
All Abuse	8.4	11.4	10.5	17.7	13.7	D, e
Physical Abuse	3.9	6.9	6.4	10.5	7.0	a, D, e
Sexual Abuse	2.6	2.5	2.5	2.6	6.3	ns
Emotional Abuse	2.6	2.5	2.1	5.7	5.4	ns
NEGLECT:						
All Neglect	7.9	17.3	16.7	21.9	10.3	A, C, D
Physical Neglect	3.1	5.8	5.9	4.7	4.3	A, C
Emotional Neglect	2.3	4.0	3.4	8.8	3.1	a, G
Educational Neglect	3.0	9.6	9.5	10.8	3.1	A, B, f
SEVERITY OF INJURY:						
Fatal	0.019	0.015	0.017	0.005	0.016	ns
Serious	5.8	10.5	10.0	14.0	8.0	A, C
Moderate	8.1	15.4	14.7	20.5	10.1	A
Inferred	1.6	1.4	1.3	2.1	4.8	ns

A Difference between "Both Parents" and "Either Mother or Father" is significant at or below the $p<.05$ level.
a Difference between "Both Parents" and "Either Mother or Father" is statistically marginal (i.e., .10>p>.05).
B Difference between "Either Mother or Father" and "Neither Parent" is significant at or below the $p<.05$ level.
C Difference between "Both Parents" and "Mother only" is significant at or below the $p<.05$ level.
D Difference between "Both Parents" and "Father only" is significant at or below the $p<.05$ level.
e Difference between "Mother only" and "Father only" is statistically marginal (i.e., .10>p>.05).
f Difference between "Mother only" and "Neither Parent" is statistically marginal (i.e., .10>p>.05).
G Difference between "Father only" and "Neither Parent" is significant at or below the $p<.05$ level.
ns No between-group difference is significant or marginal (all p's>.10).

SOURCE: *The Third National Incidence Study of Child Abuse and Neglect,* National Center on Child Abuse and Neglect, Washington, D.C., 1996

living with both parents (15.5 per 1,000). The same rate held true for all types of abuse and neglect. Children living with single parents also had a greater risk of suffering serious injury (10.5 per 1,000) than did those living with both parents (5.8 per 1,000). (See Table 4.9.)

Under the Endangerment Standard, an estimated 52 per 1,000 children living with single parents suffered some type of maltreatment, compared with 26.9 per 1,000 living with both parents. Children in single-parent households were abused at a 45 percent higher rate than those in two-parent households (19.6 versus 13.5 per 1,000) and suffered over twice as much neglect (38.9 versus 17.6 per 1,000). Children living with single parents (10.5 per 1,000) were also more likely to suffer serious injuries than those living with both parents (5.9 per 1,000). (See Table 4.10.)

FAMILY SIZE. The number of children in the family was related to the incidence of maltreatment. Additional children meant additional tasks and responsibilities for the parents; therefore, it followed that the rates of child maltreatment were higher in these families. Among children in families with four or more children, an estimated 34.5 per 1,000 under the Harm Standard and 68.1 per 1,000 under the Endangerment Standard suffered some type of maltreatment (See Figures 4.12 and 4.13.)

Surprisingly, households with only one child had a higher maltreatment incidence rate than did households with 2–3 children (22 versus 17.7 per 1,000 children under the Harm Standard, and 34.2 versus 34.1 per 1,000 children under the Endangerment Standard). (See Figure 4.12 and 4.13.) The authors thought that an only child might have been in a situation where parental expectations were all focused on that one child. Another explanation was that "only" children might have been in households where the parents were just starting a family and were relatively young and inexperienced.

FAMILY INCOME. Family income was significantly related to the incidence rates of child maltreatment. Under the Harm Standard, children in families with annual incomes less than $15,000 had the highest rate of maltreatment (47 per 1,000). The figure is almost twice as high (95.9 per 1,000) using the Endangerment Standard. Children in families earning less than $15,000 annually also sustained more serious injuries. (See Tables 4.11 and 4.12.)

Characteristics of Perpetrators

RELATIONSHIP TO THE CHILD. Most child victims (78 percent) were maltreated by their birth parents. Parents accounted for the maltreatment of 72 percent of physically abused children and 81 percent of emotionally abused children. On the other hand, almost half (46 percent) of sexually abused children were violated by someone other than a parent or parent-substitute. More than a quarter (29 per-

TABLE 4.10

Incidence rates per 1,000 children for maltreatment under the Endangerment Standard in the NIS-3 (1993) for different family structures

Endangerment Standard Maltreatment Category	Both Parents	Single Parent Either Mother or Father	Mother-only	Father-only	Neither Parent	Significance of Differences
ALL MALTREATMENT	26.9	52.0	50. 1	65.6	39.3	A, C, D, G
ABUSE:						
All Abuse	13.5	19.6	18.1	31.0	17.3	a
Physical Abuse	6.5	10.6	9.8	16.5	9.2	d
Sexual Abuse	3.2	4.2	4.3	3.1	6.6	ns
Emotional Abuse	6.2	8.6	7.7	14.6	7.1	ns
NEGLECT:						
All Neglect	17.6	38.9	37.6	47.9	24.1	A, C, D, G
Physical Neglect	10.8	28.6	27.5	36.4	17.1	A, c, D
Emotional Neglect	6.4	10.5	9.7	16.2	8.3	a
Educational Neglect	3.0	9.6	9.5	10.8	3.1	A, B,C, f
SEVERITY OF INJURY:						
Fatal	0.020	0.015	0.017	0.005	0.016	ns
Serious	5.9	10.5	10.0	14.0	8.0	A, C
Moderate	9.6	18.5	17.7	24.8	11.5	A, b
Inferred	2.1	2.5	2.0	6.0	4.7	ns
Endangered	9.3	20.5	20.4	20.7	15.1	A, C

A Difference between "Both Parents" and "Either Mother or Father" is significant at or below the p < .05 level.
a Difference between "Both Parents" and "Either Mother or Father" is statistically marginal (i.e., .10 > p > .05).
B Difference between "Either Mother or Father" and "Neither Parent" is significant at or below the p < .05 level.
b Difference between "Either Mother or Father" and "Neither Parent" is statistically marginal (i.e., .10 > p > .05).
C Difference between "Both Parents" and "Mother only" is significant at or below the p < .05 level.
c Difference between "Both Parents" and "Mother only" is statistically marginal (i.e., .10 > p > .05).
D Difference between "Both Parents" and "Father only" is significant at or below the p < .05 level.
d Difference between "Both Parents" and "Father only" is statistically marginal (i.e., .10 > p > .05)
f Difference between "Mother only" and "Neither Parent" is statistically marginal (i.e., .10 > p > .05).
G Difference between "Father only" and "Neither Parent" is significant at or below the p < .05 level.
ns No between-group difference is significant or marginal (all p's > .10).

SOURCE: *The Third National Incidence Study of Child Abuse and Neglect*, National Center on Child Abuse and Neglect, Washington, D.C., 1996

FIGURE 4.12

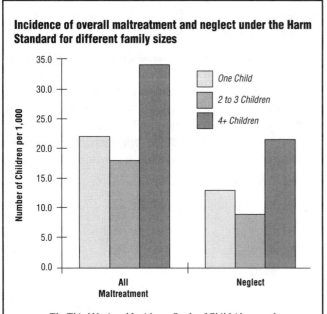

Incidence of overall maltreatment and neglect under the Harm Standard for different family sizes

SOURCE: *The Third National Incidence Study of Child Abuse and Neglect*, National Center on Child Abuse and Neglect, Washington, D.C., 1996

FIGURE 4.13

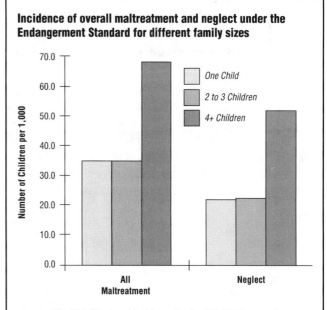

Incidence of overall maltreatment and neglect under the Endangerment Standard for different family sizes

SOURCE: *The Third National Incidence Study of Child Abuse and Neglect*, National Center on Child Abuse and Neglect, Washington, D.C., 1996

TABLE 4.11

Incidence rates per 1,000 children for maltreatment under the Harm Standard in the NIS-3 (1993) for different levels of family income

Harm Standard Maltreatment Category	<$I5K/yr	$15-29K/yr	$30K+/yr	Significance of Differences
ALL MALTREATMENT	47.0	20.0	2.1	a
ABUSE:				
All Abuse	22.2	9.7	1.6	a
Physical Abuse	11.0	5.0	0.7	a
Sexual Abuse	7.0	2.8	0.4	b
Emotional Abuse	6.5	2.5	0.5	b
NEGLECT:				
All Neglect	27.2	11.3	0.6	a
Physical Neglect	12.0	2.9	0.3	a
Emotional Neglect	5.9	4.3	0.2	ns
Educational Neglect	11.1	4.8	0.2	a
SEVERITY OF INJURY:				
Fatal	0.060	0.002	0.001	ns
Serious	17.9	7.8	0.8	a
Moderate	23.3	10.5	1.3	a
Inferred	5.7	1.6	0.1	b

a All between-group differences are significant at or below the p < .05 level.
b The highest income group ($30,000 or more) differs significantly from the others (p's < .05), but the difference between the <$15,000 group and the $15,000 to $29,999 group is statistically marginal (i.e., .10 > p > .05).
ns No between-group difference is significant or marginal (all p's > .10).

SOURCE: *The Third National Incidence Study of Child Abuse and Neglect*, National Center on Child Abuse and Neglect, Washington, D.C., 1996

TABLE 4.12

Incidence rates per 1,000 children for maltreatment under the Endangerment Standard in the NIS-3 (1993) for different levels of family income

Endangerment Standard Maltreatment Category	<$15K/yr	$15-29K/yr	$30K+/yr	Significance of Differences
ALL MALTREATMENT	95.9	33.1	3.8	*
ABUSE:				
All Abuse	37.4	17.5	2.5	*
Physical Abuse	17.6	8.5	1.5	*
Sexual Abuse	9.2	4.2	0.5	*
Emotional Abuse	18.3	8.1	1.0	*
NEGLECT:				
All Neglect	72.3	21.6	1.6	*
Physical Neglect	54.3	12.5	1.1	*
Emotional Neglect	19.0	8.2	0.7	*
Educational Neglect	11.1	4 .8	0.2	*
SEVERITY OF INJURY:				
Fatal	0.060	0.002	0.003	ns
Serious	17.9	7.9	0.8	*
Moderate	29.6	12.1	1.5	*
Inferred	7.8	2.7	0.2	*
Endangered	40.5	10.3	1.3	*

* All between-group differences are significant at or below the p < .05 level.
ns No between-group difference is significant or marginal (all p's > .10).

SOURCE: *The Third National Incidence Study of Child Abuse and Neglect*, National Center on Child Abuse and Neglect, Washington, D.C., 1996

cent) were sexually abused by a birth parent, and 25 percent were sexually abused by a parent-substitute, such as a stepparent or a father's girlfriend. In addition, sexually abused children were more likely to sustain fatal or serious injuries or impairments when birth parents were the perpetrators. (See Table 4.13.) See Chapter 6 for more information on sexual abuse.

PERPETRATORS' GENDERS. Overall, children were somewhat more likely to be maltreated by female perpetrators (65 percent) than by males (54 percent). Among children maltreated by their parents, most (75 percent) were maltreated by their mothers, and almost half (46 percent) were maltreated by their fathers. (Children who were maltreated by both parents were included in both "male" and "female" counts.) Children who were maltreated by other parents and parent-substitutes were more

likely to have been maltreated by a male (85 percent) than by a female (41 percent). Four of five children (80 percent) who were maltreated by other adults were maltreated by males, and only 14 percent were maltreated by other adults who were females. (See Table 4.14. Note that the numbers will not add to 100 percent because many children were maltreated by both parents.)

Neglected children differed from abused children with regard to the gender of the perpetrators. Because mothers or other females tend to be the primary caretakers, children were more likely to suffer all forms of neglect by female perpetrators (87 percent versus 43 percent by male perpetrators). In contrast, children were more often abused by males (67 percent) than by females (40 percent). (See Table 4.14.)

TABLE 4.13

Distribution of perpetrator's relationship to child and severity of harm by the type of maltreatment

Category	Percent Children in Maltreatment Category	Total Maltreated Children	Percent of Children in Row with Injury/Impairment. . .		
			Fatal or Serious	Moderate	Inferred
ABUSE:	100%	743,200	21%	63%	16%
Natural Parents	62%	461,800	22%	73%	4%
Other Parents and Parent/substitutes	19%	144,900	12%	62%	27%
Others	18%	136,600	24%	30%	46%
Physical Abuse	100%	381,700	13%	87%	+
Natural Parents	72%	273,200	13%	87%	+
Other Parents and Parent/substitutes	21%	78,700	13%	87%	+
Others	8%	29,700	*	82%	+
Sexual Abuse	100%	217,700	34%	12%	53%
Natural Parents	29%	63,300	61%	10%	28%
Other Parents and Parent/substitutes	25%	53,800	19%	18%	63%
Others	46%	100,500	26%	11%	63%
Emotional Abuse	100%	204,500	26%	68%	6%
Natural Parents	81%	166,500	27%	70%	2%
Other Parents and Parent/substitutes	13%	27,400	*	57%	24%
Others	5%	10,600	*	*	*
NEGLECT:	100%	879,000	50%	44%	6%
Natural Parents	91%	800,600	51%	43%	6%
Other Parents and Parent/substitutes	9%	78,400	35%	59%	*
Others	^	^	^	^	^
Physical Neglect	100%	338,900	64%	15%	21%
Natural Parents	95%	320,400	64%	16%	20%
Other Parents and Parent/substitutes	5%	18,400	*	*	*
Others	^	^	^	^	^
Emotional Neglect	100%	212,800	97%	3%	+
Natural Parents	91%	194,600	99%	*	+
Other Parents and Parent/substitutes	9%	*	*	*	+
Others	^	^	^	^	+
Educational Neglect	100%	397,300	7%	93%	+
Natural Parents	89%	354,300	8%	92%	+
Other Parents and Parent/substitutes	11%	43,000	*	99%	+
Others	^	^	^	^	+
ALL MALTREATMENT:	100%	1,553,800	36%	53%	11%
Natural Parents	78%	1,208,100	41%	54%	5%
Other Parents and Parent/substitutes	14%	211,200	20%	61%	19%
Others	9%	134,500	24%	30%	46%

+ This severity level not applicable for this form of maltreatment.
* Fewer than 20 cases with which to calculate estimate; estimate too unreliable to be given.
^ These perpetrators were not allowed by countability requirements for cases of neglect.

SOURCE: *The Third National Incidence Study of Child Abuse and Neglect,* National Center on Child Abuse and Neglect, Washington, D.C., 1996

TABLE 4.14

Distribution of perpetrator's gender by type of maltreatment and perpetrator's relationship to child

Category	Percent Children in Maltreatment Category	Total Maltreated Children	Percent of Children in Row with Perpetrator Whose Gender was . . .		
			Male	Female	Unknown
ABUSE:	100%	743,200	67%	40%	*
Natural Parents	62%	461,800	56%	55%	*
Other Parents and Parent/substitutes	19%	144,900	90%	15%	*
Others	18%	136,600	80%	14%	*
Physical Abuse	100%	381,700	58%	50%	*
Natural Parents	72%	273,200	48%	60%	*
Other Parents and Parent/substitutes	21%	78,700	90%	19%	*
Others	8%	29,700	57%	39%	*
Sexual Abuse	100%	217,700	89%	12%	*
Natural Parents	29%	63,300	87%	28%	*
Other Parents and Parent/substitutes	25%	53,800	97%	*	*
Others	46%	100,500	86%	8%	*
Emotional Abuse	100%	204,500	63%	50%	*
Natural Parents	81%	166,500	60%	55%	*
Other Parents and Parent/substitutes	13%	27,400	74%	*	*
Others	5%	10,600	*	*	*
ALL NEGLECT:	100%	879,000	43%	87%	*
Natural Parents	91%	800,600	40%	87%	*
Other Parents and Parent/substitutes	9%	78,400	76%	88%	*
Others	^	^	^	^	^
Physical Neglect	100%	338,900	35%	93%	*
Natural Parents	95%	320,400	34%	93%	*
Other Parents and Parent/substitutes	5%	18,400	*	90%	*
Others	^	^	^	^	^
Emotional Neglect	100%	212,800	47%	77%	*
Natural Parents	91%	194,600	44%	78%	*
Other Parents and Parent/substitutes	9%	18,200	*	*	*
Others	^	^	^	^	^
Educational Neglect	100%	397,300	47%	88%	*
Natural Parents	89%	354,300	43%	86%	*
Other Parents and Parent/substitutes	11%	43,000	82%	100%	*
Others	^	^	^	^	^
ALL MALTREATMENT:	100%	1,553,800	54%	65%	1%
Natural Parents	78%	1,208,100	46%	75%	*
Other Parents and Parent/substitutes	14%	211,200	85%	41%	*
Others	9%	134,500	80%	14%	7%

* Fewer than 20 cases with which to calculate, estimate too unreliable to be given
^ These perpetrators were not allowed by countability requirements for cases of neglect.

SOURCE: *The Third National Incidence Study of Child Abuse and Neglect*, National Center on Child Abuse and Neglect, Washington, D.C., 1996

CHAPTER 5
CAUSES AND EFFECTS OF CHILD ABUSE

Raising a child is not easy. Everyday stresses, strains, and sporadic upheavals in family life, coupled with the normal burdens of child care, cause most parents to feel angry at times. People who would not dream of hitting a colleague or an acquaintance when they are angry may think nothing of hitting their children. Some feel remorse after hitting a loved one; nevertheless, when they are angry, they still resort to violence. The deeper intimacy and greater commitment in a family make emotionally charged disagreements more frequent and more intense.

Murray A. Straus and Richard J. Gelles, experts in child abuse research affiliated with the Family Research Laboratory of the University of New Hampshire, Durham, believe that cultural standards permit violence in the family. The family, which is the center of love and security in most children's lives, is also the place where the child is punished, often physically.

The 1975 and 1985 *National Family Violence* surveys, conducted by Straus and Gelles, are the most complete studies of spousal and parent–child abuse yet prepared in the United States. The major difference between these two surveys and most other surveys discussed in Chapter 4 is that the data from the *National Family Violence* surveys came from detailed interviews with the general population, not from cases that came to the attention of official agencies and professionals. Straus and Gelles had a more intimate knowledge of the families and an awareness of incidences of child abuse that were not reported to the authorities. (Straus and Gelles incorporated research from the *National Family Violence* surveys and additional chapters into the book *Physical Violence in American Families: Risk Factors and Adaptations to Violence in 8,145 Families,* Transaction Publishers, New Brunswick, NJ, 1990; see below.)

CONTRIBUTING FACTORS TO CHILD ABUSE

The factors contributing to child maltreatment are complex. The *Third National Incidence Study of Child Abuse and Neglect* (NIS-3; Andrea J. Sedlak and Diane D. Broadhurst, U.S. Department of Health and Human Services, Washington, D.C., 1996), the most comprehensive federal source of information about the incidence of child maltreatment in the United States, found that family structure and size, poverty, alcohol and substance abuse, domestic violence, and community violence are contributing factors to child abuse and neglect.

Under the Harm Standard of NIS-3, children in single-parent households were at a higher risk of physical abuse and all types of neglect than were children in other family structures. Children living with only their fathers were more likely to suffer the highest incidence rates of physical abuse and emotional and educational neglect. (See Figure 5.1.) Under the Endangerment Standard, higher incidence rates of physical and emotional neglect occurred among children living with only their fathers than among those living in other family structures. (See Figure 5.2.) (See Chapter 4 for more on the NIS-3 Harm and Endangerment Standards and findings related to family structure and income.)

Sedlak and Broadhurst noted that the increase in illicit drug use since the 1986 NIS-2 study may have contributed to the increased child maltreatment incidence reported in NIS-3. Children whose parents are alcohol and substance abusers are at very high risk of abuse and neglect because of the physiological, psychological, and sociological nature of the addiction.

While several factors increase the likelihood of child maltreatment, they do not necessarily lead to abuse. It is important to understand that the causes of child abuse and the characteristics of families in which child abuse occurs are only indicators. The vast majority of parents, even in

FIGURE 5.1

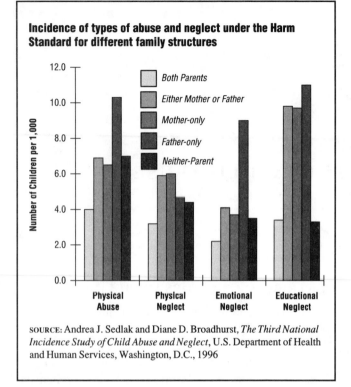

Incidence of types of abuse and neglect under the Harm Standard for different family structures

SOURCE: Andrea J. Sedlak and Diane D. Broadhurst, *The Third National Incidence Study of Child Abuse and Neglect*, U.S. Department of Health and Human Services, Washington, D.C., 1996

FIGURE 5.2

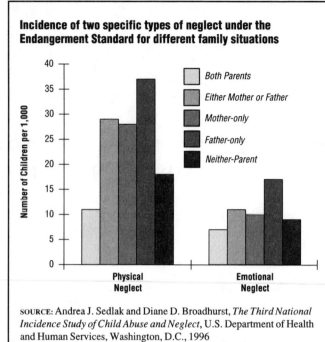

Incidence of two specific types of neglect under the Endangerment Standard for different family situations

SOURCE: Andrea J. Sedlak and Diane D. Broadhurst, *The Third National Incidence Study of Child Abuse and Neglect*, U.S. Department of Health and Human Services, Washington, D.C., 1996

the most stressful and demanding situations, and even with a personal history that might predispose them to be more violent than parents without such a history, do not abuse their children.

Murray A. Straus and Christine Smith noted, in "Family Patterns and Child Abuse" (*Physical Violence in American Families: Risk Factors and Adaptations to Violence in 8,145 Families*), that one cannot simply single out an individual factor as the cause of abuse. The authors found that a combination of several factors is more likely to result in child abuse than is a single factor by itself. Also, the sum of the effects of individual factors taken together does not necessarily add up to what Straus and Smith called the "explosive combinations" of several factors interacting with one another. Nonetheless, even "explosive combinations" do not necessarily lead to child abuse.

Socioeconomic Status

WHICH COMES FIRST—POVERTY OR ABUSE? Candace Kruttschnitt et al., in "The Economic Environment of Child Abuse" (*Social Problems,* Vol. 41, No. 2, 1994), examined the interaction between poverty and abuse and concluded that the relationships between the two are more complicated than previously thought. The researchers found that, generally, poor children were abused more severely than non-poor children and that this prevalence was the result of higher rates of both current poverty and severe abuse in black families.

Blacks were found to be more likely to hit their children with an object such as a belt than were white parents, which categorizes abuse by black parents as more severe. Sociologists have suggested that perhaps blacks are more likely to use an object to beat a child because poor, black, single mothers lack family support, or perhaps a cultural history of slavery has taught them that harsh discipline is necessary for survival. Sociologists also theorize that because more black children live in dangerous neighborhoods, black parents place greater value on conformity and obedience, in an effort to protect their children from outside dangers.

Kruttschnitt et al. also found links between spousal violence and parental criminality, and between poverty and abuse, but it is not clear if the poverty caused the violence and the criminality, or if the reverse was true. Researchers found that children who were repeatedly abused lived in very different circumstances from other children. They were more likely to live in families with a generalized history of violence, which in some cases explains their parents' criminal histories. These children were also more likely to live in families with intergenerational histories of poverty. The authors concluded that poverty is often combined with other factors that cause stress, which, in turn, results in poor parenting. Family violence may be both a cause and a result of poverty and antisocial behavior.

UNEMPLOYMENT AND SOCIOECONOMIC STATUS. The 1975 *National Family Violence Survey* found rates of child abuse that were considerably higher among families suffering from unemployment than among those in which the husband was working full-time. Families in which the husband was not working had a significantly higher rate of child abuse than other families (22.5 versus 13.9 per 100 children). This finding did not recur, however, in the 1985 survey, although wives of unemployed husbands did have a higher rate of abuse than wives of husbands working full-time (16.2 versus 11 per 100 children).

The rate of abuse in the 1985 *National Family Violence Survey* was considerably higher in families in which the husband was a blue-collar worker. Blue-collar fathers committed abuse at a rate of 11.9 per 100 children, compared with 8.9 per 100 children among white-collar workers. The abuse rate for the wives of blue-collar workers was even greater: 13.9 per 100 children versus 8.1 per 100 children among wives of white-collar workers.

Murray A. Straus and Christine Smith, in "Family Patterns and Child Abuse," proposed several factors that contribute to the class differences in the child abuse rate. Blue-collar parents tend to be more authoritarian with their children, are more likely to use physical punishment as a means of child-rearing, and generally have less understanding of child psychology. Blue-collar families are more likely to emphasize conformity and be less permissive. In addition, low-income areas of American cities have much higher rates of violence and are more crowded, increasing stress and setting a pattern of aggressive response to conflicts. Workers in the lower economic class also face greater stress because they often have less control over their employment situation, are more likely to find themselves unemployed, and have fewer resources with which to cope with these problems.

Stress

There are no "vacations" from being a parent, and parenting stress has been associated with abusive behavior. When a parent who may be predisposed toward maltreating a child must deal with a particularly stressful situation, it is possible that little time, energy, or self-control is left for the children. In times of stress the slightest action by the child can be "the last straw" that leads to violent abuse.

Often, when striking out at a child, the parent may be venting anger at his or her own situation rather than reacting to some misbehavior on the part of the child. Abused children have indicated that they never knew when their parents' anger would explode and that they were severely beaten for the most minor infractions. The child may also be hostile and aggressive, contributing to the stress.

Caring for Children with Disabilities

According to the National Clearinghouse on Child Abuse and Neglect Information, in *The Risk and Prevention of Maltreatment of Children with Disabilities* (Wash-

ington, D.C., October 2000), children with disabilities are 1.7 times more likely to suffer maltreatment than children with no disabilities.

The Clearinghouse's review of several studies revealed that children with disabilities are potentially at risk for maltreatment because society treats them as different and less valuable, thus tolerating violence against them. In addition, these children require a lot of special care and attention, and parents may not have the social support to help ease stressful situations. A lack of financial resources further exacerbates the situation.

Some parents may feel disappointment at not having a "normal" child. Others may expect too much and feel frustrated if the child does not live up to their expectations. Children under the care of non-family members are at risk for maltreatment, not only from those caregivers who abuse their power or who feel no bond with them, but from other children, especially in an institutional setting.

Toilet Training

Toilet training can be one of the most frustrating events in the lives of parents and children. Researchers are now linking it to many of the more serious, even deadly, cases of abuse in children between the ages of one and four. Some parents have unrealistic expectations, and when their children are unable to live up to these demands, the parents explode in rage. Parental stress and inability to control emotions play a role in child abuse, but they require a trigger to set off the explosion. Soiled clothes and accidents frequently serve as this trigger.

When children are brought to the emergency room with deep, symmetrical scald burns on their bottoms, health care personnel conclude that they were deliberately immersed and held in hot water. This form of abuse is nearly always committed as the result of a toilet accident. Even a one-second contact with 147-degree water can cause third-degree burns. Some parents think that immersing a child in hot water will make the child go to the bathroom.

Toileting accidents can be especially dangerous for children because the parent has to place his or her hands on the child to clean up the mess, making it easy for the parent's rage to be taken out on the child's body. This abuse is more common among less-educated, low-income mothers who mistakenly believe that children should be trained by 12–16 months of age. Better-educated parents are more likely to be aware that successful training for girls happens at around two years of age and sometimes not until age three or later for boys.

THE VIOLENT FAMILY

Spousal Conflicts

Child abuse is sometimes a reflection of other forms of severe family conflict. Violence in one aspect of family life often flows into other aspects. Parents may have an excessive dependence on physical punishment because they do not know any other way to deal with conflicts. Figure 5.3 illustrates the higher probability of wife assaults among husbands who were subjected to physical punishment as teens and who witnessed violence between their own parents.

Communication is poor among members of violent families. Abusive parents talk to their children less, and when they do, it is often in a negative manner, not in a praising, positive way that builds the self-confidence of the child. They also touch their children less. Some of this behavior is part of the individual parent's character, but much of this type of behavior has been learned from the parent's parents.

Murray A. Straus and Christine Smith, in the 1985 *National Family Violence Survey* ("Family Patterns and Child Abuse"), found that parents who were in constant conflict were also more likely to abuse their children. The researchers measured the level of husband–wife conflict over such issues as money, sex, social activities, housekeeping, and children. The child abuse rate for fathers involved in high marital conflict was 13 per 100 children, compared with 7.4 per 100 children for other men. Mothers in high-conflict relationships reported an even higher child abuse rate: 13.6 per 100 children versus 8 per 100 children among mothers in lower-conflict homes.

Spousal Verbal Aggression and Child Abuse

Husbands and wives sometimes use verbal aggression to deal with their conflicts. The 1985 *National Family Violence Survey* found that spouses who verbally attacked each other were also more likely to abuse their children. Among verbally aggressive husbands, the child abuse rate was 11.2 per 100 children, compared with 4.9 per 100 children for other husbands. Verbally aggressive wives had a child abuse rate of 12.3 per 100 children, compared with 5.3 per 100 children for other wives. The researchers believed that verbal attacks between spouses, rather than clearing the air, tended to mask the reason for the dispute. The resulting additional tension made it even harder to resolve the original source of the conflict.

Spousal Physical Aggression and Child Abuse

In "Family Patterns and Child Abuse," Straus and Smith reported that one of the most distinct findings of the two *National Family Violence* surveys is that violence in one family relationship is frequently associated with violence in other family relationships. In the 1985 survey in families in which the husband struck his wife, the child abuse rate was much higher (22.3 per 100 children) than in other families (8 per 100 children). Similarly, in families in which the wife hit the husband, the child abuse rate was also considerably higher (22.9 per 100 children) than in families in which the wife did not hit the husband (9.2 per 100 children).

FIGURE 5.3

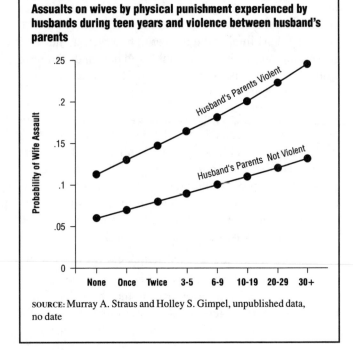

Assaults on wives by physical punishment experienced by husbands during teen years and violence between husband's parents

SOURCE: Murray A. Straus and Holley S. Gimpel, unpublished data, no date

In "Risk of Physical Abuse to Children of Spouse Abusing Parents" (*Child Abuse and Neglect,* Vol. 20, No. 7, January 1996), Susan Ross, who did further research based on the 1985 *National Family Violence Survey,* reported that marital violence is a statistically significant predictor of physical child abuse. Ross noted that the probability of child abuse by a violent husband increases from 5 percent with one act of marital violence to near certainty with 50 or more acts of spousal abuse. The percentages were similar for violent wives.

Ross found that, of those husbands who had been violent with their wives, 22.8 percent had engaged in violence toward their children. Similarly, 23.9 percent of violent wives had engaged in at least one act of physical child abuse. These rates of child abuse were much higher than those of parents who were not violent toward each other (8.5 percent for fathers and 9.8 percent for mothers). In other words, the more frequent the spousal violence, the higher the probability of child abuse.

Verbal Abuse of Children

Parents who verbally abuse their children are also more likely to physically abuse their children. In 1975, respondents to the *National Family Violence Survey* who verbally abused their children reported a child abuse rate six times that of other parents (21 versus 3.6 per 100 children). The 1985 survey found that verbally abusive mothers physically abused their children nearly 10 times more than other mothers (16.3 versus 1.8 per 100 children). Verbally aggressive fathers physically abused their chil-

TABLE 5.1

Public attitudes toward parent behavior (in percentage)

	1999	1998	1997	1996	1995	1994	1993	1992	1991	1990	1989	1988	1987
Question: How often do you think physical punishment of a child leads to injury to the child?													
Very often/often	34%	30%	32%	33%	32%	38%	38%	36%	31%	35%	35%	33%	40%
Occasionally	33	35	36	37	36	34	35	38	44	37	35	38	31
Hardly ever/never	18	19	18	23	22	22	20	20	18	19	21	23	24
Not sure	9	9	7	7	10	6	7	6	7	9	8	6	5
Question: How often do you think repeated yelling and swearing leads to long-term emotional problems for the child?													
Very often/often	74%	75%	76%	78%	75%	74%	79%	74%	75%	76%	73%	71%	73%
Occasionally	15	14	15	14	16	17	14	17	18	15	18	18	17
Hardly ever/never	5	5	4	7	6	7	5	7	5	6	6	8	7
Not sure	3	3	2	2	3	2	2	2	2	3	2	2	2
Number of respondents	*1250*	*1250*	*1253*	*1274*	*1263*	*1250*	*1250*	*1250*	*1250*	*1250*	*1250*	*1250*	*1250*

SOURCE: Deborah Daro, *Public Opinion and Behaviors Regarding Child Abuse Prevention: 1999 Survey,* Prevent Child Abuse America, Chicago, IL, November 1999

dren three and a half times as much as other fathers (14.3 versus 4.2 per 100 children).

TRENDS IN USE OF VERBAL ABUSE. Prevent Child Abuse America (PCA America) recently surveyed American parents regarding their use of verbal abuse (Deborah Daro, *Public Opinion and Behaviors Regarding Child Abuse Prevention: 1999 Survey,* Chicago, November 1999). The proportion of parents who reported having verbally abused (insulted or sworn at) their children in the last year had declined, from 53 percent in 1988 to 38 percent in 1999. Since 1997 PCA America has asked parents about their failure to meet their children's emotional needs in the past year. The percentage of parents (about half of the respondents) who reported doing so has remained the same.

ATTITUDES TOWARD THE USE OF VERBAL ABUSE. Through the years 1987–99, the majority (71–79 percent) of the respondents to PCA America's survey believed that repeated yelling and swearing leads to long-term emotional problems for the child. In 1999 three-quarters (74 percent) of the American public believed that repeated yelling and swearing very often or often emotionally harms a child, while just 5 percent thought such parental behavior is rarely or never harmful to a child's emotional well-being. (See Table 5.1.)

WOMAN BATTERING AND CHILD MALTREATMENT

Some experts believe that a link exists between woman battering and child maltreatment. According to the National Clearinghouse on Child Abuse and Neglect

Information (*In Harm's Way: Domestic Violence and Child Maltreatment,* Washington, D.C., undated), published studies have shown that there is a 30–60 percent overlap between violence against children and violence against women in the same families. (See Figure 5.4.)

Child Witnesses to Domestic Violence

The Department of Justice's *National Crime Victimization Survey* showed that, in 1993, women were physically attacked by intimate partners at an annual rate of 9.3 per 1,000 women and that children under age 12 lived in about half of those households. Findings by the National Institute of Justice's Spousal Assault Replication Program (SARP) further revealed that more than twice as many children were present in homes with domestic violence than in comparable homes in the general population. For example, in Milwaukee, Wisconsin, 8 of 10 (81 percent)

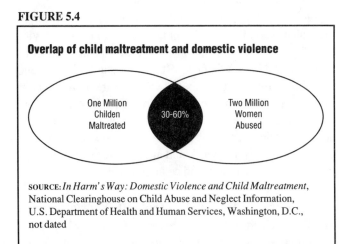

FIGURE 5.4

Overlap of child maltreatment and domestic violence

SOURCE: *In Harm's Way: Domestic Violence and Child Maltreatment,* National Clearinghouse on Child Abuse and Neglect Information, U.S. Department of Health and Human Services, Washington, D.C., not dated

of SARP households had children present, compared with just 3 of 10 (32 percent) comparison households.

Exposure to Domestic Violence and Experiencing Child Maltreatment

The Administration for Children and Families of the U.S. Department of Health and Human Services has found that children whose mothers experience partner battery are twice as likely to be abused as are children whose mothers are not victims of abuse. In addition, children who witness violence at home exhibit many of the symptoms suffered by children who are directly abused (see below). According to the Advisory Board on Child Abuse and Neglect (*A Nation's Shame: Fatal Child Abuse and Neglect in the United States,* U.S. Department of Health and Human Services, Washington, D.C., 1995), domestic violence is the single most frequent precursor to child abuse and neglect deaths in the United States.

Azmaira Hamid Maker, Markus Kemmelmeier, and Christopher Peterson, in "Long-Term Psychological Consequences in Women of Witnessing Parental Physical Conflict and Experiencing Abuse in Childhood" (*Journal of Interpersonal Violence,* Vol. 13, No. 5, October 1998), found that in distressed families, child witnesses to physical violence between parents experienced other childhood risk factors. In a survey of community college women ages 18–43, child maltreatment—specifically sexual abuse and physical abuse—were found to have coexisted with domestic violence.

Women who had witnessed parental violence as children reported being involved in violent dating relationships, both as victims and perpetrators. Witnesses of severe parental violence not only were victims of violence by their dating partners but also exhibited violence toward their dating partners. The risk factors of childhood maltreatment that coexisted with parental violence also accounted for long-term psychological problems, such as depression, antisocial behaviors, and trauma symptoms.

Effects of Domestic Violence on Children

According to John W. Fantuzzo and Wanda K. Mohr, in "Prevalence and Effects of Child Exposure to Domestic Violence" (*The Future of Children: Domestic Violence and Children,* Vol. 9, No. 3, Winter 1999), various studies have found that child witnesses to domestic violence are more likely to exhibit aggression and behavior problems. These children experience internalizing behaviors, including depression, anxiety, suicidal tendencies, and low self-esteem. They have problems with schoolwork and attain lower scores in tests that gauge verbal, motor, and cognitive skills.

Child Protective Services and Domestic Violence

When child protective services (CPS) workers have been involved with children who have witnessed domestic violence, their main concern has been the interests of the children. Critics have charged that CPS further penalizes battered women by taking their children from them when their partners have abused the children. Jeffrey L. Edleson, in "The Overlap Between Child Maltreatment and Woman Battering" (*Violence against Women,* Vol. 5, No. 2, February 1999), observed that, ironically, in child maltreatment reports, CPS records often just list the mother's name and the steps mothers should take to ensure their children's safety. Abusive males are "invisible" in CPS caseload data.

ABUSIVE MOTHERS

Straus and Smith, in "Family Patterns and Child Abuse," found that women are as likely, if not more likely, as men to abuse their children. The authors believed child abuse by women could be explained in terms of social factors rather than psychological factors. Women are more likely to abuse their children because they are more likely to have much greater responsibility for raising the children, which means that they are more exposed to the trials and frustrations of child-rearing.

Women spend more "time at risk" while tending to their children. "Time at risk" refers to the time a potential abuser spends with the victim. This would apply to any form of domestic violence, such as wife abuse and elder abuse. For example, elderly people are more likely to experience abuse from each other, not from a caregiver, if one is present. This is not because elderly couples are more violent than caregivers, but because they spend more time with each other.

To illustrate the "time at risk" factor, the authors noted the reduction in the difference in child abuse rates of mothers and fathers between the 1975 and 1985 *National Family Violence* surveys. Since fathers had taken on some responsibility for child care between these time periods, men and women had shared more equally in the "time at risk" spent with the children.

The researchers believed two other factors may contribute to the problem of high abuse rates among mothers. Generally the mother is blamed if the child misbehaves or does not do as well as expected. Since all children misbehave at some time or other, and since standards of children's accomplishments are sometimes not clear, almost all mothers may feel anxious about their roles.

Working Mothers and Stay-at-Home Mothers

A third factor that may predispose mothers to abuse their children is related to the roles society has imposed on women—that of caretakers and homemakers, roles that some women may resent. Straus and Smith advanced two theories regarding this factor. Although many more women are working outside the home than a generation ago, the attitudes among many families toward who is responsible for the children have not changed. Consequently, the working mother comes home to most of the responsibility for raising the children and maintaining the household, even though she may be just as physically, emotionally, and mentally exhausted from a day at work as is her husband. The woman may, as a result, be more vulnerable to losing control of herself when the children frustrate her.

Straus and Smith noted that, on the other hand, more women working outside of the home might instead have contributed to the decrease in the incidence of abuse between the 1975 and 1985 surveys. Mothers who work outside the home spend less "time at risk" because they are exposed to the children for less time and, therefore, have fewer opportunities for abusive confrontations. Furthermore, they can often escape the stress and frustrations that sometimes accompany child-rearing. The decrease in the abuse rate may reflect social changes: women who do not want to be homemakers no longer feel society's pressure to stay home with the children, while women who are full-time homemakers are usually there by choice.

The 1975 and 1985 *National Family Violence* surveys confirmed this second theory. The 1975 survey found that full-time homemakers had a considerably higher rate of child abuse (15.7 per 100 children) than did mothers with jobs outside the home (10.3 per 100 children). This latter rate was virtually the same as that for men (10.1 per 100 children). In the 1985 survey (by which time, in theory, women who did not want to be full-time homemakers had jobs), the child abuse rate among homemakers had dropped sharply to 11 per 100 children, almost the same rate as that for mothers with jobs outside the home (10.3 per 100 children). The authors surmised that earning a salary might have increased women's self-esteem and their power in the family.

SIBLING ABUSE

Vernon R. Wiehe, in "Sibling Abuse" (*Understanding Family Violence,* Sage Publications, Thousand Oaks, CA, 1998), claimed that abusive behavior between brothers and sisters is often considered sibling rivalry and is therefore not covered under mandatory reporting of abuse. The author conducted a nationwide survey of survivors of sibling abuse who had sought professional counseling for problems resulting from physical, emotional, and sexual abuse by a brother or sister.

The respondents were generally victims of more than one type of abuse: 71 percent reported being physically, emotionally, and sexually abused. An additional 7 percent indicated being just emotionally abused, pushing the total of emotionally abused victims to 78 percent. Emotional

abuse took the forms of "name-calling, ridicule, degradation, exacerbating a fear, destroying personal possessions, and torturing or destroying a pet."

As far as the victims of sibling incest could remember, they were sexually abused at ages five to seven. However, the author believed it was possible that the abuse started at an earlier age. The perpetrator was often an older sibling, from three to ten years older. The incest generally occurred over an extended period of time. (See Chapter 6 for more on sexual abuse.)

CHILDHOOD MALTREATMENT, DELINQUENCY, AND CRIMINAL BEHAVIOR

Consequences during Adolescence

The Office of Juvenile Justice and Delinquency Prevention of the U.S. Department of Justice, in "In the Wake of Childhood Maltreatment" (Barbara Tatem Kelley, Terence P. Thornberry, and Carolyn A. Smith, *Juvenile Justice Bulletin,* Washington, D.C., 1997), studied the relationship between childhood maltreatment and subsequent adolescent problem behaviors. The *Rochester Youth Development Study* included a sample of 1,000 seventh- and eighth-graders from Rochester, New York, public schools. The longitudinal study was conducted until the students were in grades 11 and 12.

DEMOGRAPHIC CHARACTERISTICS. Substantiated child maltreatment was reported for 14 percent of the students. While no significant differences were reported in the prevalence of maltreatment by sex or race, the youth's socioeconomic status had a bearing on the prevalence of maltreatment—20 percent of the children from disadvantaged families had been maltreated, compared with 8 percent of those from non-disadvantaged families. (A disadvantaged family was described as one in which the main wage earner was unemployed, welfare was received, or income was below the poverty level.) A marked difference in the prevalence of maltreatment involved the family structure: only 3 percent of the children who lived with both biological parents had been maltreated, while 19 percent of those in other family structures were victims of maltreatment. (See Table 5.2.)

DELINQUENCY. The Rochester researchers measured the prevalence of delinquency by examining official police records and self-reported offenses. Self-reported delinquency was determined during face-to-face interviews with the children at intervals of six months, for a total of seven interviews, using the questions in Table 5.3. Figure 5.5 illustrates the relationship between childhood maltreatment and later delinquency.

OTHER NEGATIVE OUTCOMES. The *Rochester Youth Development Study* also measured other negative outcomes during adolescence as a result of childhood maltreatment (see Figure 5.6):

TABLE 5.2

Prevalence of reported maltreatment prior to age 12 by demographic characteristics

	Reported Maltreatment	No Maltreatment
Total Sample	**14%**	**86%**
Demographic Characteristics		
Sex		
Male	13%	87%
Female	14%	86%
Race		
White	16%	84%
African American	14%	86%
Hispanic	9%	91%
Disadvantaged Family		
Yes	20%	80%
No	8%	92%
Family Structure		
Two Biological Parents	3%	97%
Other Family Structures	19%	81%

SOURCE: Barbara Tatem Kelley et al., *In the Wake of Childhood Maltreatment*, OJJDP Juvenile Justice Bulletin, August 1997

- Pregnancy—there was no difference between the maltreated and non-maltreated boys in the rates of impregnating a female. However, maltreated girls (52 percent) were more likely than non-maltreated girls (34 percent) to get pregnant.

- Drug use—the risk of drug use was about one-third higher among maltreated youth (43 percent), compared with non-maltreated youth (32 percent).

- Low academic achievement—a lower GPA (grade point average) during middle school or junior high school was evident in 33 percent of maltreated youth, compared with 23 percent of those who had no history of maltreatment. The researchers found that students performing poorly in middle school are considered to be at an increased risk for continued academic failure in high school, low educational aspirations, school dropout, and reduced educational and economic opportunities.

TABLE 5.3

Interview items for self-reported delinquency indexes

Since we interviewed you last time, have you . . .	Minor Delinquency	Moderate Delinquency	Serious Delinquency	Violent Delinquency
1. Carried a hidden weapon?				
2. Been loud or rowdy in a public place where someone complained and you got in trouble?	X			
3. Been drunk in a public place?		X		
4. Damaged, destroyed, marked up, or tagged somebody else's property on purpose?		X		
5. Set fire or tried to set fire to a house, building, or car on purpose?				
6. Gone into or tried to go into a building to steal or damage something?			X	
7. Tried to steal or actually stolen money or things worth $5 or less?	X			
8. Tried to steal or actually stolen money or things worth $5-$50?		X		
9. Tried to steal or actually stolen money or things worth $50-$100?			X	
10. Tried to steal or actually stolen money or things worth more than $100?			X	
11. Tried to buy or sell things that were stolen?				
12. Taken someone else's car or motorcycle for a ride without the owner's permission?		X		
13. Stolen or tried to steal a car or other motor vehicle?			X	
14. Forged a check or used fake money to pay for something?		X		
15. Used or tried to use a credit card, bank card, or automatic teller card without permission?		X		
16. Tried to cheat someone by selling them something that was not what you said it was or that was worthless?				
17. Attacked someone with a weapon or with the idea of seriously hurting or killing them?			X	X
18. Hit someone with the idea of hurting them?		X		X
19. Been involved in gang or posse fights?			X	X
20. Thrown objects such as rocks or bottles at people?		X		X
21. Used a weapon or force to make someone give you money or things?			X	X
22. Made obscene phone calls?		X		
23. Been paid for having sexual relations with someone?				
24. Physically hurt or threatened to hurt someone to get them to have sex with you?			X	X
25. Sold marijuana/reefer/pot?				
26. Sold hard drugs such as crack, heroin, cocaine, or LSD/acid?				
Total Number of Items	**2**	**9**	**8**	**6**

SOURCE: Barbara Tatem Kelley et al., *In the Wake of Childhood Maltreatment*, OJJDP Juvenile Justice Bulletin, August 1997

FIGURE 5.5

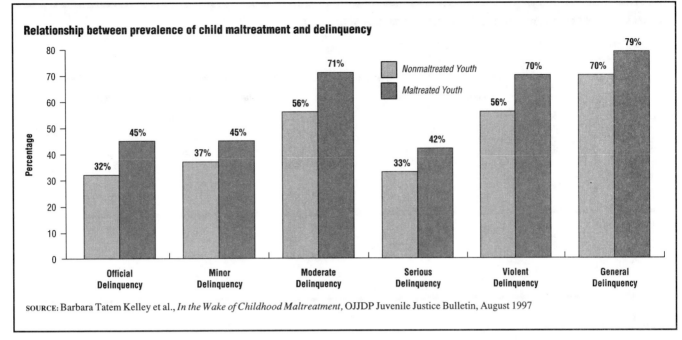

Relationship between prevalence of child maltreatment and delinquency

SOURCE: Barbara Tatem Kelley et al., *In the Wake of Childhood Maltreatment*, OJJDP Juvenile Justice Bulletin, August 1997

FIGURE 5.6

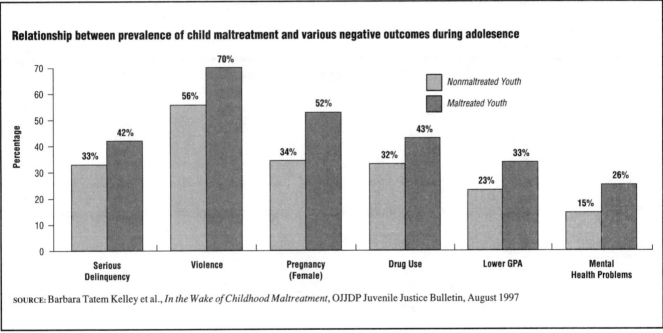

Relationship between prevalence of child maltreatment and various negative outcomes during adolesence

SOURCE: Barbara Tatem Kelley et al., *In the Wake of Childhood Maltreatment*, OJJDP Juvenile Justice Bulletin, August 1997

• Mental health problems—26 percent of childhood maltreatment victims, compared with 15 percent of non-maltreated youth exhibited externalized conduct problems (aggression, hostility, hyperactivity) and internalized problems (social isolation, anxiety, physical distress).

Inmates Report Childhood Abuse

A Bureau of Justice Statistics study (Caroline Wolf Harlow, *Prior Abuse Reported by Inmates and Probationers*, U.S. Department of Justice, Washington, D.C., 1999) found that male inmates and probationers who reported abuse generally had been 17 years old or younger when they experienced the abuse. Their female counterparts reported being abused both as children and as adults. Between 5.8 and 14.4 percent of male offenders and between 23 and 36.7 percent of female offenders reported having been physically or sexually abused before age 18. (See Table 5.4.)

Among state prisoners with past or current violent offenses, 70.4 percent of those who had experienced abuse, compared with 60.2 percent of the non-abused,

TABLE 5.4

Physical or sexual abuse before admission, by sex of inmate of probationer

Before admission	State inmates		Federal inmates		Jail inmates		Probationers	
	Male	Female	Male	Female	Male	Female	Male	Female
Ever abused	16.1%	57.2%	7.2%	39.9%	12.9%	47.6%	9.3%	40.4%
Physically[a]	13.4	46.5	6.0	32.3	10.7	37.3	7.4	33.5
Sexually[a]	5.8	39.0	2.2	22.8	5.6	37.2	4.1	25.2
Both	3.0	28.0	1.1	15.1	3.3	26.9	2.1	18.3
Age of victim at time of abuse								
17 or younger[b]	14.4%	36.7%	5.8%	23.0%	11.9%	36.6%	8.8%	28.2%
18 or older[b]	4.3	45.0	2.7	31.0	2.3	26.7	1.1	24.7
Both	2.5	24.7	1.3	14.2	1.3	15.8	0.5	12.5
Age of abuser								
Adult	15.0%	55.8%	6.9%	39.0%	12.1%	46.0%	8.5%	39.2%
Juvenile only	0.9	1.0	0.2	0.3	0.8	1.3	0.6	
Rape before admission	4.0%	37.3%	1.4%	21.4%	3.9%	33.1%	—	—
Completed	3.1	32.8	1.0	17.9	3.0	26.6	—	—
Attempted	0.8	4.3	0.3	3.2	0.7	5.6	—	—

—Not available.
[a] Includes those both physically and sexually abused.
[b] Includes those abused in both age categories.

SOURCE: Caroline Wolf Harlow, *Prior Abuse Reported by Inmates and Probationers,* Bureau of Justice Statistics, U.S. Department of Justice, Washington, D.C., 1999

TABLE 5.5

Current and past violent offenses and past alcohol and drug use, by whether abused before admission to State prison, 1997

	Percent of State prison inmates					
Offense history and drug and alcohol use	Reported being abused			Reported being not abused		
	Total	Males	Females	Total	Males	Females
Current or past violent offense	70.4%	76.5%	45.0%	60.2%	61.2%	29.1%
Current violent offense	55.7%	61.0%	33.5%	45.3%	46.1%	20.9%
Homicide	15.9	16.3	13.9	12.7	12.8	7.3
Sexual assault	15.6	18.8	2.0	6.9	7.1	0.4
Robbery	12.5	13.5	7.8	14.5	14.7	6.1
Assault	9.5	9.9	7.6	9.3	9.4	5.7
Used an illegal drug						
Ever	88.6%	88.5%	88.9%	81.8%	81.9%	77.4%
Ever regularly	76.3	75.5	79.7	67.9	67.9	65.0
In month before offense	61.4	59.7	68.6	55.3	55.3	54.0
At time of offense	39.6	38.0	46.2	30.7	30.7	32.0
Drank alcohol						
Ever regularly	66.9%	69.1%	57.5%	59.0%	59.8%	38.2%
At time of offense	41.6	43.6	33.1	36.1	36.6	23.5

SOURCE: Caroline Wolf Harlow, *Prior Abuse Reported by Inmates and Probationers,* Bureau of Justice Statistics, U.S. Department of Justice, Washington, D.C., 1999

reported serving at least one sentence for a violent crime. More than three-quarters (76.5 percent) of abused male inmates were serving at least one sentence for a violent crime, compared with 61.2 percent of male offenders with no history of abuse. Almost half (45 percent) of abused female inmates were in prison for at least one violent crime, compared with 29.1 percent of

females who experienced no childhood maltreatment. (See Table 5.5.)

The study found that a history of past abuse was associated with the commission of sexual assault and homicide, illegal drug use, and alcohol use. Nearly 76 percent of abused males and 79.7 percent of abused females had used drugs regularly. Among the non-abused correctional population, a lower proportion of men (67.9 percent) and women (65 percent) had used drugs regularly. Approximately 69 percent of abused male inmates and 57.5 percent of abused female inmates had used alcohol regularly at some time in their lives, compared with 59.8 percent of non-abused male inmates and 38.2 percent of non-abused female inmates. (See Table 5.5.)

Maltreated Girls Who Become Offenders

Researcher Cathy Spatz Widom studied a group of girls who had experienced neglect and physical and sexual abuse from ages 0–11 through young adulthood ("Childhood Victimization and the Derailment of Girls and Women to the Criminal Justice System," *Research on Women and Girls in the Justice System,* U.S. Department of Justice, Washington, D.C., September 2000). The researcher found that abused and neglected girls were almost twice as likely to have been arrested as juveniles (20 percent, compared with 11.4 percent of a matched control group of non-abused girls) and twice as likely as the control group to be arrested as adults (28.5 versus 15.9 percent). Additionally, the maltreated girls were also more than twice as likely (8.2 percent) as the non-maltreated girls (3.6 percent) to have been arrested for violent crimes. Widom, however, noted that although abused and neglected girls were at increased risk for criminal behavior, about 70 percent of the maltreated girls did not become criminals.

Abused and neglected girls who committed status offenses as minors tended to be arrested as adults (49 percent, compared with 36 percent of the non-abused girls). Status offenses are acts that are illegal only when committed by minors: for example, drinking alcohol, skipping school, or violating curfews.

Widom, together with Peter Lambert and Daniel Nagin, found that 8 percent of the maltreated girls developed antisocial and criminal lifestyles that carried over to adulthood (*Does Childhood Victimization Alter Developmental Trajectories of Criminal Careers;* paper presented at the American Society of Criminology, Washington, D.C., November 1998). Among this group, nearly 2 of 5 (38 percent) had been arrested for status offenses as juveniles, but a larger percentage had been arrested for violence (46 percent) and property crimes (54 percent). Another third (32 percent) had been arrested for drug crimes. None of the girls in the control group exhibited these tendencies.

CORPORAL PUNISHMENT

In the United States, hitting a child with "reasonable force" for purposes of discipline is not considered criminal assault. The states define corporal punishment as "the use of physical force with the intention of causing a child to experience pain, but not injury, for the purpose of cor-

TABLE 5.6

Do you approve or disapprove of spanking children?

| | Spanking—Trend | | |
	Approve	Disapprove	No opinion
1997			
National adults	65%	32	3
All parents	66%	31	3
1990			
National adults	65%	25	10
1946			
All parents	74%	24	2

SOURCE: *The Gallup Poll Monthly,* March 1997

rection or control of the child's behavior." This means that objects such as belts may be used as long as the child does not suffer injury. When states passed child abuse laws in the 1960s, provisions allowing parents to use corporal punishment helped facilitate passage of the legislation.

As of December 2000, 23 states allowed corporal punishment in public schools. In August 2000 the Committee on School Health of the American Academy of Pediatrics released its policy statement advocating the abolition of corporal punishment in all schools in the United States (*Pediatrics,* Vol. 106, No. 2). The Committee claims that each year corporal punishment is administered one million to two million times in the nation's schools. In Europe, nine countries prohibit corporal punishment both in the home and in school: Austria, Croatia, Cyprus, Denmark, Finland, Italy, Latvia, Norway, and Sweden.

Past Widespread Acceptance

The 1985 *National Family Violence Survey* found that over 90 percent of parents of children 3–4 years old used some form of corporal punishment, ranging from a slap on the hand to severe spanking. While spanking generally decreased as the child got older, 48 percent of 13-year-olds were still being physically punished.

In 1997 the Gallup Organization found that 65 percent of the general public and 66 percent of parents approved of spanking children. This proportion was the same as that for the 1990 survey. In a Gallup Poll from 1946, 74 percent of parents had approved of corporal punishment. (See Table 5.6.) In 1997 about 4 in 5 of all respondents (81–82 percent) indicated that they had been spanked as a child, about the same percentage (84 percent) as those who said so in 1947. (See Table 5.7.)

Decreasing Use of Physical Punishment

Since 1988 Prevent Child Abuse America (PCA America) has surveyed American parents regarding their use of physical punishment (Deborah Daro, *Public Opin-*

TABLE 5.7

Were you spanked as a child?

	Spanked as Child-Trend		
	Yes	No	No opinion
1997			
National adults	81%	18	1
All parents	82%	17	1
1947			
All parents	84%	15	1

SOURCE: The Gallup Poll Monthly, March 1997

FIGURE 5.7

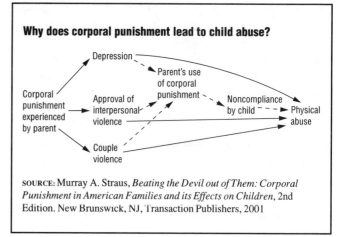

Why does corporal punishment lead to child abuse?

SOURCE: Murray A. Straus, *Beating the Devil out of Them: Corporal Punishment in American Families and its Effects on Children*, 2nd Edition. New Brunswick, NJ, Transaction Publishers, 2001

ion and Behaviors Regarding Child Abuse Prevention: 1999 Survey,* Chicago, November 1999). In 1999, 2 of 5 parents (41 percent) reported having spanked or hit their children during the last year. In comparison, in 1988, 3 of 5 parents (62 percent) indicated having disciplined their children this way.

Public Attitudes Regarding Corporal Punishment

Since 1987 the proportion of the American public surveyed by PCA America who thought physical punishment (for example, hitting or spanking) of a child very often or often harms the child has remained stable, at between 30 and 40 percent. In 1999, one-third (34 percent) believed physical punishment very often or often causes injury to a child. Another third (33 percent) thought physical punishment occasionally hurts a child. Just 18 percent felt that physical punishment hardly ever or never leads to injury to a child. (See Table 5.1.) Parents with children under age 18 tended to consider physical punishment as harmful to children (35 percent versus 33 percent of those with no children).

Corporal Punishment Increases the Risk of Physical Abuse

Murray A. Straus presented a model called "path analysis" to illustrate how physical punishment could escalate to physical abuse ("Physical Abuse," Chapter 6 in *Beating the Devil out of Them: Corporal Punishment in American Families and Its Effects on Children,* 2nd Edition, Transaction Publishers, New Brunswick, NJ, 2001). Straus theorizes that parents who have been physically disciplined as adolescents are more likely to believe that it is acceptable to use violence to remedy a misbehavior. These parents tend to be depressed and to be involved in spousal violence. When a parent resorts to physical punishment and the child does not comply, the parent increases the severity of the punishment, eventually harming the child. (See Figure 5.7.)

Corporal punishment experienced in adolescence produces the same effect on males and females. Parents who

were hit 30 or more times as adolescents were three times (24 percent) as likely as those who never received physical punishment (7 percent) to physically abuse their children. (See Figure 5.8.) Straus noted that his model also shows that three-quarters (76 percent) of parents who were hit many times (30 or more) as adolescents did not, in turn, abuse their children. He further pointed out that 8 percent of those parents who were not disciplined physically as adolescents ended up physically abusing their children.

Prevalence and Chronicity of Corporal Punishment

Murray A. Straus and Julie H. Stewart, in *Corporal Punishment by American Parents: National Data on Prevalence, Chronicity, Severity, and Duration, in Relation to Child and Family Characteristics* (Family Research Laboratory, University of New Hampshire, Durham, NH; a paper presented at the 14th World Congress of Sociology, Montreal, Canada, 1998), reported on a national survey of American parents regarding their use of corporal punishment.

Overall, based on the chronological age of the children, over a third (35 percent) of parents surveyed used corporal punishment on their infants, reaching a peak of 94 percent of parents hitting their children who were three and four years old. The prevalence rate of parents hitting their children decreased after age five, with just over 50 percent of parents hitting their children at age 12, one-third (33 percent) at age 14, and 13 percent at age 17. (See Figure 5.9.) The survey also found that corporal punishment was more prevalent among blacks and parents in the low socioeconomic level. It was also more commonly inflicted on boys, by mothers, and in the South.

Chronicity refers to the frequency of the infliction of corporal punishment during the year. Corporal punishment was most frequently used by parents of two-year-olds, averaging 18 times a year. After age two, chronicity declined, averaging six times a year for teenagers. (See Figure 5.10.)

FIGURE 5.8

FIGURE 5.9

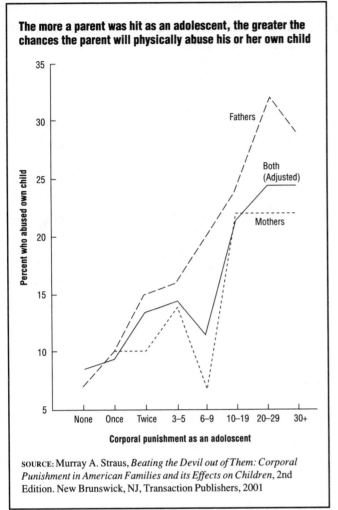

The more a parent was hit as an adoloscent, the greater the chances the parent will physically abuse his or her own child

SOURCE: Murray A. Straus, *Beating the Devil out of Them: Corporal Punishment in American Families and its Effects on Children*, 2nd Edition. New Brunswick, NJ, Transaction Publishers, 2001

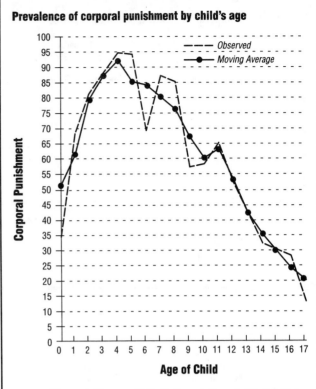

Prevalence of corporal punishment by child's age

SOURCE: Murray A. Straus and Julie H. Stewart, *Corporal Punishment by American Parents: National Data on Prevalence, Chronicity, Severity, and Duration, in Relation to Child and Family Characteristics,* Family Research Laboratory, University of New Hampshire. Durham, NH, 1998

Corporal Punishment and Antisocial Behavior of Children

Murray A. Straus, David B. Sugarman, and Jean Giles-Sims, in "Spanking by Parents and Subsequent Antisocial Behavior of Children" (*Archives of Pediatrics and Adolescent Medicine,* Vol. 151, No. 8, August 1997), analyzed over 900 children ages six to nine whose mothers reported using corporal punishment. The researchers found that, regardless of the child's socioeconomic status, sex, and ethnic group and regardless of whether or not the parents provided emotional support, mental stimulation, and satisfactory socialization environment, corporal punishment was linked to an increase in the children's antisocial behavior between the start of the study to two years later. The antisocial behavior included cheating or lying, bullying of or cruelty to others, lack of remorse for misbehavior, deliberate destruction of things, disobedience in school, and trouble in getting along with their teachers.

The researchers pointed out that frequent physical punishment does not always result in a child's exhibiting antisocial behavior. However, physical punishment, if used through the teen years, has been associated with adult behavior problems (see below).

FIGURE 5.10

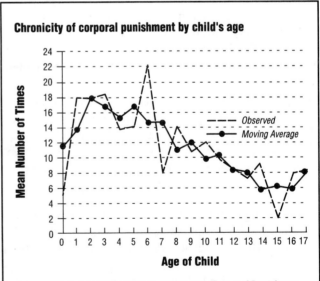

Chronicity of corporal punishment by child's age

SOURCE: Murray A. Straus and Julie H. Stewart, *Corporal Punishment by American Parents: National Data on Prevalence, Chronicity, Severity, and Duration, in Relation to Child and Family Characteristics,* Family Research Laboratory, University of New Hampshire. Durham, NH, 1988

FIGURE 5.11

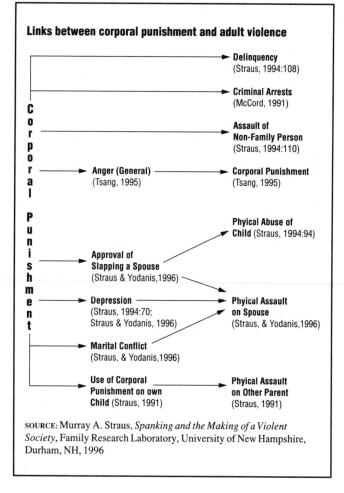

Links between corporal punishment and adult violence

SOURCE: Murray A. Straus, *Spanking and the Making of a Violent Society*, Family Research Laboratory, University of New Hampshire, Durham, NH, 1996

FIGURE 5.12

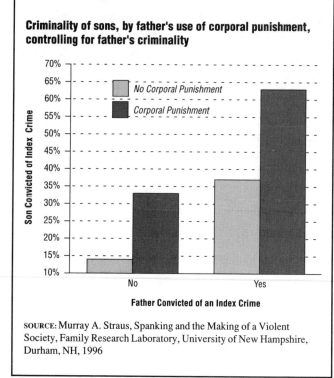

Criminality of sons, by father's use of corporal punishment, controlling for father's criminality

SOURCE: Murray A. Straus, *Spanking and the Making of a Violent Society*, Family Research Laboratory, University of New Hampshire, Durham, NH, 1996

Corporal Punishment and Criminal Violence

Murray A. Straus, in *Spanking and the Making of a Violent Society* (a report to the American Academy of Pediatrics, Elk Grove, IL, February 1996), indicated that, while corporal punishment alone does not cause a violent society, it increases the probability of societal violence. In explaining the connection between corporal punishment and criminal violence, Straus pointed out that almost all corporal punishment is carried out to control or correct behavior, and almost all assaults and about two-thirds of homicides are committed to correct a wrong action or behavior.

Straus noted that several studies have shown that the more corporal punishment experienced in middle childhood or early adolescence, the greater the probability of crime and violence. Figure 5.11 is a graphic summary of various studies that have linked corporal punishment to delinquency, criminal arrests, and assault of family and non-family members. The second arrow from the top (*Criminal Arrests,* McCord, 1991) refers to a 33-year study of individuals who experienced corporal punishment as boys. Their conviction records were examined when they reached middle age. Even after controlling for the criminality of the boys' fathers, corporal punishment

was linked to the doubling of the proportion of sons who were convicted of serious crimes. (See Figure 5.12.)

Straus noted the unintended consequences of physical punishment. Because parents are usually the first to hit an infant, the child learns to associate the first people he or she loves with those who hurt him or her. Parents who use physical punishment to train their children or to teach them about which dangerous things they should avoid are also teaching them that it is all right to hit other family members. Children also learn that the use of violence is justified when something is really important. Finally, parents teach their children that when a person is stressed out or angry, it is "understandable" if he or she resorts to hitting.

Corporal Punishment and Cognitive Development

In *Corporal Punishment by Mothers and Child's Cognitive Development: A Longitudinal Study* (Family Research Laboratory, University of New Hampshire, Durham, NH; a paper presented at the 14th World Congress of Sociology, Montreal, Canada, 1998), Straus and Mallie J. Paschall found that corporal punishment was associated with a child's failure to keep up with the average rate of cognitive development.

Straus and Paschall followed the cognitive development of 960 children born to mothers who participated in the *National Longitudinal Study of Youth*. The women were 14–21 years old at the start of the study. In 1986, when the women were between the ages of 21 and 28, those with children were interviewed regarding the way they were raising these children. The children underwent cognitive, psychosocial, and behavioral assessments. Children ages one to four were selected, among other reasons, because "the development of neural connections is greatest at the youngest ages." The children were tested again in 1990.

HIGH INCIDENCE AND LONG DURATION. About 7 in 10 (71 percent) mothers reported spanking their toddlers in the past week, with 6.2 percent hitting the child during the course of their interview for the study. Those who used corporal punishment reported using it an average of 3.6 times per week. This amounted to an estimated 187 spankings a year.

COGNITIVE DEVELOPMENT. Straus and Paschall found that the more prevalent the corporal punishment, the greater the decrease in cognitive ability. (See Figure 5.13.) Considering other studies, which showed that talking to children, including infants, is associated with increased neural connections in the brain and cognitive functioning, the researchers hypothesized that if parents are not using corporal punishment to discipline their child, they are very likely verbally interacting with that child, thus positively affecting cognitive development.

Moreover, corporal punishment has been found to affect cognitive development in other ways. It is believed that experiencing corporal punishment can be very stressful to a child. Stress hampers a child's ability to process events, which is important for his or her cognitive development. And since corporal punishment generally occurs over a long period of time, a child's bonding with his parents may be minimized to the point that he or she will not be motivated to learn from them.

OTHER FINDINGS. Straus and Paschall also found that, contrary to some beliefs that corporal punishment is acceptable if the parent provides emotional support to the child, the adverse effects of physical punishment on cognitive development remained the same whether or not there was maternal support. The results of the study also debunked the general belief among blacks that corporal punishment benefits children. The adverse consequences on cognitive development held true for all racial and ethnic groups.

IS CHILD NEGLECT A LOST CONCERN?

When most Americans think of child maltreatment, they think of abuse and not neglect. Furthermore, research literature and conferences dealing with child maltreatment have generally overlooked child neglect. The congressional hearings that took place before the passage of the landmark Child Abuse Prevention and Treatment Act of 1974 (PL 93-247) focused almost entirely on examples of physical abuse. Barely three pages of the hundreds recorded pertained to child neglect.

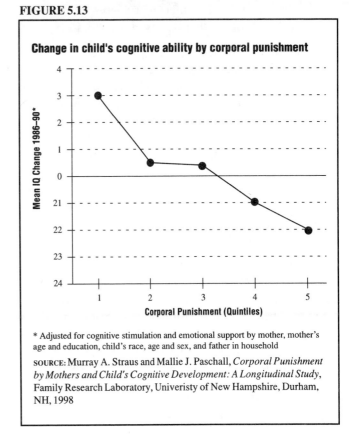

FIGURE 5.13

Change in child's cognitive ability by corporal punishment

* Adjusted for cognitive stimulation and emotional support by mother, mother's age and education, child's race, age and sex, and father in household

SOURCE: Murray A. Straus and Mallie J. Paschall, *Corporal Punishment by Mothers and Child's Cognitive Development: A Longitudinal Study*, Family Research Laboratory, Univeristy of New Hampshire, Durham, NH, 1998

Nonetheless, every year the federal government reports a very high incidence of child neglect. *Child Maltreatment 1998: Reports from the States to the National Child Abuse and Neglect Data System* (U.S. Department of Health and Human Services, Washington, D.C., 2000) found that nearly two-and-a-half times as many children were victims of neglect as of physical abuse (7.2 versus 2.9 children per 1,000). In addition, 57.3 percent of the children who died of child maltreatment died of neglect. Another 8.8 percent died of medical neglect. (See Figure 4.3 and Table 4.4 in Chapter 4.)

Child Neglect—A Major Social Problem

Neglect is an act of omission rather than commission. While the consequences of child neglect can be just as serious as abuse, neglect receives far less attention. Neglect may be evidenced in a child's appearance, such as being unkempt or being severely malnourished, but in many cases neglect leaves no visible marks. Moreover, it usually involves infants and very young children who cannot speak for themselves. (See Chapter 2 for more information on the different types of neglect.)

Martha Farrell Erickson and Byron Egeland, in "Child Neglect" (*The APSAC Handbook on Child Maltreatment,* Sage Publications, Thousand Oaks, CA, 1996), noted that child neglect is often entangled in patterns of family dysfunction as well as environmental factors such as poverty. It is therefore difficult to assess whether the child's subsequent developmental problems are results of the neglect itself or of other factors in that child's life.

The authors studied neglected children in the *Minnesota Mother–Child Project,* one of the first major studies to focus on the antecedents of child maltreatment and its long-term effects on children's development. (The antecedents of maltreatment refer to those circumstances that precede the child abuse and/or neglect, often having a causal relationship to that maltreatment.) The *Project* is a longitudinal study (many aspects of the study are still going on) that tracks the development of 267 babies born to first-time mothers who are at risk for parenting problems due to poverty, youth, low level of education, lack of support, and unstable life situations.

ANTECEDENTS OF NEGLECT The *Minnesota Mother–Child Project* has found that "neglectful" parents have a difficult time understanding their relationship with their children. They tend to see situations in black and white and therefore cannot respond to the nuances of their children's behavior during their developmental process. This may be due to the parents' own neglected situations as children themselves or to their level of intellectual functioning. Among mothers who were neglected as children, seven of nine maltreated their children during the first two years of life; most of their children suffered neglect.

The families tracked by the Minnesota study did not have social support in child-raising. Within the same at-risk group of mothers, maltreating families had more stressful life situations than non-maltreating families. Emotional neglect, or "psychologically unavailable parenting," involves a lack of responsiveness to a child's need for attention. The psychologically unavailable mothers tended to be more tense, depressed, angry, and confused. When they did interact with their children, their responses were mechanical, revealing little or no warmth.

CONSEQUENCES James M. Gaudin, Jr., in "Child Neglect: Short-Term and Long-Term Outcomes" (*Neglected Children: Research, Practice, and Policy,* Sage Publications, Thousand Oaks, CA, 1999), reported that, compared with non-maltreated and abused children, neglected children have the worst delays in language comprehension and expression. Psychologically neglected children also score lowest in IQ tests.

Emotional neglect, in its most serious form, can result in the "non-organic failure to thrive syndrome," a condition in which a child fails to develop physically or even to survive. According to Gaudin, studies found that, even with aggressive intervention, the neglected child continued to deteriorate. The cooperation of the neglectful parents, which was crucial to the intervention, usually declined as the child's condition worsened. This shows

FIGURE 5.14

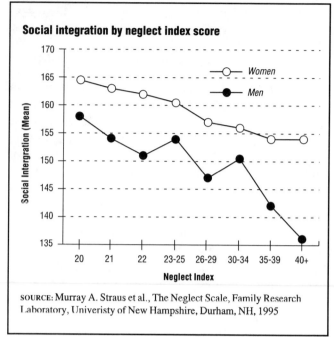

SOURCE: Murray A. Straus et al., The Neglect Scale, Family Research Laboratory, Univeristy of New Hampshire, Durham, NH, 1995

that it is sometimes not that easy to change the parental attributes that contributed to the neglect in the first place.

Erickson and Egeland found that if neglected children manage to survive, the adverse effects of neglect carry over to their future adapting abilities in the school environment and in the outside world. The adverse consequences of neglect include a lack of affection toward the parents, overdependence on teachers, a lack of enthusiasm and persistence in performing tasks, noncompliance, withdrawal and, consequently, low peer acceptance. Those who suffer emotional neglect during the first two years of life are the most likely to exhibit these adverse effects. The authors added that the effects of neglect on children's development, contrary to some beliefs, far outweigh the effects of poverty.

Murray A. Straus, E. Milling Kinard, and Linda Meyer Williams, in *The Neglect Scale* (a paper presented at the Fourth International Conference on Family Violence Research in Durham, NH, July 23, 1995), found that neglect increases the probability of low social integration, which in turn increases the probability of all types of criminal behavior, including assaults on spouses or partners. In other words, the more neglect suffered in childhood, the lower the degree of social integration, especially as the neglect victim ages. The correlation between neglect and social integration is consistent, especially for men. (See Figure 5.14.)

CHAPTER 6
CHILD SEXUAL ABUSE

A BETRAYAL OF TRUST

Many experts believe that sexual abuse is the most underreported type of child maltreatment. A victim, especially a very young child, may not know what he or she is experiencing; in many cases, the child is sworn to secrecy. Adults who may be aware of the abuse sometimes get involved in a conspiracy of silence.

Child sexual abuse is the ultimate misuse of an adult's trust and power over a child. When the abuser is particularly close to the victim, the child feels betrayed, trapped in a situation where an adult who claims to care for the child is assaulting him or her.

In July 2000 a 68-year-old former Mormon in Texas was sentenced to 68 years in prison for the sexual abuse of young girls in his church. His victims, some of them now young women in their twenties, testified that the former high priest molested them when they were very young. Although lawyers for the church claimed that the defendant's title did not mean he was a church leader, the victims indicated they looked up to the priest because of his role in the church.

In August 1999 an assistant principal and teacher at the prestigious Stuyvesant High School in New York City was arrested and eventually pleaded guilty to sexually abusing a 15-year-old female student in his office. He admitted to exposing himself to the adolescent and showing her pornographic material. Other students later told prosecutors that the educator had made sexual comments to them.

FREUD

The first person to present childhood sexual abuse as a source of psychological problems was Sigmund Freud. Early in his career, Freud proposed that the hysteria he saw in some of his patients was the result of childhood sexual abuse. He thought his patients' symptoms represented symbolic manifestations of their repressed sexual memories. Freud later changed his mind, denying that he thought sexual abuse had taken place. Instead, he proposed that young children have an unconscious sexual attachment to the parent of the opposite sex and a sense of rivalry with the parent of the same sex. This is called the Oedipus complex in males and the Electra complex in females. In other words, the adult's memories of incestuous experiences were remnants of his or her childhood desire to be seduced by an adult. Freud theorized that, under the normal psychological development process, the child starts to identify with the parent of the same sex. He claimed that if this does not occur, the individual will develop personality disorders in adulthood.

Some scholars have proposed that Freud revised his theory because he was pressured by colleagues to recant. Psychoanalyst Alice Miller claims that Freud suppressed the truth so that he, his colleagues, and men in Viennese society would be spared having to examine their own histories. Some experts believe that the testimonies Freud originally elicited from his patients were cases of incestuous abuse. Others believe that he changed his theory to preserve his concept of repression, on which he based the whole structure of psychoanalysis.

WHAT IS CHILD SEXUAL ABUSE?

Federal Definition

The Child Abuse Prevention and Treatment Act of 1974 (Public Law 93-247) specifically identified parents and caretakers as the perpetrators of sexual abuse (see Chapter 2). Sexual molestation by other individuals was considered sexual assault. However, the 1996 amendments to this law (see below) included a more comprehensive definition, one that also included sexually abusive behavior by individuals other than parents and caretakers.

The Child Abuse Prevention and Treatment Act of 1996 (PL 104-235; Sec. 111 [42 U.S.C. 5106g]) defines child sexual abuse as:

- The employment, use, persuasion, inducement, enticement, or coercion of any child to engage in, or assist any other person to engage in, any sexually explicit conduct or simulation of such conduct for the purpose of producing a visual depiction of such conduct; or

- The rape, and in cases of caretaker or interfamilial relationships, statutory rape, molestation, prostitution, or other form of sexual exploitation of children, or incest with children.

Specific Definition Varies by State

Whereas the federal government has established a broad definition of child sexual abuse, it leaves it up to state child abuse laws to specify detailed provisions. All states have laws prohibiting child sexual molestation and generally consider incest as illegal. States also specify the age of consent, or the age at which a person can consent to sexual activity with an adult—generally between the ages of 14 and 18. Sexual activity between an adult and a person below the age of consent is against the law.

TYPES OF CHILD SEXUAL ABUSE

Familial abuse, or incest, involves the use of a child for sexual satisfaction by family members—blood relatives who are too close to marry. Extrafamilial abuse involves a person outside the family. Extrafamilial predators may be strangers, but they may also be persons in a position of trust, such as family friends, teachers, and spiritual advisers.

Some researchers define incest not in terms of blood ties, but in terms of the emotional bond between the victim and the offender. Suzanne M. Sgroi, an expert on child sexual abuse, believes that the presence or absence of blood relationships is far less important than the kinship roles the abusers play. When live-in help or a parent's lover is the abuser, there may be no blood relationship, but the abuse is still taking place within the context of the family.

HOW FREQUENT IS ABUSE?

Research on the problem of child sexual abuse is contradictory and the more studies that are done, the more researchers find that the extent of the problem is difficult to measure. Because state definitions vary, the number of cases of abuse may not include acts committed by non-family members. Therefore, rates of child sexual abuse reported are generally just estimates. In 1955's *Incest Behavior* (Citadel Press, New York), S. K. Weinberg calculated the average yearly rate to be only 1.9 cases per million people.

By 1969 Dr. Vincent De Francis and the American Humane Association had found an annual rate of 40 per 1 million children. In 1996 the *Third National Incidence Study of Child Abuse and Neglect* (NIS-3) reported a rate of 3.2 per 1,000 children using the Harm Standard and 4.5 per 1,000 children using the Endangerment Standard. (See Tables 4.5 and 4.6 in Chapter 4; the chapter also explains the two NIS-3 standards.)

Some Victims May Not Be Counted

Estimates of the number of abuse cases generally do not include victims of pornographic exploitation and child prostitution. These types of child abuse have only recently become subjects of research, and while they are known to involve multimillion-dollar businesses, little is known about the numbers of child victims involved. (See below for the first research on the online victimization of youth.)

The estimates also do not include stranger abductions, often for sexual purposes, that result in the death of the child. According to the National Center for Missing & Exploited Children (NCMEC), there are about 114,600 attempted abductions of children per year by non-family members. In addition, there are more than 354,000 abductions by family members. Another 438,200 children are lost, injured, or otherwise harmed.

Is the Federal Count of Sexual Abuse Flawed?

Diana E. H. Russell and Rebecca M. Bolen, in *The Epidemic of Rape and Child Sexual Abuse in the United States* (Sage Publications, Thousand Oaks, CA, 2000), claim that the incidence of child sexual abuse reported by the *National Incidence Study of Child Abuse and Neglect* is flawed. The authors note that the federal study only counts abuse committed by parents or caretakers. Sexual abuse by persons not in the caretaking role (for example, siblings, neighbors, and acquaintances), and by peers and strangers, is not included in the study.

The Endangerment Standard of the NIS, however, counts as perpetrators those who allow sexual abuse to take place. The authors believe that this definition of child sexual abuse perpetrators is out of step with other definitions used in research. The authors also consider this practice sexist, because males related to the child are typically the molesters, and mothers are usually blamed for not protecting their children. Finally, the incidence of child sexual abuse is undercounted because only cases substantiated or indicated (see Chapter 4) by child protective services (CPS) are included in the national study.

Adults Who Disclose Sexual Abuse

Many individuals who work in the field of sexual abuse believe that, to obtain a more accurate estimate of the rate of abuse, the researcher must ask adults whether they were abused during childhood. A 1995 Gallup Poll (the most recent poll of this kind) surveyed 1,000 parents nationwide about their sexual abuse experiences as children. When asked if they had been touched in a sexual way or had been asked to touch someone in a sexual way before the age of 18, 22 percent reported that it had happened at least once. Nine percent of the respondents reported that they were forced to have sex before the age of 18. (See Table 6.1.) The questions posed by the Gallup Organization demonstrate one of the problems with studies of sexual abuse. While Gallup pollsters asked questions about touching and having sex, many studies do not ask questions about specific sexual experiences.

David Finkelhor, director of the Crimes Against Children Research Center at the University of New Hampshire, is a national authority on child sexual abuse. In "Current Information on the Scope and Nature of Child Sexual Abuse" (*The Future of Children: Sexual Abuse of Children,* Vol. 4, No. 2, Summer/Fall 1994), Finkelhor noted that surveys of adults regarding their childhood experiences (called retrospective studies) probably give the most complete estimates of the actual extent of child sexual abuse. He reviewed 19 adult retrospective surveys and found that the proportion of adults who indicated sexual abuse during childhood ranged widely, from 2 to 62 percent for females and from 3 to 16 percent for males.

Finkelhor observed that the surveys that reported higher levels of abuse were those that asked multiple questions about the possibility of abuse. Multiple questions are more effective because they provide respondents various "cues" about the different kinds of experiences the researchers are asking about. Multiple questions also give the respondents ample time to overcome their embarrassment. Many experts accept the estimate that 1 in 5 (20 percent) American women and 1 in 10 (10 percent) American men were subjected to some form of sexual abuse as children.

Do some adults exaggerate trivial incidents or fabricate experiences that inflate abuse statistics? Finkelhor believed that there is no evidence to suggest that fabrication has distorted the validity of surveys, and yet no study has ever been done that examined the actual circumstances of alleged abuse reported in any large-scale study.

While the actual numbers of sexual abuse can only be roughly estimated, experts do agree that demographic trends suggest that more children are in situations of risk than ever before. More mothers are working outside the home, more children are in day care centers, and more parents are divorcing and remarrying, bringing stepfamilies together in much greater numbers than ever before.

A Landmark Study of Child Sexual Abuse

One of the early landmark studies of child sexual abuse was conducted by sociologist Diana E. H. Russell in 1978. She surveyed 930 adult women in San Francisco about their early sexual experiences (*The Secret Trauma: Incest in the Lives of Girls and Women,* Basic Books, New York, 1986). Russell reported that 38 percent of the women had suffered incestuous and extrafamilial sexual abuse before their 18th birthday. About 16 percent had been abused by a family member.

TABLE 6.1

Now I would like to ask you something about your own experiences as a child that may be very sensitive. As you know, sometimes, in spite of efforts to protect them, children get sexually abused, molested, or touched in sexual ways that are wrong. To find out more about how often they occur, we would like to ask you about your own experiences when you were a child . . .

Before the age of 18, were you personally ever touched in a sexual way, or were you ever forced to touch, an adult or older child in a sexual way—including anyone who was a member of your family, or anyone outside your family? (If "Yes", asked:) Did it happen more than once?

Yes, it happened more than once	14%
Yes, it happened just once	8
No, it did not happen	77
No opinion	1
	100%

Before the age of 18, were you ever forced to have sex by an adult or older child—including anyone who was a member of your family, or anyone outside your family? (If "Yes", asked:) Did it happen more than once?

Yes, it happened more than once	5%
Yes, it happened just once	4
No, it did not happen	90
No opinion	1
	100%

SOURCE: The Gallup Poll Monthly, December 1995

Russell's study is still frequently cited by experts who believe that much more abuse occurs than is officially reported by government studies. They suggest the high results recorded in her study reflect the thoroughness of her preparation. While other studies have asked one question concerning childhood sexual abuse, she asked 14 different questions, any one of which might have set off a memory of sexual abuse.

In 2000, in *The Epidemic of Rape and Child Sexual Abuse in the United States* (see above), Russell and Rebecca M. Bolen revisited the prevalence rates reported in Russell's 1978 survey. The authors believed those rates to be underestimates. The 1978 survey subjects did not include two groups regarded to be at very high risk for child sexual abuse: females in institutions and those not living at home. The authors also found that some women were reluctant to reveal experiences of abuse to survey interviewers, while others did not recall these experiences.

THE VICTIMS

Gender

Virtually all studies indicate that girls are far more likely than boys to suffer sexual abuse. Under the Harm and Endangerment Standards of *The Third National Incidence Study of Child Abuse and Neglect,* girls were sexually abused about three times more often than boys. (See Tables 4.7 and 4.8 in Chapter 4.)

IS SEXUAL ABUSE OF BOYS UNDERREPORTED? Dr. William C. Holmes of the University of Pennsylvania School of Medicine claimed that sexual abuse of boys is not only common but also underreported and undertreated. In "Sexual Abuse of Boys: Definition, Prevalence, Correlates, Sequelae, and Management" (*The Journal of the American Medical Association,* Vol. 281, No. 21, December 2, 1998) Holmes reviewed 149 studies of male sexual abuse. These studies, conducted between 1985 and 1997, included face-to-face interviews, telephone surveys, medical chart reviews, and computerized and paper questionnaires. The respondents included adolescents (ninth- through twelfth-graders, runaways, non-sex-offending delinquents, and detainees), college students, psychiatric patients, American Indians, sex offenders (including serial rapists), substance-abusing patients, and homeless men. Holmes found that, overall, 1 in 5 boys had been sexually abused.

Holmes found that boys younger than 13 years of age, non-white, of low socioeconomic status, and not living with their fathers were at a higher risk for sexual abuse. Boys whose parents had abused alcohol, had criminal records, and were divorced, separated, or remarried were more likely to experience sexual abuse. Sexually abused boys were 15 times more likely than boys who had never been sexually abused to live in families in which some members had also been sexually abused.

Start and Duration of Abuse

Kathleen Kendall-Tackett and Roberta Marshall, in "Sexual Victimization of Children" (*Issues in Intimate Violence,* Raquel Kennedy Bergen, ed., Sage Publications, Thousand Oaks, CA, 1998), reported that studies have found that the age of victims at the start of the abuse could be anywhere between 7 and 13, although there had been cases of sexual abuse among children six years of age or younger. The sexual abuse may be a one-time occurrence or it may last for several years. The authors found durations of abuse ranging from 2.5 to 8 years.

In *Sexual Assault of Young Children as Reported to Law Enforcement: Victim, Incident, and Offender Characteristics* (Bureau of Justice Statistics, U.S. Department of Justice, Washington, D.C., 2000), Howard N. Snyder found that 34.1 percent of all victims of sexual assault reported to law enforcement from 1991 to 1996 were under age 12, with 14 percent (1 of 7 victims) under age six. (See Table 6.2.) (Some researchers distinguish between child sexual abuse as perpetrated by parents or caretakers and sexual assault as committed by other individuals. In this report, the term "sexual assault" included child sexual abuse.)

START AND DURATION FOR MALE VICTIMS. In his research on male child victims, Dr. William C. Holmes (see above) found that sexual abuse generally began before puberty. About 17–53 percent of the respondents reported repeated abuse, with victimization continuing over a period of less than six months to 18–48 months.

TABLE 6.2

Age profile of the victims of sexual assault

Victim age	All sexual assault	Forcible rape	Forcible sodomy	Sexual assault with object	Forcible fondling
Total	100.0%	100.0%	100.0%	100.0%	100.0%
0 to 5	14.0%	4.3%	24.0%	26.5%	20.2%
6 to 11	20.1	8.0	30.8	23.2	29.3
12 to 17	32.8	33.5	24.0	25.5	34.3
18 to 24	14.2	22.6	8.7	9.7	7.7
25 to 34	11.5	19.6	7.5	8.3	5.0
Above 34	7.4	12.0	5.1	6.8	3.5

SOURCE: Howard N. Snyder, *Sexual Assault of Young Children as Reported to Law Enforcement: Victim, Incident, and Offender Characteristics,* Bureau of Justice Statistics, U.S. Department of Justice, 2000

Race and Ethnicity

In "Sexual Abuse of Children" (*The APSAC Handbook on Child Maltreatment,* Sage Publications, Thousand Oaks, CA, 1996), Lucy Berliner and Diana M. Elliott reported that black children were more likely to be the youngest victims of sexual abuse, while Asians were more likely to be older at the onset of sexual abuse. Black and Hispanic victims were more likely than white and Asian victims to experience penetration during sexual assault. Asian children tended to be abused by a male relative, while white children were more likely to be victims of acquaintance assault.

THE PERPETRATORS

Howard N. Snyder (*Sexual Assault of Young Children as Reported to Law Enforcement: Victim, Incident, and Offender Characteristics;* see above) found that the abusers of young victims were more likely than the abusers of older victims to be family members. Nearly half (48.6 percent) of those who sexually abused children five years old and younger were family members. Another 42.4 percent of family members victimized 6- to 11-year-olds. (See Table 6.3.) More female victims (51.1 percent of those five years old and younger and 43.8 percent of those ages 6–11) were abused by family members, compared with their male counterparts (42.4 percent and 37.7 percent, respectively). (See Table 6.4.)

Fathers

David Finkelhor, in "The Sexual Abuse of Children: Current Research Reviewed" (*Psychiatric Annals: The Journal of Continuing Psychiatric Education,* April 1987), found that, while case reports from child welfare systems were dominated by sexual abuse by fathers and stepfathers, such cases actually made up no more than 7–8 percent of all sexual abuse cases. Other family members (usually uncles and older brothers) accounted for 16–42 percent, while nonrelatives known to the child

TABLE 6.3

Victim-offender relationship in sexual assault

		Offenders		
Victim age	Total	Family member	Acquaintance	Stranger
All victims	**100.0%**	**26.7%**	**59.6%**	**13.8%**
Juveniles	**100.0%**	**34.2%**	**58.7%**	**7.0%**
0 to 5	100.0	48.6	48.3	3.1
6 to 11	100.0	42.4	52.9	4.7
12 to 17	100.0	24.3	66.0	9.8
Adults	**100.0%**	**11.5%**	**61.1%**	**27.3%**
18 to 24	100.0	9.8	66.5	23.7
Above 24	100.0	12.8	57.1	30.1

SOURCE: Howard N. Snyder, *Sexual Assault of Young Children as Reported to Law Enforcement: Victim, Incident, and Offender Characteristics,* Bureau of Justice Statistics, U.S. Department of Justice, 2000

TABLE 6.4

Victim-offender relationship in sexual assault, by victim gender

		Offenders		
Victim age	Total	Family member	Acquaintance	Stranger
Female victims	**100.0%**	**25.7%**	**59.5%**	**14.7%**
Juveniles	100.0	33.9	58.7	7.5
0 to 5	100.0	51.1	45.9	3.0
6 to 11	100.0	43.8	51.4	4.8
12 to 17	100.0	24.3	65.7	10.0
Adults	100.0	11.5	61.0	27.5
18 to 24	100.0	9.8	66.4	23.8
Above 24	100.0	12.9	56.9	30.2
Male victims	**100.0%**	**32.8%**	**59.8%**	**7.3%**
Juveniles	100.0	35.8	59.2	5.0
0 to 5	100.0	42.4	54.1	3.5
6 to 11	100.0	37.7	57.7	4.6
12 to 17	100.0	23.7	68.7	7.6
Adults	100.0	11.3	63.9	24.8
18 to 24	100.0	10.7	68.4	20.9
Above 24	100.0	11.8	60.3	27.9

SOURCE: Howard N. Snyder, *Sexual Assault of Young Children as Reported to Law Enforcement: Victim, Incident, and Offender Characteristics,* Bureau of Justice Statistics, U.S. Department of Justice, 2000

TABLE 6.5

Incestuous and non-incestuous fathers' childhood experiences (N=234)

Childhood Experiences	IF	CN	Odds Ratio
Lonely	82%	46%	(5.29)
Lived apart from father	47%	36%	
Lived apart from mother	30%	17%	(2.02)
Changed living situations	43%	32%	
Resided in an institution	5%	3%	
Father alcohol problem	36%	35%	
Mother alcohol problem	11%	10%	
Problem with stealing	34%	25%	
Problem with bedwetting	30%	22%	
Problem with fire setting	21%	10%	(2.33)
Problem with school failure	52%	29%	(2.63)
Abuse History			
Severe abuse by father	54%	21%	(4.54)
Severe abuse by mother	37%	14%	(3.72)
Rejection by mother	67%	30%	(4.79)
Rejection by father	31%	6%	(6.77)
Child sexual abuse	70%	32%	(5.06)

SOURCE: Linda Meyer Williams and David Finkelhor, *The Characteristics of Incestuous Fathers,* Family Research Laboratory, Univeristy of New Hampshire, Durham, NH, 1992

TABLE 6.6

Incestuous and non-incestuous fathers' sexual victimization history (N=234)

	IF	CN
Sexually Abused in Childhood	70%	32%
Abused by Multiple Perpetrators	45%	13%
Abused by:		
Mother	12%	0%
Father	9%	0%
Brother	8%	1%
Sister	6%	3%
Male Cousin	8%	1%
Uncle	7%	0%
Female Cousin	5%	3%
Aunt	5%	0%
Grandfather	1%	0%
Non-Family Adult Male	35%	14%
Non-Family Adult Female	24%	14%
Non-Family Male Juvenile	13%	3%
Non-Family Female Juvenile	11%	4%
Stranger	16%	13%

SOURCE: Linda Meyer Williams and David Finkelhor, *The Characteristics of Incestuous Fathers,* Family Research Laboratory, Univeristy of New Hampshire, Durham, NH, 1992

(for example, neighbors, family friends, child care workers) accounted for 32–60 percent of perpetrators.

Finkelhor and Linda Meyer Williams, in *The Characteristics of Incestuous Fathers* (Family Research Laboratory, University of New Hampshire, Durham, NH, 1992), found that, generally, incestuous fathers had lonely childhoods (82 percent). Almost half (47 percent) had not lived with their own fathers and had changed living arrangements (43 percent), perhaps as a result of parental divorce or remarriage. However, their own parents' alcohol problem was no different from that of the non-abused comparison group. Incestuous fathers were far more likely to have been juvenile delinquents, to have been rejected by their parents, and to have experienced physical and sexual abuse as children. (See Table 6.5.) The researchers also found that the sex education of incestuous fathers while growing up did not come from friends or peers, but from being victims of sexual abuse. See Table 6.6 for the victimization history of incestuous fathers.

Women Who Abuse

Until recently, experts thought female sex abusers were uncommon. When women were involved in abuse, it was thought to be a situation in which a man had forced the woman to commit the abuse. Some experts postulate that women are more maternal and, therefore, less likely to abuse a child. Women are also thought to have different attitudes toward sex. While a man ties his feelings of self-worth to his sexual experiences, a woman is supposedly less concerned with sexual prowess and tends to be more empathetic toward others.

MOTHERS. Sexual abuse by mothers may remain undetected because it occurs at home and is either denied or never reported. Mothers generally have more intimate contact with their children, and the lines between maternal love and care and sexual abuse are not as clear-cut as they are for fathers. Furthermore, society is reluctant to see a woman as a perpetrator of incest, portraying the woman as someone likely to turn her pain inward into depression, compared with the man who acts out his anger in sexually criminal behavior.

WOMEN IN POSITIONS OF TRUST. Women in positions of trust have been known to sexually abuse children. In 1997, 35-year-old Mary Kay LeTourneau pleaded guilty to the sexual abuse of her 13-year-old male student. She became sexually involved with the sixth-grader in 1996, became pregnant, and gave birth to their child in 1997. The court suspended her prison sentence of 7.5 years and sentenced her instead to six months in jail, with credit for time already served. She was also required, among other things, to cease any contact with the boy and undergo a sex-offender treatment program.

In 1998 LeTourneau was rearrested after having contact with the boy and was sentenced to serve the rest of her 7.5-year prison sentence. She has since given birth to a second child fathered by the student.

CHARACTERISTICS OF ABUSING WOMEN. Some researchers have proposed that the abusive behavior of women is influenced by severe psychiatric disturbance, mental retardation, brain damage, or male coercion. C. Allen studied female offenders in *A Comparative Analysis of Women Who Sexually Abuse Children* (Final Report to the National Center on Child Abuse and Neglect, Iowa State University, 1990) and found that their lives involved particularly harsh childhoods marked by instability and abuse.

Comparing male and female offenders, Allen found that the women reported more severe incidents of physical and emotional abuse in their pasts, had run away from home more often, were more sexually promiscuous than male offenders, and had more frequent incidents of being paid for sex. Both male and female offenders reported that their victims were most often members of their own families.

Because they perceived child sexual abuse as a great social deviance, female offenders were less likely to admit guilt. They were less cooperative than men during the investigations and were angrier with informants and investigators. Following disclosure, they also appeared to experience less guilt and sorrow than male offenders.

Sibling Sexual Abusers

Sibling incest is another form of abuse that has not been well studied. Some experts, however, believe that sibling sexual abuse is more common than father–daughter incest. Vernon R. Wiehe ("Sibling Abuse," *Understanding Family Violence: Treating and Preventing Partner, Child, Sibling, and Elder Abuse,* Sage Publications, Thousand Oaks, CA, 1998) believed that the problem of sibling incest has not received much attention because of the families' reluctance to report to authorities that such abuse is happening at home; the parents' downplaying of the fact that "it" is indeed a problem; and the perception that it is normal for brothers and sisters to explore their sexuality.

The author also felt that a very serious factor is that the victim may be living with threats of real harm from the abusive sibling. Indeed, in the author's nationwide survey of survivors of sibling abuse (see also Chapter 5), the incest victims reported an interaction of physical abuse and incest, such as threats of physical harm, or even death, if the parents were told. An interaction of emotional abuse and incest might involve constant humiliation of the victim from the sibling perpetrator, such as comments that the victim was no longer a virgin.

Wiehe believed that sexual abuse by a sibling should be considered a crime of rape because the perpetrator uses aggression, force, or threats. Moreover, the consequences to the victim are the same whether the sexual abuse takes the form of fondling or intercourse.

Sexual Abusers of Boys

Dr. William C. Holmes's review of 149 studies of boys and young male adolescents who experienced sexual abuse revealed that more than 90 percent of their abusers were male ("Sexual Abuse of Boys: Definition, Prevalence, Correlates, Sequelae, and Management"; see above). However, male abusers of older male teenagers and young male adults made up 22–73 percent of perpetrators. This older age group also experienced abuse by females, ranging from 27 to 78 percent. Adolescent babysitters accounted for up to half of female sexual abusers of younger boys.

More than half of those who sexually abused male children were not family members, but were known to the victims. Boys younger than six years old were more likely to be sexually abused by family and acquaintances, while those older than 12 were more likely to be

FIGURE 6.1

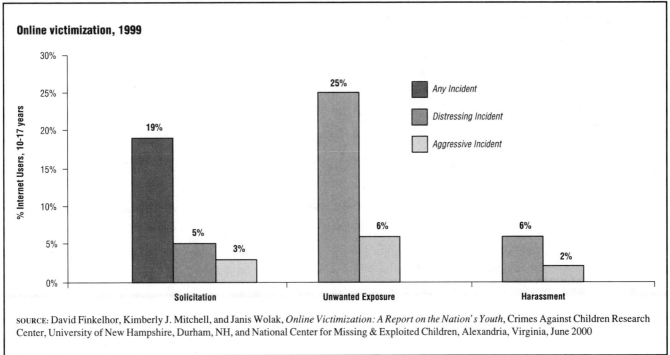

Online victimization, 1999

SOURCE: David Finkelhor, Kimberly J. Mitchell, and Janis Wolak, *Online Victimization: A Report on the Nation's Youth*, Crimes Against Children Research Center, University of New Hampshire, Durham, NH, and National Center for Missing & Exploited Children, Alexandria, Virginia, June 2000

victims of strangers. While male perpetrators used physical force, with threats of physical harm increasing with victim age, female perpetrators used persuasion and promises of special favors. One study reviewed by Dr. Holmes found that up to one-third of boys participated in the abuse out of curiosity.

Pedophiles

Until recently, a pedophile was stereotyped as a lonely, isolated man who generally sought employment that permitted contact with children. Experts now know that men or women, heterosexual or gay, married or single, may be pedophiles. In 1998 employees of a Tulsa, Oklahoma, pediatric dentist notified authorities after discovering pornographic photographs of children in his office. The father of three daughters, and youth minister in his church, the dentist had been anesthetizing young patients and photographing them in lewd positions.

PEDOPHILES ON THE INTERNET. Many pedophiles have found that the Internet gives them easy access to vulnerable children. They target and recruit potential victims through electronic conversations. In December 2000 a 26-year-old soldier who had deserted his unit in Kentucky was found hiding in the closet of a 15-year-old girl in Ohio. He was charged with corrupting a minor through sexual contact and illegally using her in pornographic materials. The adolescent had met him over the Internet. Pedophiles also contact one another through the Internet and computer online services, transmitting electronic images and sharing experiences. (See Chapter 7 for more on child pornography.)

FIRST NATIONAL SURVEY ON THE ONLINE VICTIMIZATION OF CHILDREN. In 1999 Congress directed the National Center for Missing & Exploited Children (NCMEC) to conduct the first national survey, the *Youth Internet Safety Survey,* on the risks children face on the Internet. NCMEC contracted with the Crimes Against Children Research Center of the University of New Hampshire to undertake the research.

In *Online Victimization: A Report on the Nation's Youth* (David Finkelhor, Kimberly J. Mitchell, and Janis Wolak, Crimes Against Children Research Center, University of New Hampshire, Durham, NH, and National Center for Missing & Exploited Children, Alexandria, VA, June 2000) the researchers reported that nearly one in five (19 percent) youths using the Internet in the last year had received an unwanted sexual solicitation or approach. Sexual solicitations involved requests to do sexual things the children did not want to do, while sexual approaches involved incidents in which persons tried to get children to talk about sex when they did not want to or asked them intimate questions. One in four of those solicited (5 percent of child Internet users) reported distressing incidents in which they were very or extremely afraid or upset. Another 3 percent reported aggressive solicitations in which attempts had been made to contact them through regular mail, by telephone, or in person. (See Figure 6.1; solicitations include sexual approaches.)

Twice as many females (66 percent) than males (34 percent) received a sexual solicitation or approach, and more than three-quarters were age 14 or older. Persons age 18 and over accounted for 24 percent of perpetrators

TABLE 6.7

Population estimates and confidence intervals for online victimization of youth[1]

Online Victimization	% Regular Internet Users	95% Confidence Interval	Estimated Number of Youth[2]	95% Confidence Interval[2]
Sexual Solicitations and Approaches				
• Any	19%	17%-21%	4,520,000	4,050,000–4,990,000
• Distressing	5%	4%-6%	1,190,000	930,000–1,450,000
• Aggressive	3%	2%-4%	710,000	510,000–910,000
Unwanted Exposure to Sexual Material				
• Any	25%	23%-27%	5,950,000	5,430,000–6,470,000
• Distressing	6%	5%-7%	1,430,000	1,140,000–1,720,000
Harassment				
• Any	6%	5%-7%	1,430,000	1,140,000–1,720,000
• Distressing	2%	1%-3%	480,000	310,000–650,000

[1] Estimates and confidence intervals are based on an estimated number of 23,810,000 regular Internet users between the ages of 10 and 17.
[2] Estimates and confidence intervals are all rounded to the nearest ten thousand.

SOURCE: David Finkelhor, Kimberly J. Mitchell, and Janis Wolak, *Online Victimization: A Report on the Nation's Youth*, Crimes Against Children Research Center, University of New Hampshire, Durham, NH, and National Center for Missing & Exploited Children, Alexandria, Virginia, June 2000

of sexual solicitations and approaches. Twice as many solicitors (48 percent) were under 18. About two-thirds (67 percent) of the solicitors were males, and 19 percent were females. Interestingly, one-quarter of the aggressive incidents involved female solicitors.

One in 4 children (25 percent) reported unwanted exposure to sexual material (pictures of naked people or people having sex). Six percent of the regular Internet users indicated distressing exposures in which they were very or extremely upset. (See Figure 6.1.) About 7 in 10 youths (71 percent) were exposed to unwanted sexual material while surfing the Web or doing online searches. Nearly 3 of 10 (28 percent) were exposed to sexual material while opening e-mail or e-mail links.

Based on the estimated 23.8 million regular Internet users between the ages of 10 and 17, Finkelhor et al. noted that about 4.5 million of these users had experienced sexual solicitations and approaches. Nearly 6 million had experienced unwanted exposure to sexual material. (See Table 6.7.)

The survey found that few parents and children were familiar with places to which they could report offensive Internet incidents. Although about a third (31 percent) of the parents realized there are places to report these incidents, just 10 percent could name the specific places that receive such reports. Among the children, only 24 percent had heard of places to report Internet incidents. Most (9 percent) cited their Internet service provider, while just 1 percent cited the Federal Bureau of Investigation (FBI) as a place that receives such reports. (See Figure 6.2.)

When asked by the interviewers if they knew of CyberTipline, almost 10 percent of parents and 2 percent

of youth responded that they had heard of it. CyberTipline (1-800-843-5678) was established in 1998 as a cooperative effort between the FBI and the National Center for Missing & Exploited Children to receive reports on missing children and children in harm's way.

The Clergy

The Roman Catholic Church has recently been involved in a number of incidents of sexual abuse committed by priests. In 2000 the San Francisco Catholic Archdiocese settled a lawsuit on behalf of James Aylward, paying $750,000 to a former altar boy. The 61-year-old priest admitted to having inappropriately touched young males, including the boy, for his own sexual gratification, for more than a decade.

In 1997 a Dallas, Texas, jury awarded $118 million in damages to 10 men and the family of another victim who committed suicide at 20 years of age. Rudoph Kos had sexually abused altar boys—some as young as nine—when he was a seminary student and, later, as a priest in three Dallas parishes, between 1977 and 1992. Although other priests had complained about Kos's sexual interest in boys, he was ordained in 1988. The jury found that the church not only ignored Kos's actions, but also tried to cover up the abuse.

Although the Roman Catholic Church has settled several claims against priests, not all the reports of abuse are necessarily justified. In 1995 a young man accused Cardinal Joseph Bernadin, Archbishop of Chicago, of having sexually abused him many years ago. The accuser later recanted, saying his recovered memories of abuse were not reliable enough. According to the late Cardinal Bernadin, the false accusation was worse than the cancer he had contracted. Catholic priests are not the only repre-

FIGURE 6.2

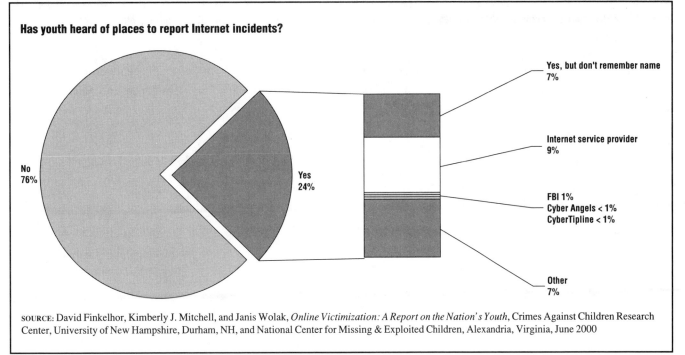

Has youth heard of places to report Internet incidents?

No 76%

Yes 24%

Yes, but don't remember name 7%

Internet service provider 9%

FBI 1%
Cyber Angels < 1%
CyberTipline < 1%

Other 7%

SOURCE: David Finkelhor, Kimberly J. Mitchell, and Janis Wolak, *Online Victimization: A Report on the Nation's Youth*, Crimes Against Children Research Center, University of New Hampshire, Durham, NH, and National Center for Missing & Exploited Children, Alexandria, Virginia, June 2000

sentatives of an organized religion to have been exposed for sexually abusing children, but the Catholic Church may get more scrutiny because priests' vows of celibacy might seem to make them more likely offenders.

THE EFFECTS OF CHILD SEXUAL ABUSE

Children and Adolescents

Many studies have been conducted to determine the effects of sexual abuse. Kathleen A. Kendall-Tackett, Linda Meyer Williams, and David Finkelhor ("Impact of Sexual Abuse on Children: A Review and Synthesis of Recent Empirical Studies," *Psychological Bulletin,* Vol. 113, No. 1, 1993) reviewed various studies on the impact of sexual abuse on children. The children studied were age 18 or younger. The most commonly studied behavior was sexualized behavior, often considered the most characteristic symptom of sexual abuse. Case studies revealed five- and six-year-old children who sexually attacked playmates, acted out sexually with family pets, compulsively masturbated, and inserted objects into their own bodies.

Table 6.8 shows the other symptoms that were frequently studied, including anxiety, depression, withdrawn behavior, aggression, school problems, and regression. Regression may involve enuresis (bed-wetting) and encopresis (passing of feces in unacceptable places after bowel control has been achieved). Posttraumatic stress disorder (PTSD) is a reaction to a traumatic experience, such as sexual abuse, that manifests itself by the reliving of the trauma, nightmares, memory impairment, insomnia, and

psychological numbness. Poor self-esteem is common among abuse victims, but it is difficult to compare abused children with non-abused children because poor self-esteem can stem from so many different sources.

However, when sexually abused children were compared with other children receiving psychological help for problems other than abuse, the sexually abused children were actually less symptomatic than the other children except for sexualized behavior and PTSD.

The authors compiled the percentages of children who were reported for different symptoms and found that an average of 20–30 percent of victims manifested any particular symptom. Only PTSD was reported in a majority of the victims, although the researchers noted that half of the children included in this calculation were alleged victims of severe ritualistic abuse. (See Table 6.8.) When the victims of ritualistic abuse were removed from the data, the percentage with PTSD dropped to 32 percent, near the level of other symptoms.

When the studies were further divided by children's ages, the researchers found that certain symptoms manifested themselves at different points in the child's life. For children 18 months and younger, the signs of possible sexual abuse included urinary and bowel problems, inappropriate fear of adults, fear of being abandoned, failure to thrive, excessive crying, and sleep disturbances.

For preschoolers, the most common symptoms were anxiety, nightmares, general PTSD, internalizing, externalizing, and sexualized behavior. School-age children were most often affected by fear, neurotic and general

TABLE 6.8

Percentage of sexually abused children with symptoms

Symptom	% with symptom	Range of %s	No. studies	N
Anxiety	28	14–68	8	688
Fear	33	13–45	5	477
Posttraumatic stress disorder				
Nightmares	31	18–68	5	605
General	53	20–77	4	151
Depression				
Depressed	28	19–52	6	753
Withdrawn	22	4–52	5	660
Suicidal	12	0–45	6	606
Poor self-esteem	35	4–76	5	483
Somatic complaints	14	0–60	6	540
Mental illness				
Neurotic	30	20–38	3	113
Other	6	0–19	3	533
Aggression				
Aggressive/antisocial	21	13–50	7	658
Delinquent	8	8	1	25
Sexualized behavior				
Inappropriate sexual behavior	28	7–90	13	1,353
Promiscuity	38	35–48	2	128
School/learning problems	18	4–32	9	652
Behavior problems				
Hyperactivity	17	4–28	2	133
Regression/immaturity	23	14–44	5	626
Illegal acts	11	8–27	4	570
Running away	15	2–63	6	641
General	37	28–62	2	66
Self-destructive behavior				
Substance abuse	11	2–46	5	786
Self-injurious behavior	15	1–71	3	524
Composite symptoms				
Internalizing	30	4–48	3	295
Externalizing	23	6–38	3	295

SOURCE: Kathleen A. Kendall-Tackett, Linda Meyer Williams, and David Finkelhor, *Impact of Sexual Abuse on Children: A Review and Synthesis of Recent Empirical Studies*, Psychological Bulletin, vol. 113, no. 1, 1993. Copyright 1993 by the American Psychological Association. Reprinted with permission.

TABLE 6.9

Percentage of children with symptoms by age group

Symptom	% of subjects (No. studies/No. subjects)			
	Preschool	School	Adolescent	Mixed
Anxiety	61 (3/149)	23 (2/66)	8 (1/3)	18 (4/470)
Fear	13 (1/30)	45 (7/58)	—	31 (2/389)
Posttraumatic stress disorder				
Nightmares	55 (3/183)	47 (7/17)	0 (1/3)	19 (2/402)
General	77 (1/71)	—	—	32 (3/80)
Depression				
Depressed	33 (3/149)	31 (2/66)	46 (3/129)	18 (2/409)
Withdrawn	10 (1/30)	36 (1/58)	45 (2/126)	15 (3/446)
Suicidal	0 (1/37)	—	41 (3/172)	3 (2/397)
Poor self-esteem	0 (1/25)	6 (1/17)	33 (1/3)	38 (4/438)
Somatic complaints	13 (2/54)	—	34 (1/44)	12 (2/442)
Mental illness				
Neurotic	20 (1/30)	38 (1/58)	24 (1/25)	
Other	0 (1/37)	19 (1/58)	16 (2/69)	3 (1/369)
Aggression				
Aggressive/antisocial	27 (3/154)	45 (1/58)	—	14 (3/446)
Delinquent	—	—	8 (1/25)	
Sexualized behavior				
Inappropriate sexual behavior	35 (6/334)	6 (1/17)	0 (1/3)	24 (7/999)
Promiscuity	—	—	38 (2/128)	—
School/learning problems	19 (2/107)	31 (1/58)	23 (2/69)	17 (2/418)
Behavior problems				
Hyperactivity	9 (2/55)	23 (2/75)	0 (1/3)	
Regression/immaturity	36 (4/159)	39 (2/75)	0 (1/3)	15 (2/389)
Illegal acts	—	—	27 (1/101)	8 (3/469)
Running away	—	—	45 (3/172)	4 (3/469)
General	62 (1/17)	—	—	28 (1/49)
Self-destructive behavior				
Substance abuse	—	—	53 (2/128)	2 (3/658)
Self-injurious behavior	—	—	71 (2/128)	1 (1/369)
Composite symptoms				
Internalizing	48 (1/69)	—	—	24 (2/226)
Externalizing	38 (1/69)	—	—	23 (2/226)

SOURCE: Kathleen A. Kendall-Tackett, Linda Meyer Williams, and David Finkelhor, *Impact of Sexual Abuse on Children: A Review and Synthesis of Recent Empirical Studies*, Psychological Bulletin, vol. 113, no. 1, 1993. Copyright 1993 by the American Psychological Association. Reprinted with permission.

mental illness, aggression, nightmares, school problems, hyperactivity, and regressive behavior. Adolescents' most common behaviors included depression, withdrawal, self-destructive behaviors, illegal acts, and running away. (See Table 6.9.) The authors theorized that sexual behavior in preschoolers may be submerged during the school-age period and may then resurface in adolescence in the form of promiscuity or sexual aggression.

SOME SHOW NO SYMPTOMS. Kendall-Tackett et al. found that a substantial proportion of victims appeared to be asymptomatic (without any of the symptoms) measured by the studies. Different studies have found between 21 and 49 percent of the children to be asymptomatic. Experts have offered various explanations for why so many children exhibited no symptoms: the researchers have not used sufficiently sensitive measures or have not looked for the right symptoms; the children have not yet manifested their symptoms and will do so after their victimization has more meaning for them; or asymptomatic children are less affected or not at all affected by the abuse.

The findings of different studies indicated that abuse characterized by a closely related perpetrator, high frequency of sexual contact, long duration, use of force, penetration, lack of maternal support at the time of disclosure, and a victim's negative outlook or coping style led to increased symptoms. Strong maternal support was the most important factor in reducing symptoms over time.

PROBLEMS CAN BE MASKED OR EVEN OVERCOME. In "Treating Abused Adolescents" (*The APSAC Handbook on Child Maltreatment,* Sage Publications, Thousand Oaks, CA, 1996) Mark Chaffin, Barbara L. Bonner, Karen Boyd Worley, and Louanne Lawson noted that little is known about why some children and teenagers are able to overcome the effects of sexual abuse. Nonetheless, this ability to overcome can be explained in part by a lack of severe or frequent abuse, and in part by "attribution"—whether the blame for the abuse is placed on oneself or on others.

Those who use internal attribution (blame themselves) experience depression, greater distress, low self-esteem, and feelings of helplessness because they did not control the situation. On the other hand, those capable of external attribution (blaming someone or something else) manage to come away from sexual abuse with their emotions intact, rationalizing that they live in a dangerous world and were randomly and unavoidably victimized. It is the latter, Chaffin et al. maintained, who can more easily overcome the psychological effects of sexual abuse.

ADOLESCENT FEMALES. Jacqueline L. Stock, Michelle A. Bell, Debra K. Boyer, and Frederick A. Connell, in "Adolescent Pregnancy and Sexual Risk-Taking among Sexually Abused Girls" (*Family Planning Perspectives,* Vol. 29, No. 5, September/October 1997), found that female adolescents who had been sexually abused were 3.1 times as likely as those who had not been sexually abused to report that they had ever been pregnant. Moreover, female victims of sexual abuse were also more likely to have had intercourse by the time they were 15 years old, to have not used birth control during their last intercourse, and to have had more than one sexual partner.

Adults

The issue of the effects of child sexual abuse on adults has become very controversial. Many therapists who specialize in helping adults confront child sexual abuse have developed lists of symptoms so inclusive, critics charge, that based on those criteria, everyone must have been abused. Eating disorders, distorted self-image, depression, low self-esteem, and multiple personality disorder (MPD; now clinically referred to as Dissociative Identity Disorder, or DID) are some of the more commonly cited symptoms.

In "Sexual Abuse of Children" (*The APSAC Handbook on Child Maltreatment;* see above), Lucy Berliner and Diana M. Elliott reported that sexual abuse during childhood is a major risk factor for a variety of problems

in adulthood. They also noted, however, that the problems are not uniform. Some experience no coping problems or mild coping problems, and others feel overwhelmed and unable to cope. Research on the long-term effects of childhood sexual abuse has focused on women, but the authors explained that adult male victims suffer as well. Men tend to externalize their pain through anger or abuse toward others. Women generally internalize their distress and suffer from depression, self-hatred, and anxiety.

Berliner and Elliott also describe another coping mechanism called dissociation. Often seen in adult survivors of sexual abuse, dissociation is a sort of psychic numbing thought to be a defense against abuse-related memories. Survivors who can dissociate abuse-specific thoughts, effects, and memories are able to reduce their importance in their lives. This manner of avoidance, when used to deal with traumatic events, has been associated with amnesia, multiple personalities, and a diminishing ability to appropriately cope with other problems. (See Chapter 8 for a discussion of the controversy about therapists' diagnosis of abuse.)

Dr. William C. Holmes's review of studies of male child sexual abuse ("Sexual Abuse of Boys: Definition, Prevalence, Correlates, Sequelae, and Management"; see above) found that only 15–39 percent of victims who responded to the studies thought that they were adversely affected by the sexual abuse. The victims stressed that the adverse effects were linked to the use of force, a great difference in victim-perpetrator age, or cases in which the perpetrator was much older, or the victim was very young. However, Holmes noted that negative clinical results (in contrast to what the studies' subjects reported) included posttraumatic stress disorder, major depression, paranoia, aggressive behavior, poor self-image, poor school performance, and running away from home.

Holmes also found a connection between sexual abuse and subsequent substance abuse among male victims. Sexually abused males were also more likely to have sex-related problems, including sexual dysfunction, hypersexuality, and the tendency to force sex on others. He surmised that the discrepancy between the respondents' perceptions of the negative consequences of their sexual victimization and those discovered in clinical outcomes may be due to several factors. Holmes observed that perhaps abused males believe they have failed to protect themselves as society expects them to do. Instead of owning up to their failure, they resort to not giving much gravity to their experiences. Moreover, if the victims had experienced pleasure while being abused, they may be confused about their feelings about it.

Diane N. Roche, Marsha G. Runtz, and Michael A. Hunter studied female undergraduate students who had suffered child sexual abuse ("Adult Attachment: A Mediator Between Child Sexual Abuse and Later Psychological

Adjustment," *Journal of Interpersonal Violence,* Vol. 14, No. 2, February 1999). The researchers found that, overall, the women who were victims of child sexual abuse were less secure and more fearful in their adult relationships, compared with the control group. Moreover, those who suffered family abuse exhibited more negative attachment relationships than those abused by non-family offenders.

According to the authors, when a child is abused by a family member, he or she loses trust in what should have been a safe relationship. The abuse interrupts the child's developing sense of self. This development, which, under normal circumstances, continues to early adulthood, is derailed. Consequently, the victim's damaged perception of self may keep him or her from sustaining healthy relationships.

Adult Sexual Revictimization

Carolyn M. West, Linda M. Williams, and Jane A. Siegel reinterviewed victims of child abuse an average of 17 years after their abuse ("Adult Sexual Revictimization among Black Women Sexually Abused in Childhood: A Prospective Examination of Serious Consequences of Abuse," *Child Maltreatment,* Vol. 5, No. 1, February 2000). The research subjects were black women, ages 19–31, who were 10 months to 12 years of age at the time of the abuse. The researchers found that 30 percent of the women experienced revictimization as adults, with physical force during childhood abuse as the only predictor of adult abuse. The women reported between one and six episodes of revictimization, with the majority (79 percent) experiencing one incident of abuse and 18 percent indicating two such incidents.

The researchers found that revictimized women were three times more likely to have engaged in prostitution (27 percent, compared with 8 percent of nonrevictimized women) and to be one-and-a-half times as likely to have been involved in partner violence (73 percent, compared with 48 percent of nonrevictimized women). Although revictimized women did not have first consensual intercourse at younger ages, or more sexual partners compared with their nonrevictimized counterparts, they tended to have more health problems. They had more problems conceiving and experienced more vaginal infections, sexually transmitted diseases, and painful intercourse.

A PIONEER IN THE STUDY OF DEVIANT SEXUAL BEHAVIOR

A critical step in bringing a scientific focus to the study of sexual deviance was achieved in the late-1950's by Kurt Freund, a psychiatrist born in what is now the Czech Republic, when he created a method to test male response to erotic stimuli. With Freund's phallometric device, which some experts have compared to a lie detector, the penis is put into a tube. The tube is sealed, and the man is shown slides or movies of adult men and women and of boys and girls. The air displacement from the tube shows increases in penile volume, which are recorded so the tester can see which images caused the greatest penile reactions. This was the first of many such testing mechanisms since developed. Freund, who died in October 1996, was among the first to conclude that child molesters were incapable of changing their sexual outlook; today, treatment programs are based on his presumption.

RITUAL CHILD ABUSE

A Study of Ritual Abuse Reports and Evidence

Concerned over allegations of ritual child abuse during the 1980s and early 1990s, especially since the much-publicized McMartin Preschool case (see Chapter 7), the federal government commissioned four studies to investigate the characteristics and sources of such allegations (Gail S. Goodman, Jianjian Qin, Bette L. Bottoms, and Phillip R. Shaver, *Characteristics and Sources of Allegations of Ritualistic Child Abuse,* Final Report to the National Center on Child Abuse and Neglect, Washington, D.C., 1994). For comparison, the investigators also looked into allegations of religion-related abuse (for example, withholding of medical care, abuse by religious officials, and corporal punishment "to beat the devil out of the children").

The first study surveyed clinicians who might have worked with ritual and religion-related abuse cases. A total of 720 clinical psychologists, psychiatrists, and social workers provided information on 1,548 such cases. These cases had been reported to them by victims who were either adult survivors or children. About 31 percent of clinicians each reported one or two cases of ritual abuse. More than 1 percent reported having more than 100 cases each.

Claims of the adult ritual cases were the most extreme and involved more severe types of abuse, such as murder, cannibalism, and baby breeding for ritual sacrifice. However, no hard evidence of these incidents could be found. Moreover, victims in adult ritual cases were most likely to be diagnosed with multiple personality disorders. The only evidence reported in ritual abuse cases was the patient's disclosure during hypnotherapy and, in a few cases, the presence of scars. Goodman et al. noted, however, that even when scars were found, it was not determined whether the victims themselves had caused them.

Overall, the clinicians accepted the allegations of abuse, as well as the characteristics of both ritual and religion-related cases. They reported finding evidence of harm and abuse in religion-related cases, as well as very rare cases of ritual abuse of children involving satanic themes that are perpetrated by one or two people. However, they reported that hard evidence for satanic ritual abuse, especially that involving large cults, was "scant to nonexistent."

In the second study, Goodman et al. surveyed different agencies that were involved with child abuse allegations: offices of district attorneys, departments of social services, and law enforcement agencies. About 23 percent (1,079 respondents) reported that they had encountered at least one ritual or religion-related case, while three-quarters (77 percent) reported no cases. More than 2 percent reported having seen more than 100 victims of alleged ritual abuse.

As with the clinicians, the various agencies reported that victims of alleged ritual abuse cases experienced severe abuse. In addition, ritual cases involved more types of abuse than religion-related cases. The agencies also found that allegations of ritual abuse involved multiple perpetrators and victims, with relatively high numbers of female perpetrators and male victims. Most religion-related cases were committed by parents or persons in a position of trust, while ritual abuses were committed by acquaintances or strangers. The agencies believed the allegations of both ritual abuse and religion-related abuse, although they were more likely to accept the validity of allegations of religion-related abuse than of ritual abuse.

The third study examined repression and recovery of memories of early abuse, analyzing 490 cases from the first study. Of these cases, 43 were repressed memory (RM) cases and 447 were nonrepressed memory (NRM) cases. RM cases were characterized by more types of abuse and a larger number of perpetrators than those not based on RM. More than two-thirds (68 percent) of RM cases were diagnosed with multiple personality disorder. The alleged abuse started earlier and lasted longer and was more likely to involve ritual abuse than non-RM cases. According to Goodman, there was no evidence to indicate the existence of the satanic ritual abuse scenarios that allegedly occurred in many of the RM cases. (See Chapter 8 for more on repressed memory.)

The fourth study examined children's knowledge of satanic topics. Some professionals believe that children are incapable of reporting ritual abuse if they have not experienced the abuse. On the other hand, other professionals feel that children's suggestibility makes them vulnerable to making false reports of such abuse. The researchers investigated whether children have the necessary knowledge base to make up details of ritual abuse.

Of the children surveyed, those ages 3–12, while knowing about the devil and crime, did not have any knowledge of activities associated with satanic sexual abuse. The researchers noted that the fact that younger children had little knowledge of ritual abuse does not mean their reports of satanic abuse were true. The researchers felt it meant that children were unlikely to have made up such reports. They also warned that the results of the fourth study must be interpreted cautiously. For ethical reasons, the children were not asked about satanic ritual abuse. Instead, they were asked about God, the devil, heaven, hell, symbols, and pictures.

An Expert's Opinion

Kenneth V. Lanning, a Supervisory Special Agent with the Federal Bureau of Investigation (FBI) and one of the foremost national experts on child molestation, claims that satanic or ritual abuse is rare and that the FBI has never found evidence or credible witnesses indicating the existence of satanists who ritually abuse children sexually. In *Investigator's Guide to Allegations of Ritual Child Abuse* (Federal Bureau of Investigation, Washington, D.C., 1992) Lanning wrote,

> Any professional evaluating victims' allegations of "ritual abuse" cannot ignore or routinely dismiss the lack of physical evidence (no bodies or physical evidence left by violent murders); the difficulty in successfully committing a large-scale conspiracy crime (the more people involved in any crime conspiracy, the harder it is to get away with it); and human nature (intragroup conflicts resulting in individual self-serving disclosures are likely to occur in any group involved in organized kidnapping, baby-breeding, and human sacrifice). If and when members of a destructive cult commit murders, they are bound to make mistakes, leave evidence, and eventually make admissions in order to brag about their crimes or to reduce their legal liability.

CHAPTER 7
CHILD ABUSE AND THE LAW

JUVENILE COURTS

As early as the mid-17th century in colonial America, adults accused of child abandonment, excessive physical abuse, and of depriving their children of basic necessities faced criminal trials. But it was not until 1899 that a statewide (Illinois) juvenile court system was created to prosecute abusive adults in civil trials. Today all 50 states have authorized juvenile family courts to intervene in child abuse cases, and all 50 states consider child abuse of any kind a felony and a civil crime. A felony could result in a prison term; a loss of a civil suit could result in the payment of a fine or in losing custody of the child. (While many states have distinct and separate juvenile courts, some states try juvenile or family cases in courts of general jurisdiction, where child protection cases are given priority over other cases on the court's docket.)

Government child protective services (CPS) initiate a civil court proceeding (after consultation with CPS lawyers) if it seeks to remove the child from the home, provide in-home protective services, or require the abuser to get treatment. Criminal proceedings are initiated by a government prosecutor if the abuser is to be charged with a crime, such as sexual abuse.

In civil child protection cases the accused has the right to a closed trial (a hearing with no jury and closed to the public), in which court records are kept confidential, although a few states permit jury trials. On the other hand, in criminal child protection cases the person charged with abuse is entitled to the Sixth Amendment right to an open trial (a jury trial opened to the public), which can be waived only by the defendant.

In 1967, *In re Gault* (387 U.S.1) substantially changed the nature of juvenile courts. Initially, children were not subject to constitutional due process rights or legal representation, and judges presiding over these courts were given unlimited power to protect children from criminal harm. *Gault* established that children—whether they have committed a crime or are the victims of a crime—are entitled to due process and legal representation. These rights, however, are interpreted differently among the states.

Court-Appointed Special Advocate (CASA)

In the past, for many abused and neglected children who could not be reunited with their families, foster care became a permanent placement. In the 1970s David W. Soukup, presiding judge of the King County Superior Court in Seattle, Washington, realized that judges did not always have enough information to make the right decision to serve the best interests of the child.

Traditionally the child's advocate in court had been the guardian *ad litem,* an attorney appointed by the court. The lawyers, however, usually did not have the time or training to conduct a thorough review of each child's case. Judge Soukup recruited and trained community volunteers to serve as the children's long-term guardians *ad litem.* The role of the Court-Appointed Special Advocate (CASA) was born on January 1, 1977, and Seattle's program has since been adopted nationwide.

The role of CASA volunteers varies in different states. They either act as or work with the guardians *ad litem.* Each trained volunteer works with only one or two children at a time, thereby enabling him or her to research and monitor each case thoroughly.

PROBLEMS FOR THE PROSECUTOR

For the prosecutor's office, child abuse can present many problems. The foremost is that the victim is a child. This becomes an even greater problem when the victim is very young (from birth to age six), since the question of competency arises (see below). In "What Young Children Recall: Issues of Content, Consistency, and Coherence"

(*Memory and Testimony in the Child Witness,* Sage Publications, Thousand Oaks, CA, 1995) R. Fivush and J. Shukar found that children under the age of six, who often face multiple interviews, can be inconsistent in recalling and retelling past events. Different settings and interview techniques can result in children remembering different details at different times.

The prosecutor may also worry about the possible harm the child may suffer, having to relive the abuse and being interrogated by adversarial defense attorneys. If the child is an adolescent making accusation of sexual abuse, the defendant's attorney may accuse the teenage victim of seducing the defendant or willingly taking part in the acts.

Other factors prosecutors must consider include the slowness of the court process and the possibility that the case may be delayed, not just once, but several times. This is hard enough for adults to tolerate, but it is particularly difficult for children. The delay prolongs the child's pain. Children may become more reluctant to testify or may even no longer be able to accurately retell their stories. There is a far greater difference between a 31-year-old testifying about something that happened when he or she was 26 and an 11-year-old retelling an event that happened at six years of age. Prosecutors are also obliged to keep the child's best interests in mind and to try and preserve the family.

Prosecuting Child Sexual Abuse

Prosecuting a child sexual abuse case is particularly challenging. A child who has been physically abused or neglected will often display unmistakable signs of the abuse, such as broken bones. Sexual abuse does not necessarily leave such visible marks. So the abuse is less likely to have been noticed by others, and more difficult to verify once an accusation has been made.

Many other difficulties exist. For example, physical abusers will sometimes admit to having "disciplined" their children by striking them, or have actually been seen committing abusive acts in public. Sexual abusers almost never admit to their actions when confronted, and their abuse always takes place in secret. Another major difficulty is that young children who have little or no knowledge of sex may have trouble understanding, let alone explaining in a court room, what was done to them.

DISCLOSURE

What should parents do when their children claim to have been abused? It may come as an offhand remark, as if the child is testing to see what a parent's reaction will be. Perhaps the child is engaged in sexualized behavior (a common symptom of sexual abuse) and then adds that this is what a parent, stepparent, relative, or a teacher at school has done.

A major preschool sexual abuse case against Margaret Kelly Michaels, a teacher at the Wee Care Day Nursery Maplewood, New Jersey, began when a boy at the pediatrician's office who was having his temperature taken rectally remarked that his teacher had been doing the same thing to him while he napped at school. The remark ultimately led to Michaels being charged with various forms of sexual abuse, and a nine-month trial at which several children testified. (See below for outcome of trial.)

Sometimes a parent realizes that something is wrong when the child's behavior changes. Some young children have an especially hard time expressing themselves verbally and may instead begin having sleep difficulties, such as nightmares and night terrors; eating problems; a fear of going to school (if that is the site of the abuse); regression; acting out, such as biting, masturbating, or sexually attacking other family members; and withdrawing. However, these behavior changes do not necessarily mean that the child is being sexually abused. Children may also express themselves in their drawings.

The abuse may have occurred for a long time before children tell. Why do children keep the abuse a secret? Children who reveal their abuse through the nonverbal ways listed above may be afraid to speak out because they believe the threats of death or punishment made by their abusers. Child Abuse Listening and Mediation (CALM), a California counseling organization, lists some of the reasons children do not tell:

- Children feel responsible for what has happened to them.

- Children fear adults will not believe them.

- Children believe threats from the offender.

- Children do not know how to describe what has happened to them.

- Children are taught to be respectful of adults.

- Children fear getting an adult in trouble or disobeying an adult who has requested secrecy.

  According to CALM, children tell:

- When they come in contact with someone who appears to already know.

- When they come in contact with someone who does not appear to be judgmental, critical, or threatening.

- When they believe a continuation of the abuse will be unbearable.

- When physical injury occurs.

- When they receive sexual abuse prevention information.

- If pregnancy is a threat.

- When they come into contact with someone who may protect them.

If parents believe their child, particularly if the abuser is not a family member, their first reaction may be to file charges against the alleged perpetrator. Parents rarely realize how difficult and painful the process can be. Some experts claim that children psychologically need to see their abuser punished, while others feel children are victimized by the court process, only this time by the very people who are supposed to protect them.

THE CHILD'S STORY

Some experts believe children do not lie about abuse. They point out that children cannot describe events unfamiliar to them. For example, the average six-year-old has no concept of how forced penetration feels or how semen tastes. Experts also note that children lie to get themselves out of trouble, not into trouble, and reporting sexual abuse is definitely trouble. Children sometimes recant, or deny that any abuse has happened, after they have disclosed it. Perhaps the reaction to the disclosure was unfavorable or the pain and fear of talking about the experience was too great. If the child recants under interrogation in a court of law, it is extremely damaging to the case and encourages claims that children make false accusations.

Not a Lie but Not the Truth Either

Kenneth V. Lanning, a Supervisory Special Agent of the Federal Bureau of Investigation (FBI), claimed that children rarely lie about sexual abuse ("Criminal Investigation of Suspected Child Abuse—Criminal Investigation of Sexual Victimization of Children," *The APSAC Handbook on Child Maltreatment,* Sage Publications, Thousand Oaks, CA, 1996). However, some children may recount what they believe in their mind to be the truth, although their accounts may turn out to be inaccurate. Lanning gave the following explanations for these inaccuracies:

- The child may be experiencing distorted memory due to trauma.

- The child's story might be a reflection of normal childhood fears and fantasy.

- The child may have been confused by the abuser's use of trickery or drugs.

- The child's testimony may be influenced by the suggestive questions of investigators.

- The child's account might reflect urban legends and cultural mythology.

The Pressure of the Judicial System

Once the child becomes enmeshed in the courts, his or her testimony may become muddled. Children, by definition, are immature in their physical, reasoning, and emotional development. In "Early and Long-Term Effects of Child Sexual Abuse" (*Professional Psychology,* No. 21, 1990) David Finkelhor, an expert on child sexual abuse, pointed out that the child's story may decrease in validity as the abuse becomes a distant past. Therapists who believe children do not invent abuse feel that if a child's story changes, then psychological progress is being made because the child is dealing with the emotional trauma. For the courts, however, changing stories raise doubts.

Often, the goals of the therapist and the judicial system are at odds. The therapist's goal is to protect the best interests of the child. If, to encourage the child to speak out, a therapist asks leading questions (questions that suggest a specific answer—"Did daddy take his clothes off?"—rather than, "What did daddy look like? What was he wearing?"), the purpose is to help the child remember painful events that need to be expressed. The courts, however, look at such questions as leading the witness. Cases have fallen apart when it appeared that therapists put words in the children's mouths. Critics charge that an alleged abuse may go to trial because an overzealous therapist or investigator has implanted the occurrence of abuse into the child's impressionable mind.

By the time a case makes it to the courtroom, most children are under a great deal of stress. Many will have undergone a thorough genital/rectal examination by a physician and relentless interrogations by innumerable strangers. A child may have been interviewed over 30 times by therapists, lawyers, the police, CPS workers, and the parents. Some of these people may have experience with sexual abuse cases; many may not, and their goals will be very different. How can a child possibly be able to handle this? Nonetheless, our legal system demands this process in order to give every accused person a fair trial and a chance to be cleared of the charges.

Sexual abuse cases are different from most trials in that the question is not just who did it, but did it actually happen? In cases where there is frequently no physical evidence of the crime, it is crucial for the jury to hear the children testify. Many people, however, feel that children are not able to present credible evidence to a jury. Testimony by others, such as the parents, is often excluded by hearsay rules (rules that prevent a witness from repeating in court those statements someone else has made about the case).

THE CHILD AS A COMPETENT WITNESS

Traditionally, judges protected juries from incompetent witnesses, which in early America were considered to include women, slaves, and children. Children in particular were believed to live in a fantasy world, and their inability to understand terms like "oath," "testify," and "solemnly swear" denied them the right to appear in court. In 1895 the U.S. Supreme Court, in *Wheeler v.*

United States (159 U.S. 523), established the rights of child witnesses. The Court explained,

> There is no precise age which determines the question of competency. This depends on the capacity and intelligence of the child, his appreciation of the difference between truth and falsehood, as well as of his duty to tell the former. The decision of this question rests primarily with the trial judge, who sees the proposed witness, notices his manner, his apparent possession or lack of intelligence, and may resort to any examination which will tend to disclose his capacity and intelligence as well as his understanding of the obligation of an oath. To exclude [a child] from the witness stand would sometimes result in staying the hand of justice.

As a result of this ruling, the courts formalized the *Wheeler* decision, requiring judges to interview all children to determine their competency. It was not until 1974 that the revised Federal Rules of Evidence abolished the competency rule so that children may testify at trial in federal courts regardless of competence.

In state courts, judges sometimes still apply the competency rule regardless of state laws that may have banned it. In the 1987 Margaret Kelly Michaels case (see below), the judge chatted with each child witness before he or she testified, holding a red crayon and asking questions like, "If I said this was a green crayon, would I be telling the truth?"

THE CONFRONTATION CLAUSE

It is difficult for children to deal with the fear and intimidation of testifying in open court. The person who has allegedly abused and threatened them may be sitting before them, while the serious nature of the court can be intimidating to them. The use of videotape and closed-circuit television have become common methods to relieve the pressure on the child who must testify. Currently 35 states and the federal government recognize the right to use videotaped testimony taken at depositions or preliminary hearings for children under age 18. In addition, 34 states and the federal government recognize the right to use closed-circuit television testimony.

Using closed-circuit television or video tape testimony has been challenged on the grounds that the defendant's Sixth Amendment constitutional right permits him or her to confront an accuser face to face. The Confrontation Clause of the Sixth Amendment states, "In all criminal prosecutions, the accused shall enjoy the right . . . to be confronted with the witnesses against him."

Several court rulings in the last decade have upheld the introduction of closed-circuit television, but only when it was used carefully and with full recognition of the rights of the accused. Those who disagree with these rulings claim that this method unfairly influences the jury to think that the accused is guilty simply because the procedure is permitted, and, worse, it deprives the defendant of his or her constitutional right to confront the accuser face to face.

State Rulings On the Confrontation Clause

STATE V. LOMPREY. In 1992 Mark Lomprey appealed a conviction for sexually abusing his niece (*State of Wisconsin v. Lomprey,* 496 N.W.2d 172 [Wis.App. 1992]). The defendant maintained that his right to cross-examine the child in a videotaped interview that was shown to the court was denied because when he entered the room, she curled herself up into a ball ("withdrew into her shell") and refused to speak. The trial court made two more efforts to provide both sides with opportunities to interrogate the child, but she would not respond. She was so withdrawn that the defendant's attorney did not even attempt to question her. The appeals court found that the child's behavior was "in fact, a statement." A statement includes "nonverbal conduct of a person if it is intended by him as an assertion." The court found that the child asserted through her conduct that she feared the defendant.

COMMONWEALTH V. WILLIS. Leslie Willis, who was indicted for the sexual abuse of a five-year-old child, claimed that the child was an incompetent witness and should therefore not be allowed to testify in his trial. The trial judge conducted a private hearing to determine the child's competency, but the child was unresponsive.

The prosecution proposed that, pursuant to the Kentucky statute allowing a child abuse victim age 12 or younger to testify by videotape or closed-circuit television, the trial should proceed using such method. The state statute permits such testimony if there is "substantial probability that the child would be unable to reasonably communicate because of serious emotional distress produced by the defendant's presence." The trial judge ruled to exclude the child's testimony because he was of the opinion that the provisions of the Kentucky statute allowing such testimony were unconstitutional. He held the statute not only violated the Sixth Amendment Confrontation Clause (see above) and Section Eleven of the Kentucky Constitution "to meet the witnesses face to face," but also the separation of powers doctrine of the state constitution.

Without the testimony of the child witness to the alleged crime, the case could not go to trial. Therefore, the prosecution appealed the case. The Kentucky Supreme Court, in *Commonwealth v. Willis* (Ky., 716 S.W.2d 224 [1986]), upheld the state law permitting the child to testify by videotape or closed-circuit television. It ruled that the law did not violate the defendant's state and federal rights of confronting his witness. The court pointed out that the defendant's right to hear and see the witness testify remained intact. He could "object to and seek exclusion of all portions of a tape which he consider[ed] unfair or unduly prejudicial." He also had the right of cross-examination through consultation with his lawyer. Moreover, the jury could assess the credibility of the witness.

The court also ruled that the state law did not violate the separation of powers doctrine of the Kentucky Constitution, because the law left it up to the judge to use his discretion in applying the law. The court concluded,

> The strength of the State and Federal Constitutions lies in the fact that they are flexible documents which are able to grow and develop as our society progresses. The purpose of any criminal or civil proceeding is to determine the truth. [The law] provides such a statutory plan while protecting the fundamental interests of the accused as well as the victim.

Federal Rulings on the Confrontation Clause

COY V. IOWA. In June 1988 the U.S. Supreme Court ruled on a case similar to *Commonwealth v. Willis.* An Iowa trial court, pursuant to a state law enacted to protect child victims of sexual abuse, allowed a screen to be placed between the two child witnesses and the alleged abuser. The lighting in the courtroom was adjusted so that the children could not see the defendant, Coy, through the screen. However, Coy was able to dimly see the children and hear them testify. The trial judge cautioned the jury that the presence of the screen was not an indication of guilt. Coy was convicted.

In *Coy v. Iowa* (397 N.W.2d 730, 1986) Coy appealed to the Iowa Supreme Court, arguing that the screen denied him the right to confront his accusers face to face as provided by the Sixth Amendment. In addition, he claimed that due process was denied because the presence of the screen implied guilt. The Iowa Supreme Court, however, upheld the conviction of the trial court, ruling that the screen had not hurt Coy's right to cross-examine the child witnesses, nor did its presence necessarily imply guilt.

The U.S. Supreme Court, however, in a 6-2 decision, reversed the ruling of the Iowa Supreme Court and remanded (sent back) the case to the trial court for further proceedings. In Coy v. Iowa (487 U.S. 1012, 1988), the High Court maintained that the right to face-to-face confrontation was the essential element of the Sixth Amendment's Confrontation Clause. It held that any exceptions to that guarantee would be allowed only if needed to further an important public policy. The Supreme Court found no specific evidence in this case that these witnesses needed special protection that would require a screen.

The two dissenters, Justice Harry A. Blackmun and Chief Justice William Rehnquist, argued that the use of the screen is only a limited departure from the face-to-face confrontation, justified by a substantially important state interest that does not require a case-by-case scrutiny.

MARYLAND V. CRAIG. In June 1990, in a 5–4 decision, the U.S. Supreme Court upheld the use of one-way closed-circuit television. In *Maryland v. Craig* (497 U.S. 836) a six-year-old child alleged that Sandra Craig had committed perverted sexual practices and assault and battery on her in the pre-kindergarten run by Craig. In support of its motion to permit the child to testify through closed-circuit television, the state presented expert testimony that the child "wouldn't be able to communicate effectively, would probably stop talking and would withdraw, and would become extremely timid and unwilling to talk."

The High Court decision, written by Justice Sandra Day O'Connor, noted that, although "it is always more difficult to tell a lie about a person 'to his face' than 'behind his back,'" the Sixth Amendment Confrontation Clause does not guarantee *absolute* right to a face-to-face meeting with the witness. The closed-circuit television does permit cross-examination and observation of the witness's demeanor. "We are therefore confident," Justice O'Connor declared, "that use of the one-way closed-circuit television procedure, where necessary to further an important state interest, does not impinge upon the truth-seeking or symbolic purposes of the Confrontation Clause."

Justice Antonin Scalia, dissenting, felt that the Constitution had been juggled to fit a perceived need when the Constitution explicitly forbade it. He stated, "We are not free to conduct a cost-benefit analysis [comparison of the benefits] of clear and explicit constitutional guarantees and then to adjust their meaning to comport [agree] with our findings."

HEARSAY EVIDENCE

Together with the Sixth Amendment Confrontation Clause, hearsay rules are intended to prevent the conviction of defendants by reports of evidence offered by someone they would be unable to challenge. Certain exceptions to the ban on hearsay have always been allowed. A dying person's reported last words are often permitted in court, for example. Whether or not to accept the hearsay evidence from a child's reports of abuse to a parent has been frequently debated.

Hearsay evidence is especially important in cases of child sexual abuse. Cases often take years to come to trial, by which time a child may have forgotten the details of the abuse or may have made psychological progress in dealing with the trauma. The parents may be reluctant to plunge the child back into the anxious situation suffered earlier. Hearsay evidence can be crucial in determining the validity of sexual abuse charges in custody cases. In these cases juries need to know when the child first alleged abuse, to whom, under what circumstances, and whether the child ever recanted.

In *Ohio v. Roberts* (448 U.S. 56, 1979) the U.S. Supreme Court established the basis for permitting hearsay: the actual witness has to be unavailable and his or her statement has to be reliable enough to permit another person to repeat it to the jury. Many judges have chosen to interpret unavailability on physical standards rather than the emotional unavailability that children who are afraid to testify may exhibit. Furthermore, legal experts insist that the reliability of a statement does not refer to whether the statement appears to be truthful, but only that it has sufficient reliability for the jury to decide whether it is true.

Hearsay Exceptions

Some courts consider spontaneous declarations or excited utterances made by a person right after a stressful experience as reliable hearsay. Courts also allow statements children have made to physicians and other medical personnel for purposes of medical treatment or diagnosis. Josephine A. Bulkley, Jane Nusbaum Feller, Paul Stern, and Rebecca Roe cited the example of the case *State v. Nelson* (406 N.W.2d 385 [Wis. 1987], *cert. denied* 110 S. Ct. 835, 1990), in which the court permitted a psychologist to repeat his patient's statements because the child believed she was being treated by the doctor ("Child Abuse and Neglect Laws and Legal Proceedings," *The APSAC Handbook on Child Maltreatment,* Sage Publications, Thousand Oaks, CA, 1996). The authors pointed out that some states have concluded that younger children do not understand that seeing a psychologist will help make them better. Therefore, the child's statements to the physician cannot be considered as statements made to obtain a medical diagnosis or treatment.

The Greenbrook Preschool case (reported in *On Trial: America's Courts and Their Treatment of Sexually Abused Children,* Beacon Press, Boston, 1989), with all identifying details changed to protect the families, was lost largely because of the judge's strict interpretation of hearsay. The parents of the children were not permitted to tell the jury anything the children had revealed in conversations during the year between the discovery of the abuse and the trial. Illogical court testimony ensued.

At one point, the defense asked one of the parents to relate a conversation she had had with the school's teacher and director. "I asked if they [the teacher and director] had any explanation for the sexual detail that Laurie had gone into." (The jury had no knowledge of the sexual detail because the court had not permitted Laurie's mother to talk about it.) The defense objected, and the judge sustained the objection, saying, "The jury will not assume that she went into sexual detail because that would be hearsay."

The Validity of Hearsay Evidence

In *United States v. Inadi* (475 U.S. 387, 1986) the U.S. Supreme Court clarified its intentions on hearsay evidence that did not concern child sexual abuse. The Court explained that "unavailability" [of a witness] was not a required criterion for the admission of hearsay. In fact, the High Court wrote that some statements "derive much of their value from the fact they are made in a context very different from trial and, therefore, are usually irreplaceable as substantive evidence." The Arizona Supreme Court, in *State v. Robinson* (735 P.2d 801, 1987), permitted hearsay evidence from a 10-year-old girl to her psychologist. The court stated,

> An additional factor of great weight in this case is the unlikelihood that more trustworthy or probative evidence could have been produced by [the child's] in-court testimony. A young child's spontaneous statements about so unusual a personal experience, made soon after the event, are at least as reliable as the child's in-court testimony, given months later, after innumerable interviews and interrogations may have distorted the child's memory. Indeed, [her] statements are valuable and trustworthy in part because they were made in circumstances very different from interrogation or a criminal trial.

WHITE V. ILLINOIS. In *White v. Illinois* (502 U.S. 346, 1992) the U.S. Supreme Court dealt with both the hearsay rules and the Confrontation Clause of the Sixth Amendment. Randall White was charged with sexually assaulting a four-year-old girl, S. G., in the course of a residential burglary. The child's screams attracted the attention of her babysitter, who witnessed White leaving the house. S. G. related essentially the same version of her experience to her babysitter, her mother (who returned home shortly after the attack), a policeman, an emergency room nurse, and a doctor. All of these adults testified at the trial. S. G. did not testify, being too emotional each time she was brought to the courtroom.

White was found guilty and appealed on the grounds that, because the defendant had not been able to face the witness who had made the charges of sexual assault, her hearsay testimony was invalid under the Confrontation Clause. The High Court, in a unanimous decision, rejected linking the Confrontation Clause and the admissibility of hearsay testimony.

S. G.'s statements fulfilled the hearsay requirements in that they were either spontaneous declarations or made for medical treatment and therefore, in the eyes of the High Court, "may justifiably carry more weight with a [court] than a similar statement offered in the relative calm of the courtroom." The Supreme Court concluded that whether the witness appeared to testify had no bearing on the validity of the hearsay evidence. Furthermore, because the hearsay statements in this case fit the "medical evidence" and "spontaneous declaration" exceptions, its decision upheld hearsay evidence as valid.

This decision, coupled with the *Inadi* decision (see above), has affected hundreds of child abuse cases. More prosecutors can now risk taking on abuse cases without having to rely on a frightened child's testimony to reveal the full story.

EXPERT WITNESSES

Videotaping and closed-circuit television permit juries to see and hear child witnesses, but it does not mean that the juries will understand or believe them. Prosecutors often request permission to bring in an expert witness to clarify an abused child's behavior, particularly to explain why a child might have waited so long to make an accusation or why the child might withdraw an accusation made earlier.

The danger of bringing in an expert witness is that the expert often lends an unwarranted stamp of authenticity to the child's truthfulness. If an expert states that children rarely lie about sex abuse, that expert might be understood by the jury to be saying that the defendant must be guilty, when in fact the expert has no way of knowing if that is the case. In some highly contested cases, expert witnesses swayed the jury in their decision. In the Margaret Kelly Michaels case (see below), an expert witness explained how the children's problems were symptomatic of their abuse. In the Eileen Franklin case (see Chapter 8), the expert witness convinced the jury of the validity of repressed memory and explained that inconsistencies in Franklin's story were symptoms of her trauma.

Rules Governing the Use of Expert Testimony

For expert testimony to be acceptable in court, the statements made must be very general and explain only psychological tendencies, never referring specifically to the child witness. For example, a Wisconsin court permitted testimony on why a victim does not always report sexual abuse right away, while a Kentucky court reversed a decision when a social worker testified that the child's behavior was a sign of "sexual abuse accommodation syndrome" (accepting the abuse and not reporting it) and that few children invent such allegations.

The U.S. Court of Appeals, in *U.S. v. Azure* (801 F.2d 336, 1986), reversed the conviction of the defendant because an expert's testimony was too specific. During trial an expert witness had testified that the alleged victim was believable. According to the court, "by putting his stamp of believability on [the young girl's] entire story, [the expert] essentially told the jury that [the child] was truthful in saying that [the defendant] was the person who sexually abused her. No reliable test for truthfulness exists and [the expert witness] was not qualified to judge the truthfulness of that part of [the child's] story."

In *State v. Milbradt* (756 P.2d 1372, 1988) the Oregon Supreme Court strongly condemned expert testimony on the truthfulness of children. The court wrote,

> We have said before, and we will say it again, but this time with emphasis—we really mean it—no psychotherapist may render an opinion on whether a witness is credible in any trial conducted in this state. The

assessment of credibility is for the [court] and not for psychotherapists.

Nonetheless, the court felt that expert witness testimony was acceptable if:

- The expert testimony remains general.

- It is necessary in order to answer charges from the defense.

- The child is young.

- The alleged perpetrator is a family member, making it more likely that an explanation of delayed reporting and recantation is necessary.

Expert Witnesses Differ

M. A. Mason, in "A Judicial Dilemma: Expert Witness Testimony in Child Sex Abuse Cases" (*Psychiatry and Law,* Vol. 42, 1991), analyzed 122 appellate court cases of child sexual abuse. She found that some experts cited the consistency of a child's accounts as evidence of abuse, while other experts cited inconsistency as a sign of authenticity. Other researchers have found that in some cases supposedly expert testimony has been offered by a child protective services employee after being on the job for six months and knowing only a few articles pertinent to the case. It would appear that in some trials, neither the jury nor the "experts" are aware that sexualized behavior, inappropriate knowledge of sex, and inconsistent accounts are frequently found in non-abused children who have been exposed to suggestive sexual influences.

INNOVATIONS IN THE COURT

Anatomically Detailed Dolls

Many legal professionals use dolls with sexual organs made to represent the human anatomy to help children explain what has happened to them in court. Advocates of the use of dolls report that they make it easier to get a child to talk about things that can be very difficult to discuss. Even when children know the words, they may be too embarrassed to say them out loud to strangers. The dolls allow these children to point out and show things difficult or even impossible for them to say. Some experts claim dolls work because children find them easier to use, as they are age-appropriate and familiar to them.

Lori S. Holmes, Training Coordinator for Corner-House, a child abuse evaluation and training center in Minneapolis, Minnesota, noted that the use of anatomical dolls helps the child demonstrate internal consistency. A child who has made allegations of abuse can show the interviewer exactly what happened to him or her, thus confirming the verbal disclosure ("Using Anatomical Dolls in Child Sexual Abuse Forensic Interviews," *American Prosecutors Research Institute Update,* Vol. 13, No. 8, 2000).

There are, however, potential problems in using dolls. Critics of this method believe that dolls suggest fantasy to children, and the exaggerated sexual organs on a doll (they are proportionately larger than life-size) may suggest improper sexual activity. Since most children's dolls do not have such sexual parts, the appearance of such parts on a doll might bring to a child's mind things he or she might not have thought of otherwise. According to the "affordance phenomenon," children will experiment with any opportunities provided by a new experience. Some experts believe that what might appear to be sexual behavior, like putting a finger in a hole in the doll, may have no more significance than a child putting a finger through the hole in a doughnut. Such exploratory play can have disastrous effects when it is misinterpreted as the re-creation of sexual acts.

CHILDREN INTERACT WITH DOLLS DIFFERENTLY. In the 1990s most research of children's interaction with anatomically detailed dolls was concentrated on white, middle-class children. Lane Geddie, Brenda Dawson, and Karl Weunsch, in "Socioeconomic Status and Ethnic Differences in Preschoolers' Interactions with Anatomically Detailed Dolls" (*Child Maltreatment,* Vol. 3, No. 1, February 1998), found that cultural differences may influence the manner in which children interact with dolls.

A study of a sample of non-abused preschoolers confirmed the findings of previous studies that non-abused children are not likely to exhibit sexualized behavior with dolls. However, the researchers found that black children who were of low socioeconomic status were more likely to demonstrate sexualized behavior with the dolls.

Black families are more likely than white families to have older siblings and other family members supervising the children. This means the children are exposed to a variety of experiences, such as watching an explicit movie with an older sibling. Children in low-income families are also more likely to share their parents' bedroom, which may account for inadvertent exposure to parental relations and nudity. This study shows that professionals have to be cautious in their interpretations of children's interaction with anatomically detailed dolls.

Videotaped Interviews

Videotaping, like closed-circuit television, is another technical innovation that some experts have hoped will increase a child's opportunity to present the truth. A videotape of the pre-trial interviews shows the jury how the child behaved and whether the interviewer prompted the child. Often prepared soon after the abuse, videotaped interviews preserve the child's memory and emotions when they are still fresh. Because a videotaped interview presents an out-of-court statement, which the alleged abuser cannot refute face to face, it can only be admitted as a hearsay exception.

Many states have enacted laws that permit videotapes under certain circumstances. In Kentucky, Texas, and Louisiana, a videotape is permitted if it is of the child's first statement, the questioning was by someone other than an attorney, and both the interviewer and the child are available for cross-examination at the trial. Videotaping can cut down on the number of interviews the child must undergo, and prosecutors indicate that this method encourages guilty pleas.

Videotapes can be powerful tools to deal with the problem of the child who recants his or her testimony when put on the witness stand. The case can still be prosecuted, with the jury witnessing the child's opposing statements. Experts believe that a videotape statement containing sufficient details from the child and elicited through non-leading questions makes for very compelling evidence.

Many state laws permit the use of videotaped testimony taken at a deposition or preliminary hearing instead of live testimony at a trial. Depositions (testimonies given under oath to be used in court at a later date), however, can be as demanding and difficult as a trial. They often take place in small rooms, forcing the child and defendant closer together than they might have been in a courtroom. The judge might not be there to control the behavior of the defendant or his attorney. Individuals who might offer the child support, such as victim advocates, may not be permitted to attend.

Furthermore, if the prosecutor claims the child is unable to handle the emotional trauma of the witness stand, the child may have to undergo medical or psychiatric tests by the state or defense attorney in order to permit videotaped testimony. This could be as traumatic as going through with a personal appearance at the trial. Some states permit the child to sit behind a one-way mirror so that the defendant can see the child and communicate with the defense attorney, but the child is shielded from direct confrontation.

Critics of videotaping have suggested other possible problems:

- It is possible that people "perform" for the camera instead of communicating.

- Victims are placed under subjective scrutiny by juries when every gesture, change in voice or speech pattern, and eye movement are judged.

- There is no accountability for the videotapes. Multiple copies of tapes are sometimes made and given to various attorneys and witnesses. Some tapes are used at training sessions, often without concealing the victims' names.

JUDICIAL REFORMS

Concerned about how long it takes to resolve child abuse cases, many communities are taking things into their own hands. For example, in St. Paul, Minnesota, the police department has assigned a special investigator to review abuse reports at the CPS agency. This investigator determines which cases will need criminal justice intervention and which will not.

The National Council of Juvenile and Family Court Judges (NCJFCJ) developed and published *Resource Guidelines Improving Court Practices in Child Abuse and Neglect Cases* (Reno, NV, 1995). This publication provides step-by-step recommendations on how to improve court practice. Begun in 1995, the nationwide initiative by the NCJFCJ, the Victims Act Model Courts, seeks to shorten children's time in foster care and bring about an early permanent resolution of maltreatment cases.

FALSE ACCUSATIONS OF CHILD SEXUAL ABUSE

The willingness of people to believe children's accusations of sexual abuse has varied greatly over the 20th century. At one time, people were simply unwilling to believe that sexual abuse of children was happening, or happening with any frequency. Once society accepted the fact that child sexual abuse was occurring regularly, responses to accusations of child sexual abuse went from disbelief to almost total acceptance by experts, who claimed children do not lie about these things. By the 1990s, however, responses had swung back to doubt, especially when the accusations are made as part of a divorce/custody battle between parents.

Edwin Mikkelsen et al. examined studies of sexual abuse allegations to determine how many initial reports were later determined to be false. They found rates that ranged from 2 to 8 percent of abuse cases referred to child abuse clinics, to 6 percent of emergency room referrals, to much higher rates (36.4 percent to 55.5 percent) in cases arising out of custody disputes ("False Sexual Abuse Allegations by Children and Adolescents: Contextual Factors and Clinical Subtypes," *American Journal of Psychotherapy,* Vol. 46, No. 4, 1992).

Mikkelsen et al. defined four types of false allegations, although many cases involve a combination of the four types.

Subtype I is the most common and appears in the context of a custody dispute. This is the conscious manipulation on the part of one parent or caregiver to obtain custody of children from another parent or caregiver. The parent may coerce the child into alleging abuse. In these cases, the description of the abuse may be on a more sophisticated level than a child would be expected to know at that age. In one case an 11-year-old boy related sexual activity but could not explain the meaning of the sophisticated language he used to describe it.

Subtype II is an allegation that results from the accuser's psychological disturbance. The accuser may be a child or a parent/caregiver. When it comes from a child, the child is unable to differentiate fantasy from reality; in a parent, it is a delusional (a strong belief maintained despite evidence to the contrary) process in an individual who otherwise appears to be functioning adequately. For example, a mother who had been sexually abused by her 14-year-old brother when she was 12, became convinced her own daughter was being abused by her brother when the children reached the ages of 12 and 14, respectively.

Subtype III is an allegation that is a conscious manipulation by the child. In these cases, the child makes an allegation as a means to obtain a specific goal out of vindictiveness or desire for revenge or rage. Children who are in a living situation they dislike are the most common accusers. An example is a child who lives with a parent and stepparent and would rather live with the other natural parent.

Subtype IV is iatrogenic (induced in a client/patient by a professional, such as a therapist or social worker). For example, a pediatrician in England insisted she could detect sexual abuse based on subtle physical symptoms that she could see even when the person did not claim they had been abused. Based on this, charges were made against several parents in one English village.

Suing Child Protective Services

In 1993 David Tyner III was accused by his wife of sexually abusing their four-year-old daughter. The couple was in the process of divorce. CPS did not uncover any abuse but continued to prohibit the father from seeing his children. Tyner sued CPS for mishandling the investigation.

In June 2000 the Washington Supreme Court, in *Tyner v. the State of Washington Department of Social and Health Services, Child Protective Services* (No. 67602, Supreme Court of Washington, June 15, 2000, Filed 2000 Wash. LEXIS 387), ruled that CPS could be sued for negligent handling of investigations. The court held that "CPS owes a duty of care to a child's parents, even those suspected of abusing their own children, when investigating allegations of child abuse." The court reinstated a jury verdict of more than $200,000 against the department.

Suing the Police

In September 2000 the Washington Supreme Court, in *Rodriquez v. City of Wenatchee* (No. 69614-4, Sup Ct Washington, Sept. 2000 Wash. LEXIS 578), unanimously ruled that the police can be held financially liable for negligence in child abuse investigations. This first court decision of its kind stemmed from a lawsuit filed by Pastor Robert Robertson, his wife, and others accused of child molestation.

In 1994 a nine-year-old foster child was placed in the home of Bob Perez, Wenatchee's chief sex-crimes investigator. The following year the girl told her foster father about being sexually abused by her parents. After the parents were convicted, the child made allegations of a sex-ring involving the Robertsons and 43 adults since 1988. Based on the girl's testimony and that of her 13-year-old friend and a former member of Robertson's church, Robertson, his wife, and 19 others were arrested on 30,000 counts of sexual abuse against 60 children. In December 1995 the Robertsons were acquitted. In 1996 Perez's foster daughter recanted, denying her sexual abuse allegations and saying that Perez had pressured her. Her friend had also recanted her testimony. In a September 2000 hearing, the Washington Supreme Court reinstated the $30 million lawsuit brought by the Wenatchee defendants.

• THE REGISTRATION OF SEX OFFENDERS

The Jacob Wetterling Act

The Jacob Wetterling Crimes Against Children and Sexually Violent Offender Registration Act (PL 103-322; also known as the Jacob Wetterling Act), was signed into federal law on September 13, 1994, as part of the Violent Crime Control and Law Enforcement Act of 1994 (PL 103-322). The act provides funding to states to establish registration systems for sex offenders. States must require abusers who have committed a criminal offense against a minor to register every year for 10 years after release from prison, parole, or probation. Sexually violent predators must report their addresses to the state every 90 days until it is determined they are no longer threats to public safety. Sexually violent predators include those who have committed sexually violent crimes, as well as those who may not have committed sexual crimes but suffer from mental abnormalities or personality disorders that may predispose them to commit predatory or violent sex offenses.

Jacob Wetterling was an 11-year-old boy kidnapped near his home in St. Joseph, Minnesota, by an armed, masked man on October 22, 1989. His abduction was similar to a case involving a boy from a nearby town who was kidnapped and sexually assaulted earlier that year. Jacob has never been found, but police believed the cases were linked and encouraged the creation of a database so that police departments could share information.

Megan's Law

"Megan's Law" (PL 104-145), signed May 17, 1996, amended the Jacob Wetterling Act by requiring states to release information on registered sex offenders if needed to protect the public. In 1994 the nation's first notification law was enacted in New Jersey after seven-year-old Megan Kanka was raped and murdered by a convicted sex offender who lived across the street from her family. Since then every state has enacted legislation ("Ashley's Law" in Texas and Polly Klass's Law in California, for instance) that requires the registration and tracking of sex offenders.

The Pam Lychner Act

The Pam Lychner Sexual Offender Tracking and Identification Act (PL 104-236), signed on October 3, 1996, also amended the Jacob Wetterling Act by requiring the Federal Bureau of Investigation (FBI) to establish a National Sex Offender Registry (NSOR) to help state-to-state tracking and management of released sex offenders. It further allows the FBI to conduct sex offender registration and community notification in states that do not have "minimally sufficient" systems in place for such purposes. The Pam Lychner Act was named after a victim's rights activist who was killed in an airplane crash in 1988.

CHILD PORNOGRAPHY LAWS

Child pornography is the depiction of a child under the age of 18 engaged in sexually explicit behavior. The Child Pornography Prevention Act of 1996 (PL 104-208) added a definition of child pornography, stating that an actual minor need not be used in creating a depiction in order for the depiction to constitute child pornography. In October 1998, in an effort to further protect children from sexual predators who target minors through the Internet, Congress enacted the Protection of Children From Sexual Predators Act (PL 105-314). The bill provides punishment for any individual who knowingly contacts, or tries to contact, children under 18 in order to engage in criminal sexual activity, or who knowingly transfers obscene material to children.

Pornography on the Internet

Congressional debate continues on how the government should enforce obscenity standards in cyberspace. Some policy makers believe any obscenity standards could interfere with free speech and would be difficult to enforce, while others believe this is an issue relating to child protection, not to the First Amendment.

In October 1998 Congress enacted the Child Online Protection Act (COPA; PL 105-277), which amends the Communications Act of 1934 (47 U.S.C. 201) "to require persons who are engaged in the business of distributing, by means of the World Wide Web, material that is harmful to minors to restrict access to such material by minors, and for other purposes." Material harmful to minors includes pictures, articles, images, and video and audio recordings that are considered obscene.

Persons liable to COPA violations include all those who place such obscene material on the Internet for public access. The person may be a Web site administrator who creates and maintains a Web site, a content provider such as an online bookstore or magazine, or a content contributor who writes or creates graphics for communications media. Persons offering Web material considered harmful to minors may be prosecuted even if their businesses do not make profits. COPA requires all commercial sites on the Internet to obtain from users credit card numbers or adult identification numbers. Violation of COPA entails heavy fines ($50,000–$150,000 per day) and up to six months in jail.

COPA, however, exempts the following persons from liability:

- A telecommunications carrier who provides telecommunications service.

- A person who provides an Internet access service.

- A person who provides an Internet information location tool.

- A person engaged in the transmission, storage, retrieval, hosting, formatting, or translation (or any combination of these functions) of a communication made by another person, without alteration or deletion of some parts of the communication content.

COPA was set to be enforced on November 20, 1998, but that same day, commercial World Wide Web providers and Web site users who used the materials described by COPA filed a complaint with the U.S. District Court for the Western District of Pennsylvania, challenging the constitutionality of the law. The plaintiffs argued that they would be forced to either establish age-verification barriers or delete from their Web sites materials that may be perceived to violate COPA. The plaintiffs asked the court to issue a temporary restraining order prohibiting the U.S. Attorney General from enforcing COPA.

In *American Civil Liberties Union et al. v. Janet Reno, Attorney General of the United States* (Civil Action No. 98-5591, 1998) Federal District Judge Lowell A. Reed, Jr., issued a preliminary injunction against the enforcement of COPA. Judge Lowell ruled,

> The Supreme Court has repeatedly stated that the free speech rights of adults may not be reduced to allow them to read only what is acceptable for children.

> While the public certainly has an interest in protecting its minors, the public interest is not served by the enforcement of an unconstitutional law. Indeed, to the extent that other members of the public who are not parties to this lawsuit may be affected by the statute, the interest of the public is served by the preservation of the status quo until such time that this Court . . . may more closely examine the constitutionality of this statute.

On February 1, 1999, with the restraining order he imposed against COPA set to expire, Judge Reed again issued a preliminary injunction against the enforcement of the law. On June 22, 2000, the U.S. Court of Appeals for the Third Circuit, in *American Civil Liberties Union et al. v. Reno* (No.99-1324), affirmed Judge Reed's ruling.

PROSECUTION FOR DRUG USE DURING PREGNANCY

In November 1997 the South Carolina Supreme Court, in *Whitner v. South Carolina* (492 S.E.2d 777, 778 [S.C. 1997]), ruled that pregnant women who use drugs can be criminally prosecuted for child maltreatment. The court found that a viable (potentially capable of surviving outside the womb) fetus is a "person" covered by the state's child abuse and neglect laws. The ruling was handed down in a case appealed by Cornelia Whitner, who was sentenced to eight years in prison in 1992 for pleading guilty to child neglect. This was the first time the highest court of any state upheld the criminal conviction of a woman charged with such an offense. Whitner's infant tested positive for cocaine.

In March 1998 Malissa Ann Crawley, charged with the same criminal offense, began serving a five-year prison sentence in South Carolina. In June 1998 the U.S. Supreme Court refused to hear an appeal by Whitner and Crawley.

Whitner's lawyer had argued that if a woman could be prosecuted for child abuse for having used drugs while pregnant, what was to keep the law from prosecuting her for smoking or drinking or even for failing to obtain prenatal care? Other critics claim that women who are substance abusers, fearing prosecution, might not seek prenatal care and counseling for their drug problem, which would further endanger the child.

Mandatory Reporting of Child Abuse by Pregnant Women

Many states require the mandatory reporting of substance-abusing pregnant women and newborns exposed to drugs. Social services agencies then come to the mother's aid, sometimes removing the infant from her custody on a temporary or permanent basis. Currently South Dakota has a statute that mandates the reporting of "child abuse" by substance-ingesting pregnant women to law enforcement instead of to social services. Failure to report such cases of child abuse would constitute a crime punishable by up to six months in prison.

SECRECY LAWS

In some states programs and laws designed to protect children from abuse have inadvertently protected abusers. New York State had previously strictly forbidden the release of information about previous allegations of child abuse, even if the allegations were substantiated. The state also required that records of unsubstantiated allegations be destroyed. Without the ability to review case histories, it was impossible to establish patterns of abuse.

New York's strict confidentiality provisions were loosened in February 1996, dramatically changing the way the state's CPS system worked. "Elisa's Law" forbids the destruction of any abuse records for 10 years after the child has turned 18. It also enables officials to inquire into previous allegations involving child abuse, whether they have been substantiated or not.

Elisa's Law was named for six-year-old Elisa Izquierdo, who died after years of abuse at the hands of her mother and stepfather. It was prompted by public outcry after Elisa's neighbors and teachers protested that authorities ignored their repeated warnings that the girl was in danger. The New York Civil Liberties Union argues that the law violates individuals' privacy rights and harms those who are falsely accused.

MAJOR PRESCHOOL ABUSE CASES

In the 1980s and early 1990s alleged incidents of mass molestation of preschool children in the United States triggered hysteria not only among the parents of the children involved in the cases but also among the public. Some of these cases continued into the late 1990s and even into 2000. While these cases are unusually famous, they demonstrate many of the typical issues and problems that the legal system faces in dealing with child abuse cases.

The McMartin Preschool Case

The McMartin Preschool case is often considered as the case that started a string of cases involving preschool sexual abuse. In 1983 a parent of a child enrolled at the McMartin Preschool in Manhattan Beach, California, was told by hospital personnel that her son had signs of rectal trauma, including evidence of sodomy (anal penetration). The mother went to the police, who then arrested Raymond Buckey, the preschool director's adult grandson. Police sent letters to 200 parents of current and former students, informing them of the molestation investigation. Soon other parents claimed to remember strange happenings, such as their children sometimes coming home in underwear and clothes that were not their own. There were also behavior changes for which the parents could find no explanation.

The children began to tell stories about being drugged, sodomized, penetrated with sharp objects, and used in a game called "Naked Movie Star." When they were asked why they had kept it a secret, sometimes for years, they said that every once in a while one of the gerbils or rabbits that the school kept as pets was killed in front of them as a warning of what would happen to them. In addition, they claimed to have been coached on how to deal with the nightmares they might have. "You sit up in bed and say, 'I promise I'll never tell anybody what happened to me.' And the monsters will go away."

The McMartin Preschool trial is a good example of how a case can be mishandled by everyone involved and eventu-

ally fall apart regardless of the strength or weakness of the evidence of abuse. When the case finally went to trial, the children were eight to 12 years old and were recounting events that occurred when they were three to five years old. Prosecutors claimed that defense attorneys used delaying tactics, because they knew that the longer it had been since the abuse, the easier it was to confuse the children.

The McMartin pretrial hearings included videotaped interviews with the children conducted by a child sex abuse expert. Defense attorneys, however, used the tape as proof of how interrogators had misled the children with their questions. The district attorney himself admitted that his predecessors had made serious mistakes.

As the trial wore on, the allegations grew more fantastic (drinking blood in a church, riding in a van with a half-dead baby). The children turned out to be unreliable witnesses and many recanted their earlier statements. By the end of the pretrial hearing—four years and $6 million later—charges (originally 354 counts and 41 child witnesses) were dropped against all but two of the defendants: Ray Buckey and his mother, Peggy McMartin Buckey. The first trial ended with acquittals on some counts and a jury deadlocked on other charges. In 1990 when Ray Buckley was retried, the jury was deadlocked on all counts. The prosecutor decided not to retry him. Ray and Peggy had already spent five and two years in jail, respectively.

The Fells Acres Case

In 1984 a five-year-old boy told his uncle that Gerald Amirault, the son of the owner of the Fell Acres Day School in Malden, Massachusetts, had touched his private parts. He also told his mother of other incidents of abuse. Police notified parents about the situation, instructing them to question their children and watch for behaviors related to sexual abuse. Forty-one children, ages three to six, eventually told stories of being raped by a clown, of being forced to watch animals being killed, and of having their pictures taken naked. Although the children testified about a "secret" or "magic" room they visited daily, no child could show the police the location of the room, nor could the police find it. Violet Amirault and her children, Cheryl Amirault LeFave and Gerald, were convicted of sexual abuse. The mother and daughter received a sentence of 8–20 years, and Gerald, 30–40 years.

Violet and Cheryl were released in 1995 after the Massachusetts Superior Court overturned their convictions because the seating arrangement of the child witnesses (facing the jury but not the defendants) violated their right to "face-to-face" confrontations with their accusers as guaranteed by Article 12 of the Massachusetts Declaration of Rights. Two years later the state's highest court reinstated their convictions, claiming that the accused had not offered sufficient proof that justice had been miscarried. Violet Amirault died of cancer later that year.

In June 1998 a Superior Court judge overturned Cheryl's conviction, noting that the accusers, now teenagers, who have never recanted their allegations of abuse, could not testify. The judge claimed that, due to investigators' leading interview methods, it could not be determined if the accusers were telling the truth. In October 1999, after eight years in prison, Cheryl Amirault LeFave was set free. Her conviction for child molestation stood, but the court commuted her sentence to time served.

On September 20, 2000, Gerald Amirault appeared before the Massachusetts Advisory Board of Pardons to petition for commutation (reduction) of his sentence. Governor Paul Cellucci, who will receive a written recommendation from the board, has the power to deny or grant commutation. Cellucci's recommendation must then be ratified by the Governor's Council. As of January, 2001, Gerald awaits the decision of the board.

The Margaret Kelly Michaels Case

In 1985 a four-year-old boy was being examined at a pediatrician's office. When the nurse took his temperature rectally, the boy remarked that his teacher had did the same thing to him while he napped. The mother went to the authorities. Police charged Margaret Kelly Michaels, the boy's teacher at the Wee Care Day Nursery in Maplewood, New Jersey, with child molestation. A child sexual abuse expert advised the parents of the preschool children to look for changes in their children's behavior as evidence of abuse.

In 1988 Michaels was found guilty of 115 counts of sexual abuse against 19 children, and sentenced to 47 years in prison. She was charged with inserting objects, including serrated eating utensils, into the children's genital organs, forcing them to eat a cake made of feces, and playing the piano naked. The state's evidence consisted of the children's allegations during the pretrial period. No medical evidence was found, and none of the other teachers noticed the alleged abuse that supposedly went on for seven months.

In 1993 the New Jersey Appellate Division reversed the conviction, remanding the case for a retrial. The court concluded,

> Certain questions [by investigators] planted sexual information in the children's minds and supplied the children with knowledge and vocabulary, which might be considered inappropriate for their age. Children were encouraged to help the police "bust this case wide open." Peer pressure and even threats of disclosing to the other children that the child being questioned was uncooperative were used.

The New Jersey Supreme Court affirmed the appellate court's ruling and ordered a hearing to determine if the children's testimony was tainted. The prosecution decided to drop the case. In 1994 Michaels was released after serving five years in prison.

CHAPTER 8
FALSE MEMORIES?

Some mental health professionals believe that the mind can reject unpleasant ideas, desires, and memories by banishing them into the unconscious. This theory of repression explains why a victim of a traumatic experience, such as childhood sexual abuse, may not remember the incident. It is also referred to as the mind's defense mechanism against horrible experiences. The memory of the unpleasant occurrence supposedly remains repressed until it is triggered by some event.

Revelations of abuse have been made primarily by white, well-educated, middle-class women (there are some men, but women predominate). Often the individual experiencing some distress or anxiety in her life turns to a psychotherapist, who then suggests that the patient's problems stem from childhood sexual abuse that has been repressed. Critics charge that the numbers of women having allegedly suffered childhood sexual abuse is vastly exaggerated and that the issue of sexual abuse has become a politicized, feminist cause.

Throughout the 1980s the numbers of children reported to have been sexually abused steadily increased. Many experts claim that 1 in 5 (20 percent) of American women and 1 in 10 (10 percent) of American men have been subjected to some form of sexual abuse as children. (See Chapter 6.) Just as accusations of alleged ritual abuse in day care centers have come under scrutiny, a major controversy has developed over the validity of repressed memories of childhood sexual abuse that are recovered in adulthood through therapy.

MEMORY

How memory works and its reliability play a major part in the controversy of recovered memory. Historically the workings of the mind and memory have been described according to contemporary technology. Thus, during the Industrial Revolution, the brain was likened to a machine; after the invention of the telephone, to a switchboard; after the invention of the movies, to a camera; and after the first computer, Univac, to a computer.

Elizabeth F. Loftus (a memory expert and leading opponent of the recovered-memory movement) wrote in *The Myth of Repressed Memory: False Memories and Allegations of Sexual Abuse* (St. Martin's Press, New York, 1994) that if repression consists of avoiding in one's consciousness the terrible past experiences that come back to a person, then she believed in repression. However, Loftus could not accept that the mind could block out experiences of recurrent traumas, with the person unaware of them, and then recovering them years later.

Generally, research has found that children who have suffered serious psychological trauma do not repress the memory; rather, they can never forget it. Survivors of concentration camps or children who have witnessed the murder of a parent never forget. In fact, they may seek therapy to help suppress the horrible memories so they can go on with their lives.

Evidence in the Brain

Research has tried to find evidence of false memory in the brain. Daniel L. Schacter et al. (*Neuron*, August 1996) showed volunteers an initial list of words and then a second list incorporating words that were similar but had not appeared in the original list. More than half the words the volunteers "remembered" were not on the first list. Using positron emission tomography scans (PET scans measure changes in blood flow, and blood flow indicates neural activity), Schacter found that parts of the brain involved in memory (the hippocampus) became active regardless of whether the memories were true or false.

In the cases of true memories, however, an area that processes information about sounds of recently heard words also lit up. False memories, on the other hand, showed more activity in portions of the brain that had been found to struggle to recall the context of an event.

Implanting Memories

Many scientific studies have shown that false memories can be implanted in a person's mind, leading the subject to "remember" events that never happened. Hypnosis has especially been cited for producing "memories" that may or may not be true. Once these memories have been introduced, they become as real to that person as what happened the previous week.

A major split has occurred between researchers and clinicians over the role of memory. Memory researchers have shown that false memories can be implanted fairly easily in the laboratory. Elizabeth F. Loftus has experimented with implanting the traumatic memory of being lost in a shopping mall. She had the older brother of a 14-year-old boy tell his brother that at age five the boy had gotten lost at the mall. Two days later the boy remembered his feelings; on the third day he recalled a conversation with his mother; on the fourth day he described the older man who found him; on the fifth day he remembered the mall and a conversation with the stranger. Within two weeks he had a complete, detailed memory of being lost when he was five and, when questioned, was convinced that it was a true memory.

Recovered-memory advocates insist that while it may be easy to implant memories of common emotions (in this case, that of being lost), it is not possible to implant memories of something unusual like sexual abuse. Researchers cannot experiment with implanting sexual abuse memories because of the obvious ethical considerations and possible repercussions.

In an unusual situation, Richard Ofshe, social psychologist and expert on cults, successfully implanted a memory of abuse in Paul Ingram's mind. In 1988, Paul Ingram, a conservative, religious family man, was charged by his children with extensive sexual and satanic abuse. After months of interrogations and pressure from a psychologist and police detectives, Ingram began to confess to all kinds of horrific behavior. As his children brought up new charges, he would search his memory until he finally "remembered" and could even supply details of the events.

Richard Ofshe, who had been hired by the prosecution, did not believe Ingram's memories were genuine. Ofshe told Ingram he had spoken to one of Ingram's sons and one of his daughters, and they related the time Ingram forced them to have sex in front of him. This was one of the few charges that had not been brought against Ingram, and never was, but within a day Ingram submitted a written confession with details of the memory of the event. When Ofshe informed Ingram he was mistaken, Ingram protested, saying that the event was as real as anything else.

Although Ingram was not sure about his memories, he was convinced that his daughters would never lie and that he had a dark side he had not known. His pastor, who was counseling his daughters, told him that the abuse had indeed happened. The pastor exorcised him and admonished him to pray to God to bring back memories of his evil acts. Later on Paul claimed remembering the abuse. Before Dr. Ofshe could submit his report to the prosecution, Ingram pleaded guilty to the charges of rape.

Richard Ofshe reported to the prosecution that "my analysis of this interrogation is that it is quite likely that most of what Mr. Ingram reports as recollections of events are products of social influence rather than reports based on his memory of events." Ingram later realized his false recollections and withdrew his guilty plea. The Washington State Supreme Court rejected his appeal. Ingram received a 20-year prison sentence, which is equivalent to life imprisonment in Washington.

Ingram applied for pardon. Memory experts, Elizabeth Loftus and Richard Ofshe, as well as the county prosecutor, sheriff, and his son testified on his behalf. Lawrence Wright, who investigated and wrote about Ingram's case in the New Yorker magazine, also offered testimony. In 1996 Ingram's request for pardon was denied. With the help of his supporters who established the Ingram Organization, Paul Ingram currently seeks pardon from Washington Governor Gary Locke.

ARE THERE SYMPTOMS THAT INDICATE REPRESSED MEMORIES OF CHILDHOOD SEXUAL ABUSE?

The accepted symptoms of childhood abuse vary widely (see Chapters 5 and 6), so nearly everyone is liable to find clues to suggest he or she was abused in the past. For example, Ellen Bass and Laura Davis, in *The Courage to Heal: A Guide for Women Survivors of Child Sexual Abuse* (HarperCollins, New York, 1988), claimed that Sigmund Freud was right about his first theory (see Chapter 6) that the physical symptoms of hysteria in his patients were indicative of childhood sexual abuse.

The Courage to Heal has often been described as the "bible" of the recovered-memory movement, a survivor's guide for adult victims of child sexual abuse. The authors ask women readers how often they suffer the following symptoms, which they consider signs of childhood sexual abuse:

- You feel that you are bad, dirty, or ashamed.

- You feel powerless, like a victim.

- You feel that there is something wrong with you deep down inside or that if people really knew you, they would leave.

- You feel unable to protect yourself in dangerous situations.

- You have no sense of your own interest, talents, or goals.

- You have trouble feeling motivated.

- You feel you have to be perfect.

On one side of the repressed-memory controversy are some clinical therapists who believe that repressed sexual trauma can be determined from a checklist of symptoms such as stated above and that treatment is required to uncover the abuse. They believe that memories rediscovered through hypnosis and other recovery techniques are true and that they must be acknowledged in order for treatment to be successful. They are concerned that questioning the validity of these memories provides offenders with an easy way to avoid responsibility for their actions. On the other hand, some more skeptical experimental psychologists wonder how therapists can be so sure of their diagnosis from a list of symptoms that could be the result of many different conditions.

Many mental health professionals point out that the public should be wary not only of unscrupulous therapists but also of those who have no training in mental health. For example, they point out that the authors Bass and Davis (see above) are not licensed therapists. Bass was a creative writing teacher, and Davis was a student in one of her writing workshops.

Looking for Answers to Symptoms

When an anxious, unhappy patient seeks help, she (most patients are female) is looking for an explanation for what are often vague symptoms that do not appear to have a source. According to accounts from patients, the therapist may ask, "Your symptoms sound like you were sexually abused as a child. What can you tell me about this?" Some therapists feel it is imperative to ask about sexual abuse in the first meeting with every new patient.

When presented with questions like these, if the patient repeatedly reports no memories, she may feel she is letting down the therapist, and that she does not have a valid reason to be in therapy. On the other hand, if the patient does recover repressed memories, then she gains a comprehensive reason for all her problems that originate outside of herself, absolving her of responsibility. In addition, she earns approval and sympathy from her therapist.

Critics of repressed memory theories suggest that therapists who believe in repressed memory may encourage a patient to "remember" that she had been sexually abused in childhood. For example, some of these therapists have been known to recommend that a patient cut off all ties with the families to speed up recovery. This leaves the patients highly dependant on their therapists for emotional support and vulnerable to suggestion, sometimes for many years.

Michael Yapko, a clinical psychologist and a memory expert, believes that many therapists do not really understand how easy it is to convince people that they remember events that never actually happened. He fears that many therapists who believe in repressed memory and treat their patients based on these personal beliefs and philosophy, rather than an objective assessment of the facts. (*Suggestions of Abuse: True and False Memories of Childhood Sexual Abuse*, Simon and Schuster, New York, 1994.) However, Carolyn Zerbe Enns warns against condemning all therapists just because some are poorly informed or unscrupulous. She noted that there are real victims out there who have survived abuse and may fear that others may not believe them. On the other hand, Enns noted that therapists who try to force their patients to remember things are abusing their power and may hurt rather than help their patient. ("Counselors and the Backlash: 'Rape Hype' and 'False Memory Syndrome,'" *Journal of Counseling and Development*, Vol. 74, March/April 1996.)

Dissociative Identity Disorder (DID)

Some psychologists, including many recovered-memory therapists, believe sexual abuse can be so psychologically destructive that the victim, in order to save herself (or himself) from total insanity, splits her personality into separate parts, each one of which is assigned a particular aspect of life to control. This condition was originally labeled multiple personality disorder (MPD), but it has now been clinically replaced with the term Dissociative Identity Disorder (DID).

Other scientists disagree, however. For example, Daniel L. Schacter (*Searching for Memory: The Brain, the Mind, and the Past*, BasicBooks, New York, 1996) questioned how a patient could dissociate so much of her past, and yet function in society for years without her problems being obvious in her behavior before she consults a therapist. Schacter argued that patients who have really experienced many episodes of dissociation should also have a documented history of the manifestations of such disorder before ever having recovered repressed memories of long-term abuse.

DOES DISSOCIATIVE IDENTITY DISORDER REALLY EXIST? In the 1970s the publication and the making into a movie of the book, *Sybil*, helped popularize multiple personality disorder (MPD). Considered a rare mental condition, reported cases of MPD increased from fewer than 50 cases prior to the publication of the book to over 40,000 cases by 1995. Yet in 1998 evidence came to light which cast doubt on whether Sybil herself truly had MPD. Recovered tapes of interviews by the book's author, Flora

Rheta Schreiber, with Sybil's psychoanalyst, Dr. Cornelia Wilbur, revealed the doctor describing her use of hypnosis and sodium pentathol (a type of "truth serum") to "help develop" Sybil's other personalities, details which had been left out of the book and subsequent movie.

SCIENTIFIC PROOF OF REPRESSED MEMORY?

While some repressed memory experts such as Lenore Terr (see below) dismiss all laboratory experiments on memory as invalid, others have tried to scientifically prove that memories can be forgotten. Linda Meyer Williams, of the Family Research Laboratory of the University of New Hampshire, Durham, NH, studied the recall of women who had been abused in childhood, for whom there were medical records proving the abuse ("Recall of Childhood Trauma: A Prospective Study of Women's Memories of Child Sexual Abuse," *Journal of Consulting and Clinical Psychology*, Vol. 62, No. 6, 1994). Other studies attempting to prove memory repression have relied on the subjects' own assertions that they had suffered past traumas and then had forgotten them.

Williams used data gathered between 1973 and 1975 on 206 girls (ages 10 months to 12 years) who had been examined for sexual abuse in a city hospital emergency room. In 1990 and 1991, 129 of these women were included in a study that was, they were told, a follow-up on the lives and health of women who had received health care as children at the hospital. The women, now between the ages of 18 and 31, were not told of their history of child sexual abuse, although some women suspected the reason for their hospital visit.

Of the 129 women, 38 percent failed to report the sexual abuse documented by the hospital; however, of this group, 68 percent reported other childhood sexual abuses. Williams doubted that the women were simply unwilling to discuss the abuse because other personal subjects, such as abortions, prostitution, or having sexually transmitted diseases, were not withheld.

Twelve percent (15 respondents) of the total sample reported that they were never abused in childhood. Williams suggested that this was an undercount of the likely number of women who had forgotten childhood abuse. Because the abuse these women suffered was known to at least one other person (the person who brought the child to the hospital), it was less likely to have been repressed than abuse that was always kept a secret.

Williams concluded that if it is possible that victims do not remember having been abused, their recovery of repressed memory later on in life should not come as a surprise. In fact, 16 percent of the women who recalled the sexual victimization that brought them to the hospital, reported there were periods of time when they "forgot" the abuse.

In a second paper on the same research ("Recovered Memories of Abuse in Women with Documented Child Sexual Victimization Histories," *Journal of Traumatic Stress*, October 1995), Williams described the interviews with some of the women who had forgotten. It is not clear whether the women were truly amnesiac or whether the abuse was simply not a part of their conscious lives for a period of time.

Most reported that they recalled the abuse when a television movie or some other event jogged their memory. None had turned to the help of a therapist to uncover repressed memories. Williams suggested that these women (inner-city, mainly black, women) did not have the financial resources or knowledge to seek out professional help.

A Rebuttal

Critics of Williams's conclusions pointed out that one of the reasons women in the study had forgotten their abuse was that the trauma had occurred in infancy. (Experts contend that events that happen before the acquisition of language at two to three years of age are forgotten because there is no way to express the event.) Williams disagreed, noting that, while 55 percent of those who had been abused at three years or younger had no memory of the occurrence, 62 percent of those who were 4 to 6 years old also did not remember.

In addition, critics questioned how Williams could be certain that those who claimed not to remember were actually telling the truth. The researchers never confronted the women who did not report abuse by showing them their hospital records.

The American Psychological Association Report

The American Psychological Association (APA) assembled a group of clinicians and researchers to produce "The Final Report of the APA Working Group on the Investigation of Memories of Childhood Abuse" (1996). The group was split between practitioners who supported the concept of recovered memories and scientists who studied memory. The report included a list of final conclusions, which stated that most abused children remember all or part of their abuse; however, it is possible for the victims to remember long-time memories of abuse that have been forgotten. The group also reported that it is also possible to construct convincing false memories, but there are gaps in understanding the processes that lead to accurate and inaccurate memories of childhood abuse. The bulk of the 293-page report, however, was a battle between the clinicians and scientists, each citing research and evidence to support their group's position.

BELIEFS OF CLINICIANS

Most experts skeptical of repressed memory do not claim that it is impossible to forget traumatic events, but they are suspicious of how frequently repressed memory appears to occur, especially when it is brought out in therapy, hypnosis, or through self-help books and recovery groups. Michael Yapko (*Suggestions of Abuse: True and False Memories of Childhood Sexual Trauma*, Simon and Schuster, New York, 1994), concerned about the possible disastrous repercussions of misdiagnosing sexual abuse, conducted a survey of therapists' attitudes.

Approximately one-third of respondents agreed and 12 percent agreed strongly that the mind is comparable to a computer that records actual happenings. About one in 10 therapists believed that "memory is not significantly influenced by suggestion." Forty-one percent believed that childhood memories, even the earliest ones, are accurately stored and can be recovered. Another 43 percent agreed that persons who do not have many memories of their childhood could very well have had a somehow traumatic childhood.

More than half of the therapists (57 percent) admitted that they did nothing to differentiate true memories from false memories in their patients' accounts. Yapko was concerned that if a therapist is blinded to the true problems, he cannot help his client with the real issues in the client's life. (Yapko's book opens with the account of a patient who suffered such severe posttraumatic stress from his experiences in Vietnam that he committed suicide. Only after his death did his wife search the records and discover that her husband had never served in Vietnam.)

Researchers on hypnosis do not agree on whether it is a reliable method of memory retrieval or whether it increases the tendency to accept suggested memories or create false ones that are accepted by the patient as real. Yet three-quarters of Yapko's respondents thought of hypnosis as a tool for facilitating accurate recall, while 83 percent thought hypnosis helps to lift repressed memory into conscious awareness. Nearly half (47 percent) believed that therapists can rely more on the details of a traumatic experience if these details have been retrieved through hypnosis. Nearly two-thirds (64 percent) agreed that hypnosis could be used to create false memories, but more than a quarter (27 percent) did not think false memories could be generated by hypnosis.

VERIFICATION

It has been questioned whether the repressed-memory movement would have attained epidemic proportions had psychotherapists verified their patients' "memories" of past abuse. Many psychotherapists wonder why some of their colleagues have not only failed to corroborate their patients' stories, but have accepted them as realities. The False Memory Syndrome Foundation claims that, in not a single case of alleged childhood abuse that has come to its attention, has the therapist sought the patient's pediatri-

cian's records, and in only a few of the 2,800 cases was there any attempt to consult school records, other family members, or any independent sources. David Spiegel, in the *Harvard Mental Health Letter* (September 1998), observed that repressed memory, whether retrieved with or without the help of hypnosis, cannot be proven to be true without external verification.

A report by the Council on Scientific Affairs by the American Medical Association states, "The AMA considers recovered memories of childhood sexual abuse to be of uncertain authenticity, which should be subject to external verification. The use of recovered memories is fraught with problems of potential misapplication" (Sub. Res. 504, A-93; Modified by: CSA Rep. 5-A-94).

INFORMED CONSENT

Before a patient undergoes surgery or a medical diagnostic procedure, he or she is informed of the purpose of the procedure, the expected outcome, as well as the possible risks and side effects. The patient is then asked to sign a consent form. Some people who advocate a similar informed consent for those seeking therapy are proposing the passage of informed consent legislation. In October 1999 Indiana became the first state to pass a law requiring mental health services providers to obtain consent from their patients.

Allen Feld believes that informed consent is necessary in psychotherapy because some patients who have consulted therapists for contemporary problems or for specific symptoms have instead been exposed to therapy to which they have not agreed ("Perspectives on Informed Consent," Parts 1 and 2, *False Memory Syndrome Foundation Newsletter*, Vol. 9, Nos. 3 and 4, May/June and July/August, 2000). Therapies involving patients' exploration of their pasts have resulted in many cases of "recovered" memories of childhood abuse, particularly sexual abuse.

Feld believes that with informed consent, the therapist takes into consideration the reason why the patient seeks therapy. He or she then discusses with the patient the course of treatment to be implemented, his or her experiences with the treatment proposed, and the outcomes and possible risks associated with the therapy. If the therapist thinks that exploring the client's past is necessary, the patient should be told about the implications of such therapy.

RECOVERED-MEMORY THERAPY

Some critics claim that recovered-memory therapists are convinced their patients cannot heal until they confront their memories. They often suggest that the patient sue the offending parent in court. Critics charge that such therapy does not heal and often destroys.

In 1996 psychologist Elizabeth F. Loftus presented a study of the Washington State Crime Victims Compensation Program to the Southwestern Psychological Association. Loftus found that all 30 claimants in the study were still in therapy three years after their first recovered memory; 18 were still in therapy after five years. While only three thought about suicide or attempted suicide before recovering their first memory, 20 killed themselves after therapy. Two had been hospitalized prior to their first recovered memory, compared with 11 after they retrieved memories. Before therapy, 25 had been employed; after therapy, only three still had jobs. Of the 23 who had been married, 11 divorced. Seven lost custody of their children.

SATANIC ABUSE

In addition to repressed memories of incest, the recovered-memory movement has had increasingly frequent reports of ritual, or satanic, abuse. Satanic rituals allegedly include ritual rape and impregnation, murdering of babies, and drinking of blood. During the mid-1980s recovered-memory therapists linked Dissociative Identity Disorder (see above) with satanic abuse and started finding more and more patients who, through hypnosis, revealed remarkably similar horrific tales of satanic cult abuse.

Kenneth V. Lanning of the Federal Bureau of Investigation has studied the sexual victimization of children since 1981. Lanning is concerned that society has created an environment where victims are rewarded and comforted in direct proportion to the severity of their claims of abuse. The FBI has never found evidence of a national or international conspiracy of satanists. Those who believe these reports of satanism respond that the FBI is part of the conspiracy to cover up the evidence. Satanic cults have been blamed for the deaths of between 50,000 and 60,000 people every year, although the annual total of homicides averages fewer than 25,000. Law enforcement has not found any evidence of satanic abuse—no bones, no fetuses, no reliable eyewitnesses.

In her report to the Southwestern Psychological Association on a study of the Washington State Crime Victims Compensation Program (see above), Elizabeth F. Loftus stated that, of the 30 claimants, nearly all (29) reported memories of satanic abuse, with seven months being the average age of the onset of abuse. The claimants reported 150 murders, and 29 remembered physical torture and mutilation. However, none of the medical records of these patients corroborated these claims.

Tales of satanic abuse are so improbable that many supporters of recovered memory fear these claims may harm the image of the movement. Richard Ofshe and Ethan Watters, in *Making Monsters: False Memories, Psychotherapy, and Sexual Hysteria* (Scribners, New York, 1994), described allegations of satanic abuse as a pure product of suggestion and predicted it will become the Achilles heel (the weak spot that will lead to the downfall) of the recovered-memory movement.

GOING TO COURT

Suing Alleged Abusers

Between 1983 and 1996 many individuals who had "recovered" memories of childhood sexual abuse sued their alleged abusers, many at the instigation of their therapists. During those years a total of 517 civil (85 percent) and criminal (15 percent) suits based on repressed memory were filed. After a sharp rise in 1992, the year the False Memory Syndrome Foundation (FMSF) was created (see below), there has been a steep drop since 1994. (See Figure 8.1.) An informal tally of cases by the FMSF has found that two-thirds of the civil suits had been dropped, dismissed, or concluded in favor of the alleged abusers.

While the courts readily accepted some early cases of child sexual abuse, courts in more and more states are becoming increasingly suspicious of accounts of outrageous abuse. Therapists are being held liable for malpractice not only by their patients, but often by third parties (usually the accused parents of someone who has allegedly recovered memories of sexual abuse).

The Case of Eileen Franklin

In 1990 George Franklin was convicted of murdering his daughter Eileen's friend 20 years earlier. Eileen initially claimed to have recovered memories of her father's murderous act after they came to her in hypnosis while in therapy. Later on she changed her story, reporting that one day in 1989 the play of sunlight and shadow on her six-year-old daughter's face brought back the image of her playmate on the day she was murdered. Eileen suddenly remembered herself as a nine-year-old watching her father kill her friend.

Lenore Terr, a clinical professor of psychiatry, was an influential expert witness at this first criminal trial in the United States involving recovered memory. Terr, who supports the idea of repressed memory, later wrote about Eileen's story in the book, *Unchained Memories: True Stories of Traumatic Memories, Lost and Found* (BasicBooks, New York, 1994).

Harry MacLean, who reported on the case in his book, *Once Upon a Time: A True Story of Memory, Murder, and The Law* (HarperCollins, New York, 1993), claimed that Terr had repeatedly distorted the facts to suit her purpose. Terr claimed to offer a dramatic proof of Eileen's truthful testimony when she described the "body memory" (a physical manifestation of trauma that the conscious mind has forgotten) of Eileen's repressed trauma. According to Terr, Eileen had a habit of pulling her hair out, resulting in a balding spot on her scalp. Eileen

FIGURE 8.1

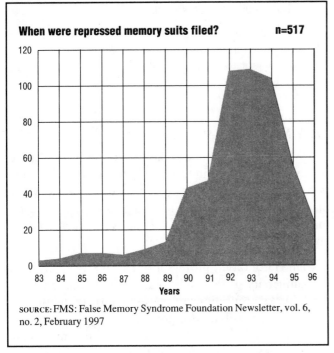

When were repressed memory suits filed?   n=517

SOURCE: FMS: False Memory Syndrome Foundation Newsletter, vol. 6, no. 2, February 1997

had allegedly seen her father murder her friend with a blow to the head using a large rock.

According to MacLean, in his interviews with Eileen's mother, sisters, school friends, and teachers, none could remember Eileen's pulling out her hair or having a bleeding spot on her scalp. Ofshe and Watters (*Making Monsters*, see above) found more than 40 photos taken of Eileen during the relevant period that were wrongly withheld from the defense and which showed no trace of a bald spot.

In November 1995 a federal appeals court overturned George Franklin's murder conviction. By this time Franklin had served almost seven years of a life sentence. The court found that the trial had been tainted by the improper allegation that Franklin had confessed and by the exclusion of crucial evidence: Eileen had been hypnotized by her therapist, Kirk Barrett, prior to the first trial, making her testimony unreliable. The court ordered a retrial. On July 2, 1996, the prosecution dropped the charges, citing the problem of Eileen's hypnosis which, by California law, would probably prevent her from testifying. In addition, new DNA evidence showed that it was impossible for Franklin to have committed a second murder his daughter had accused him of, which she claimed happened when she was 15.

In June 1997 George Franklin filed a civil suit in federal court against his daughter, her therapist Barrett, Lenore Terr, and county officials, claiming violation of his civil rights. The suit alleged, among other things, that Eileen, Barrett, and county officials conspired to deny Franklin the due process of law and violated his Fifth, Sixth, and Four-

teenth Amendment rights to confront witnesses against him. Lenore Terr and the district attorney were also being sued because they gave false testimony about recovered memories that was not based on scientific research.

In July 2000 the court threw out George Franklin's case against the county officials, leaving just his claim against his daughter's conspiracy with the therapist Kirk Barrett.

Suing the Therapist

In what was one of the longest (13 weeks) malpractice trials in the American justice system, a jury awarded Elizabeth Carlson of Minnesota more than $2.5 million in 1996. Carlson had accused Dr. Diane Bay Humenansky of "negligent psychotherapy by using hypnosis, misinformation, coercion, threats, and suggestions to implant false memories of childhood abuse" (*Carlson v. Humenansky*, District Ct., Ramsey Co., Minnesota, Case No. CX 93-7260). The patient claimed that under Dr. Humenansky's treatment, she became convinced she had developed "alters" or multiple personalities to help her cope with sexual abuses by her parents, relatives, and neighbors.

Carlson reported that during her more than two years of therapy, she felt worse and worse. Humenansky gave her books to read on incest, multiple personality disorder, and satanic abuse. Carlson also started believing that she was part of an intergenerational satanic cult. When Carlson and other patients met without the doctor, they were shocked to discover that they shared remarkably similar memories of abuse and had alternate personalities with the same names and traits. Since then eight other former patients have sued Humenansky.

THIRD-PARTY SUITS. The courts now often hold therapists liable to a third party, usually the patient's accused parent, when they implant or reinforce false memories in their patients. *The False Memory Syndrome Foundation (FMSF) Legal Survey* found that, as of December 1998, 158 malpractice suits had been brought by a third party against a negligent mental health provider. The FMSF believes that the total number of lawsuits is probably larger.

Social worker Susan L. Jones, while treating Joel Hungerford's daughter Laura, convinced her that her anxiety attacks were the result of sexual abuse by her father. Jones not only advised Laura to cease contact with her father but also convinced the patient to file a complaint of aggravated felonious sexual assault against Hungerford. In addition Jones contacted the police regarding the alleged assault and aided the prosecution in indicting Hungerford.

Hungerford sued Jones for the misdiagnosis and negligent treatment of his daughter's condition. Jones claimed that she owed Hungerford no duty of care, meaning that since she had treated Laura Hungerford, not Joel Hungerford, Joel Hungerford could not claim that her treatment had hurt him. On December 18, 1998, in *Joel Hungerford v. Susan L. Jones* (No. 97-657, 1998 N.H. LEXIS 94), the New Hampshire Supreme Court, in this case of "first impression" (with no existing precedent), ruled,

> [W]e hold that a therapist owes an accused parent a duty of care in the diagnosis and treatment of an adult patient for sexual abuse where the therapist or the patient, acting on the encouragement, recommendation, or instruction of the therapist, takes public action concerning the accusation. In such instances, the social utility of detecting and punishing sexual abusers and maintaining the breadth of treatment choices for patients is outweighed by the substantial risk of severe harm to falsely accused parents, the family unit, and society.

The Statute of Limitations

One of the legal issues contested in cases of repressed memory is how long the statute of limitations should run, since typically the victim has allegedly repressed the memories for many years. The NOW (National Organization for Women) Legal Defense and Education Fund supports survivors' right to bring a civil suit against their perpetrators at any time. NOW claims that research has shown that due to the trauma of abuse, victims may not be aware of their experiences until they have become adults.

A recent trend in court actions has been to question the validity of repressed memories and, therefore, the necessity for an extended statute of limitations. In 1996 the U.S. Supreme Court declined to review a Wisconsin Supreme Court case (*Pritzlaff v. Archdiocese of Milwaukee* 194 Wis.2d 303, 533 N.W.2d 780, 1995), thereby letting the state court's decision stand. The Wisconsin court had pointed out that when cases of environmental injury or malpractice are brought after a delay, there is a specific physical injury which can be objectively traced back to a particular cause. In this case the plaintiff could only claim "emotional" and "psychological" damage that had allegedly happened 27 years earlier. The court did not think it would be able to accurately reveal the truth.

AN EXCEPTION. In 1991 Paula Hearndon sued her stepfather, Kenneth Graham, for sexually abusing her from 1968 to 1975 (when she was between the ages of 8 and 15). According to Hearndon, the traumatic amnesia she experienced due to the abuse lasted until 1988. Due to Florida's four-year statute of limitation, the lawsuit did not proceed.

However, in September 2000 the Florida Supreme Court, in a 5-2 decision, ruled that memory loss resulting from the trauma of childhood sexual abuse should be considered an exception to the statute of limitations (*Hearndon v. Graham*, No. SC92665, September 14, 2000, Sup Ct Fla, 2000 Fla. LEXIS 1844).

The court, while observing that disagreements about recovered memory exist, stated,

> It is widely recognized that the shock and confusion resultant from childhood molestation, often coupled with authoritative adult demands and threats for secrecy, may lead a child to deny or suppress such abuse from his or her consciousness.

WHY MAKE THE ACCUSATIONS?

Why would someone make such terrible accusations if they were not true? In fact, one of the arguments in support of repressed memories is exactly that: No one would make up something so horrible and painful. If one accepts that premise, however, there is no way for an alleged abuser to prove his or her innocence.

Dr. Harold Lief, professor of psychiatry emeritus at the University of Pennsylvania, proposes that a person might make accusations of abuse to attract attention, to place the responsibility for problems on someone else, to have one simple answer for all of life's problems, and to punish oneself or someone else. Critics worry that women are drawn to the recovered-memory movement because of its cult-like atmosphere and the concern and attention the women receive from making their revelations. Investigators who have attended self-discovery weekends report that the person who can tell the most horrifying tale of abuse (satanic rituals are especially effective) gets the most love and attention.

Critics of recovered-memory therapy charge that therapists create total dependence in their patients, thereby ensuring payment for treatment for years to come. Much of this has been covered by insurance. However, with the recent changes to managed care plans, there may be much less money available for therapy. Some predict that the combination of managed care and the increasing number of malpractice lawsuits and retractors (patients who have withdrawn claims of sexual abuse) will accomplish what professional conflict has not—put an end to the issue of recovered memory.

THE PARENTS

When a child accuses her parent/parents of sexual abuse, she is very likely ruining their lives. A daughter who decides to confront her abuser has usually been prepared by her therapist or by her readings to expect that her parents will disavow any knowledge of abuse—a symptom, according to her therapist, that her parents are "in denial."

Very often families are split as family members are forced to take sides. Nineteen-year-old Beth Rutherford of Springfield, Missouri, consulted a church counselor due to job stress. By the end of her two-and-a-half-year therapy with Donna Strand, she had recovered "memories" of being impregnated twice by her minister father and of his performing a coat-hanger abortion on her. Fearful of their father, Beth and her middle sister fled to another state, while her youngest sister went into hiding. Court findings revealed that Beth was still a virgin and that her father had had a vasectomy. In 1996 the Missouri church where Strand was a counselor paid the Rutherford family $1 million as a court settlement (*Rutherford v. Strand et al.*, Circuit Ct., Green Co., MO, No. 1960C2745).

Nothing short of murder is considered so heinous as child sexual abuse and once someone has been accused, it is extremely difficult for that person to clear his name. Even after a person is cleared of a child sexual abuse crime, he or she may still have to live under a cloud of suspicion.

The False Memory Syndrome Foundation

As part of the backlash against the growing number of cases of repressed memory, an organization of parents claiming to have been falsely accused of child sexual abuse was formed in 1992. The False Memory Syndrome Foundation (FMSF) was founded by Pamela Freyd, whose daughter had accused her father of childhood abuse. (The daughter, Jennifer Freyd, is a psychologist at the University of Oregon who specializes in memory.) The FMSF publishes a newsletter six times a year and organizes conferences to support falsely accused parents. The Foundation distributes information on what it sees as a dangerous movement in psychotherapy to encourage and accept all claims of childhood abuse without verification.

The FMSF and other experts who question the validity of repressed memory do not question whether sexual abuse occurs—it questions how often. Furthermore, they are concerned that false accusations will throw doubt on genuine cases of abuse.

Ironically, just as their children have often recounted remarkably similar stories of abuse, parents have amazingly similar stories of how their children have remembered the abuse, disclosed it to the family, demanded acceptance of the alleged abuse, and then cut off all communication with the family, turning instead to the therapist and support groups. In cases in which the child has retracted her accusations, some families have seen the renewed contact with their child as a gift. Others cannot forgive the pain the child has caused them and have been reluctant to welcome the accuser back into the family.

Some mental health professionals have dismissed the FMSF as an extreme organization. The Foundation has been accused of protecting child abusers and attempting to discredit the psychiatric profession. They claim that rather than work toward improving therapy, the FMSF sided with those people considered extreme on its scientific board. (The board includes acknowledged experts such as Elizabeth F. Loftus, Richard Ofshe, and Paul McHugh.) In their view, recovered-memory therapy is the practice of a very small group of therapists. On the other hand, for the families torn apart by what they insist are false memories, the FMSF has been a lifeline to others suffering the same accusations.

A LONGITUDINAL STUDY OF MEMORY AND CHILDHOOD ABUSE

Between 1986 and 1998 Catherine Cameron conducted a long-term study of child sexual abuse survivors (*Resolving Childhood Trauma*, Sage Publications, Thousand Oaks, CA, 2000). The researcher interviewed 72 women, ages 25–64, over a 12-year period. The women comprised a group of sexual abuse survivors who sought therapy for the first time in the 1980s. On average, it had been 30 years since their first abuse occurred (36 years for those who suffered amnesia). The women were in private therapy, were better educated, and were more financially well off than most survivors. Twelve imprisoned women were included in the survey. They came from a low socioeconomic background, were serving long sentences, and had had only brief group therapy sessions, lasting less than a year.

Cameron sought to study amnesia as both an effect and a cause—what was it about the abuse that resulted in amnesia and how did the amnesia affect the victim later on in life? Twenty-five women were amnesiac, having no awareness of the abuse until recently. Twenty-one were non-amnesiac, unable to forget their abuse, and 14 were partially amnesic about their abuse. The imprisoned women were not assigned a specific category because they were part of a therapy group.

About 8 of 10 of the amnesic and partially amnesic women believed that they did not remember the sexual abuse because the memories were too painful to live with (82 percent) and they felt a sense of guilt or shame (79 percent). More than half of each group believed the amnesia served as a defense mechanism resulting from their desire to protect the family (58 percent) and love for, or dependence on, the perpetrator (53 percent). About three-quarters (74 percent) thought the amnesia occurred because they felt no one would believe them or help them. More than one-third (37 percent) thought the amnesia had come about because they needed to believe in a "safe" world.

During the years between the abuse and the recall of the abuse, the amnesiacs reported experiencing the same problems as the non-amnesiacs, including problems with relationships, revictimization, self-abuse, and dependency on alcohol. However, because the amnesiacs had no conscious knowledge of their childhood abuse, they could not find an explanation for their problems. The author claims that the conflict between the amnesia and memories that needed release left the amnesic victims depressed and confused.

Cameron addressed the allegations that some therapists implant false memories of sexual abuse in their clients. She noted that 72 percent of the amnesic women in her study had begun to recall their abuse prior to seeking therapy. Once the survivors in her study confronted their traumatic past, they took charge of how they wanted their therapy handled. Cameron also observed that, since it is evident that recovered memories of childhood abuse are common, they should not be labeled as "false memories" nor accepted as "flawless truth," but should instead be explored by proponents of the opposing views.

IMPORTANT NAMES AND ADDRESSES

American Bar Association
Center on Children and the Law
740 15th St. NW
Washington, DC 20005
(202) 662-1740
FAX (202) 662-1755
(800) 285-2221
E-mail: ctrchildlaw@abanet.org
URL: http://www.abanet.org/child

American Humane Association
Children's Division
63 Inverness Dr. East
Englewood, CO 80112-5117
(303) 792-9900
FAX (303) 792-5333
(800) 227-4645
E-mail: children@americanhumane.org
URL: http://www.americanhumane.org

Center for the Future of Children
The David and Lucile Packard Foundation
300 Second St., #200
Los Altos, CA 94022
(650) 948-7658
FAX (650) 948-6498
URL: http://www.futureofchildren.org

Child Welfare League of America
440 First St. NW, 3rd Floor
Washington, DC 20001-2085
(202) 638-2952
FAX (202) 638-4004
E-mail: jjohnson@cwla.org
URL: http://www.cwla.org

Children's Defense Fund
25 E St. NW
Washington, DC 20001
(202) 628-8787
FAX (202) 662-3510
E-mail: cdfinfo@childrensdefense.org
URL: http://www.childrensdefense.org

Children's Healthcare Is a Legal Duty, Inc. (CHILD, Inc.)
P.O. Box 2604
Sioux City, IA 51106
(712) 948-3500
FAX (712) 948-3704
E-mail: childinc@netins.net
URL: http://www.childrenshealthcare.org

Crimes Against Children Research Center
126 Horton Social Science Center
University of New Hampshire
Durham, NH 03824
(603) 862-1888
FAX (603) 862-1122
URL: http://www.unh.edu/ccrc

False Memory Syndrome Foundation
1955 Locust St.
Philadelphia, PA 19103-5766
(215) 940-1040
FAX (215) 940-1042
(800) 568-8882
URL: http://www.fmsfonline.org

Family Research Laboratory
126 Horton Social Science Center
University of New Hampshire
Durham, NH 03824
(603) 862-1888
FAX (603) 862-1122
E-mail: dmcole@cisunix.unh.edu
URL: http://www.unh.edu/frl

Family Violence and Sexual Assault Institute
7120 Herman Jared Drive
Fort Worth, TX 76180
(817) 485-2244
FAX (817) 485-0660
E-mail: dwforkids@earthlink.net
URL: http://www.fvsai.org

Juvenile Justice Clearinghouse
P.O. Box 6000

Rockville, MD 20849-6000
FAX (301) 519-5600
(800) 638-8736
E-mail: askncjrs@ncjrs.org
URL: http://www.ncjrs.org

Kempe's Children Center
1825 Marion St.
Denver, CO 80218
(303) 864-5252
FAX (303) 864-5302
E-mail: kempe@kempecenter.org
URL: http://www.kempecenter.org

National Center for Missing & Exploited Children
Charles B. Wang International Children's Building
699 Prince Street
Alexandria, VA 22314-3175
(703) 274-3900
FAX (703) 274-2220
Hotline and CyberTipline (800) 843-5678
URL: http://www.missingkids.org

National Center for Prosecution of Child Abuse
American Prosecutors Research Institute
99 Canal Center Plaza, #510
Alexandria, VA 22314
(703) 739-0321
FAX (703) 549-6259
URL: http://www.ndaa-apri.org/apri/APRIPrograms.html

National Child Abuse Hotline
(800) 422-4453

National Child Pornography Tipline
(800) 843-5678

National Clearinghouse on Child Abuse and Neglect Information
330 C St. SW
Washington, DC 20447

(703) 385-7565
FAX (703) 385-3206
(800) 394-3366
E-mail: nccanch@calib.com
URL: http://www.calib.com/nccanch

National Council of Juvenile and Family Court Judges
Family Violence Project Resource Center
University of Nevada
1041 N. Virginia St.
P.O. Box 8970
Reno, NV 89507
(702) 784-6012
FAX (702) 784-6628
(800) 527-3223
E-mail: admin@ncjfcj.unr.edu
URL: http://www.ncjfcj.unr.edu

National Council on Child Abuse and Family Violence
1155 Connecticut Ave. NW, #400
Washington, DC 20036
(202) 429-6695

FAX (202) 467-4924
URL: http://www.nccafv.org

National Resource Center on Child Maltreatment Organization
Child Welfare Institute
1349 W. Peachtree St. NE, #900
Atlanta, GA 30309-2956
(404) 876-1934
FAX (404) 876-7949
E-mail: nrccm@gocwi.org
URL: http://gocwi.org/nrccm

National Resource Center on Child Sexual Abuse
107 Lincoln St.
Huntsville, AL 35801
(205) 534-6868
FAX (205) 534-6883
(800) 543-7006
URL: http://www.reeusda.gov/pavnet/pm/pmnatrss.htm

National Runaway Switchboard
(800) 621-4000

Office on Child Abuse and Neglect (OCAN)
Children's Bureau
U.S. Department of Health and Human Services
200 Independence Ave. SW
Washington, DC 20201
(202) 619-0257
URL: http://www.acf.dhhs.gov/programs/cb

Prevent Child Abuse America
200 S. Michigan Ave., 17th Floor
Chicago, IL 60604-2404
(312) 663-3520
FAX (312) 939-8962
E-mail: mailbox@preventchildabuse.org
URL: http://www.preventchildabuse.org

UNICEF
333 East 38th St.
New York, NY 10016
(212) 686-5522
FAX (212) 867-5991
E-mail: information@unicefusa.org
URL: http://www.unicefusa.org

RESOURCES

The National Child Abuse and Neglect Data System (NCANDS) of the U.S. Department of Health and Human Services (DHHS; Washington, D.C.) is the primary source of national information on child maltreatment known to state child protective services (CPS) agencies. The latest findings from NCANDS are published in *Child Maltreatment 1998: Reports from the States to the National Child Abuse and Neglect Data System (2000). The Third National Incidence Study of Child Abuse and Neglect* (NIS-3; 1996) is the single most comprehensive source of information about the incidence of child maltreatment in the United States. The NIS-3 findings are based on data collected not only from CPS but also from community institutions (such as day care centers, schools, and hospitals) and other investigating agencies (such as public health departments, police, and courts). The National Clearinghouse on Child Abuse and Neglect Information of the DHHS provided an assortment of helpful publications used in the preparation of this book, including *The Risk and Prevention of Maltreatment of Children with Disabilities* (2000) and *In Harm's Way: Domestic Violence and Child Maltreatment* (undated).

Other federal government publications used for this book include *Sexual Assault of Young Children as Reported to Law Enforcement: Victim, Incident, and Offender Characteristics* (Bureau of Justice Statistics, Washington, D.C., 2000); *National Drug Control Strategy: 2000 Annual Report* (Office of National Drug Control Policy, Washington, D.C., 2000); *Child Welfare Outcomes 1998: Annual Report* (DHHS, 2000); *International Trafficking in Women to the United States: A Contemporary Manifestation of Slavery and Organized Crime* (Central Intelligence Agency, Washington, D.C., 1999); *Prior Abuse Reported by Inmates and Probationers* (Bureau of Justice Statistics, 1999); *Blending Perspectives and Building Common Ground: A Report to Congress on Substance Abuse and Child Protection* (DHHS, 1999); "In the Wake of Childhood Maltreatment," *Juvenile Justice Bulletin*

(U.S. Department of Justice, Washington, D.C., 1997); *Child Protective Services: Complex Challenges Require New Strategies* (U.S. Government Accounting Office, Washington, D.C., 1997); "Family Violence Education in Medical School-Based Residency Programs—Virginia, 1995" (*Morbidity and Mortality Weekly Report*, 1996), and "Investigator's Guide to Allegations of Ritual Child Abuse" (FBI, Washington, D.C., 1992). The U.S. Advisory Board on Child Abuse and Neglect published *A Nation's Shame: Fatal Child Abuse and Neglect in the United States* (DHHS, 1995). Gail S. Goodman et al. researched the *Characteristics and Sources of Allegations of Ritualistic Child Abuse* (1994) for the National Center on Child Abuse and Neglect, an agency recently replaced by the Office on Child Abuse and Neglect.

The National Center for Prosecution of Child Abuse of the American Prosecutors Research Institute (VA) partnered with the National Clearinghouse on Child Abuse and Neglect Information in undertaking the State Statutes Project. *Statutes at-a-Glance* (2000) was part of this project. *Online Victimization: A Report on the Nation's Youth* (Crimes Against Children Research Center, University of New Hampshire, NH, and National Center for Missing & Exploited Children, VA, 2000) discussed the findings of the first *Youth Internet Safety Survey*. The American Humane Association (CO) produced "Freedom from Economic Exploitation–A Basic Children's Right" (*Protecting Children: The Rights of Children*, 2000). *No Safe Haven: Children of Substance-Abusing Parents* (NY, 1999), by the National Center on Addiction and Substance Abuse at Columbia University, discussed the association between substance abuse or addiction and child maltreatment. The Child Welfare League of America (Washington, D.C.) published *Alcohol and Other Drug Survey of State Child Welfare Agencies* (1998), and Prevent Child Abuse America published *Public Opinion and Behaviors Regarding Child Abuse Prevention: 1999 Survey* (1999). The Gale Group thanks the National Center for Prosecution of Child Abuse, Crimes Against Children Research Center, National Center for Missing & Exploited Children, and Prevent Child Abuse America for permission to use graphics from their publications.

The Family Research Laboratory (FRL) at the University of New Hampshire, Durham, NH, is a major source of studies on domestic violence. Murray A. Straus, Richard J. Gelles, Linda Meyer Williams, David Finkelhor, Kathleen Kendall-Tackett, and many others associated with the laboratory have done some of the most scientifically rigorous researches in the field of abuse. Studies released by the FRL investigate all forms of domestic violence, many based on its two major surveys: the *National Family Violence Survey* (1975) and the *National Family Violence Resurvey* (1985). Much of the research from these two surveys has been gathered into *Physical Violence in American Families: Risk Factors and Adaptations to Violence in 8,145 Families* (Straus and Gelles; Christine Smith, editor, Transaction Publishers, NJ, 1990).

Murray A. Straus, E. Milling Kinard, and Linda Meyer Williams studied the correlation of childhood neglect and social integration in *The Neglect Scale* (1995). Kathleen Kendall-Tackett and Roberta Marshall reported on the "Sexual Victimization of Children" (*Issues in Intimate Violence*, Sage Publications, CA, 1998). Additional sexual abuse research can be found in *Characteristics of Incestuous Fathers* (David Finkelhor and Williams, 1992) and in "Current Information on the Scope and Nature of Child Sexual Abuse" (Finkelhor, *The Future of Children: Sexual Abuse of Children*, 1994).

Murray A. Straus and Julie H. Stewart reported on *Corporal Punishment by American Parents: National Data on Prevalence, Chronicity, Severity, and Duration, in Relation to Child and Family Characteristics* (1998). Straus and Mallie J. Paschall prepared *Corporal Punishment by Mothers and Child's Cognitive Development: A Longitudinal Study* (1998). Straus, David B. Sugarman, and Jean Giles-Sims studied the link between corporal punishment and increased antisocial behavior among children in "Spanking by Parents and Subsequent Antisocial Behavior of Children" (*Archives of Pediatrics and Adolescent Medicine*, 1997). Straus further studied the connection between corporal punishment and criminal violence in *Spanking and the Making of a Violent Society* (1996). Murray A. Straus published the second edition of *Beating the Devil out of Them: Corporal Punishment in American Families and Its Effects on Children* (Transaction Publishers, NJ, 2001). Chapter 6 ("Physical Abuse") was used in this book. Dr. Murray A. Straus and the Family Research Laboratory have kindly granted permission to use graphics from their publications.

Many journals published useful articles on child maltreatment that were used in the preparation of this book.

Diane N. Roche et al. studied female victims of child abuse in "Adult Attachment: A Mediator Between Child Sexual Abuse and Later Psychological Adjustment" (*Journal of Interpersonal Violence*, Vol. 14, No. 2, 1999). Azmaira Hamid Maker et al. researched the "Long-Term Psychological Consequences in Women of Witnessing Parental Physical Conflict and Experiencing Abuse in Childhood" (*Journal of Interpersonal Violence*, Vol. 13, No. 5, 1998). Jeffrey L. Edleson reported on "The Overlap Between Child Maltreatment and Woman Battering" (*Violence Against Women*, Vol. 5, No. 2, 1999). William C. Holmes provided current data on "Sexual Abuse of Boys: Definition, Prevalence, Correlates, Sequelae, and Management" (*The Journal of the American Medical Association*, Vol. 281, No. 21, 1998). Brett Drake and Susan Zuravin discussed "Bias in Child Maltreatment Reporting: Revisiting the Myth of Classlessness" (*American Journal of Orthopsychiatry*, Vol. 68, No. 2, 1998).

David E. Hall et al. reported on the "Evaluation of Covert Video Surveillance in the Diagnosis of Munchausen Syndrome by Proxy: Lessons From 41 Cases" (*Pediatrics*, Vol. 105, No. 6, 2000). In "Child Fatalities From Religion-motivated Medical Neglect" (*Pediatrics*, Vol. 101, No. 4, 1998), Seth M. Asser and Rita Swan reviewed the deaths of children in faith-healing religious sects. Jacqueline L. Stock et al. provided information on "Adolescent Pregnancy and Sexual Risk-Taking Among Sexually Abused Girls" (*Family Planning Perspectives*, The Alan Guttmacher Institute, Vol. 29, No. 5, 1997). Frances A. Althaus discussed "Female Circumcision: Rite of Passage or Violation of Rights" (*International Family Planning Perspectives*, The Alan Guttmacher Institute, Vol. 23, No. 3, 1997). Other helpful journals include *Child Abuse and Neglect*, *Psychological Bulletin*, *Journal of Counseling and Development*, *Social Problems*, *Journal of Consulting and Clinical Psychology*, and the *Journal of Traumatic Stress*.

The American Professional Society on the Abuse of Children (APSAC), in *The APSAC Handbook on Child Maltreatment* (1996), brought together a variety of child abuse experts to discuss ongoing controversies in their fields, as well as to challenge long-held assumptions and conclusions. APSAC's interdisciplinary journal, *Child Maltreatment*, reports on current scientific information and technical innovations in child maltreatment research. The Center for the Future of Children of the David and Lucile Packard Foundation publishes information on major issues related to children's well-being. Information from *Domestic Violence and Children* (1999), *Protecting Children from Abuse and Neglect* (1998), and *Sexual Abuse of Children* (1994) were used in this publication. The Center for the Future of Children graciously granted permission to use graphics from its publications.

Helpful books used for this publication include *The Epidemic of Rape and Child Sexual Abuse in the United*

States by Diana E. H. Russell and Rebecca M. Bolen (Sage Publications, CA, 2000), *Neglected Children: Research, Practice, and Policy* by Howard Dubowitz, editor (Sage Publications, CA, 1999); *Understanding Family Violence: Treating and Preventing Partner, Child, Sibling, and Elder Abuse* by Vernon R. Wiehe (Sage Publications, CA, 1998); *The Book of David: How Preserving Families Can Cost Children's Lives* by Richard J. Gelles (Basic-Books, NY, 1996); *Wounded Innocents: The Real Victims of the War Against Child Abuse* by Richard Wexler (Prometheus Books, NY, 1995); and *The Secret Trauma: Incest in the Lives of Girls and Women* by Diana E. H. Russell (BasicBooks, NY, 1986).

Books used for information on recovered memory include *Resolving Childhood Trauma: A Long-Term Study of Abuse Survivors* by Catherine Cameron (Sage Publications, CA, 2000), *Searching for Memory: the Brain, the Mind, and the Past* by Daniel Schacter (BasicBooks, NY, 1996); *The Myth of Repressed Memory: False Memories and Allegations of Sexual Abuse* by Elizabeth F. Loftus (St. Martin's Press, NY, 1994); *Suggestions of Abuse: True and False Memories of Childhood Sexual Abuse* by Michael Yapko (Simon and Schuster, NY, 1994); *Making Monsters: False Memories, Psychotherapy, and Sexual Hysteria* by Richard Ofshe and Ethan Watters (Scribners, NY, 1994); *Unchained Memories: The Stories of Traumatic Memories, Lost and Found* by Lenore Terr (Basic-Books, NY, 1994); *Once Upon a Time: A Story of Memory, Murder, and the Law* (HarperCollins, NY, 1993); and *The Courage to Heal: A Guide for Women Survivors of Child Sexual Abuse* by Ellen Bass and Laura Davis (HarperCollins, NY, 1988).

The Gale Group thanks the False Memory Syndrome Foundation for granting permission to reproduce graphics from its *False Memory Syndrome Foundation Newsletter*. *Child Newsline* of UNICEF graciously provided us with articles and graphics relating to child abuse worldwide. Other UNICEF publications used in the preparation of this book include *The Progress of Nations 2000* (NY, 2000) and *The State of the World's Children 2000* (NY, 2000). As always, we are grateful to the Gallup Organization for continued permission to use its surveys.

INDEX

Page references in italics refer to photographs. References with the letter t following them indicate the presence of a table. The letter f indicates a figure. If more than one table or figure appears on a particular page, the exact item number for the table or figure being referenced is provided.

A

Academic achievement, 54, 55(*f*5.6)
Accidental *vs.* abuse-related injuries, 23*f*
Adolescents, 53–55
Adoption Assistance and Child Welfare Act of 1980, 23–25
Adults
    effects of child sexual abuse on, 73–74
    sexual revictimization, 74
Advocates, court-appointed special, 77
Age
    corporal punishment chronicity by, 59(*f*5.10)
    corporal punishment prevalence by, 58, 59(*f*5.9)
    perpetrator's, 35–36, 37*f*
    victim's, 33–34, 35*f*, 35*t*, 40, 41*f*, 66*t*
American Academy of Pediatrics (AAP), 22
American Civil Liberties Union et al. v. Janet Reno, Attorney General of the United States, 87
American Humane Association, 31
American Medical Association, 95
American Society for the Prevention of Cruelty to Animals, 3
Amirault, Gerald, 88–89
Amirault, Violet, 88–89
Anatomically detailed dolls, 83–84
Antisocial behavior and corporal punishment, 59
Apprenticeships, 1
Archdiocese of Milwaukee, Pritzlaff v., 98
Asymptomatic victims of sexual abuse, 72–73
Azure, United States v., 83

B

Bass, Ellen, 92

Battered child syndrome, 3–4
Behavior problems, 11
Berliner, Lucy, 73
Besharov, Douglas J., 28
Bias in reporting abuse, 30
Black/African Americans, 48
Bolen, Rebecca M., 64, 65
Boys, sexual abuse of, 65–66
Broadhurst, Diane D., 47
Buckey, Raymond, 88

C

Cameron, Catherine, 99–100
CAPTA. *See* Child Abuse Prevention and Treatment Act
Carlson v. Humenansky, 97
Caseworkers and caseload, Child Protective Services, 25
Catholic Church, 70–71
Causes of abuse, 47–49
Characteristics of abused children, 10–13
CHILD, Inc., 12
Child Abduction and Serial Murder Investigative Resource Center, 4
Child abuse and forensic pediatrics curriculum, 22
Child Abuse Prevention, Adoption, and Family Services Act, 32
Child Abuse Prevention and Treatment Act (CAPTA), 4, 5*f*, 9–10, 63–64
Child labor, 2, 5–6, 6*f*
Child molesters, 74
Child Online Protection Act (COPA), 86–87
Child pornography laws, 86–87
Child Pornography Prevention Act, 86
Child Protective Services
    accountability, 26–27
    court involvement with, 23
    domestic violence and, 52
    family preservation, 23, 25
    investigation process, 27–28
    steps followed by cases, 24*f*
    suing, 85
    weaknesses in, 25
Child soldiers, 4
Child welfare organizations, 3

Child witnesses to domestic violence, 51–52
Children
    as property, 1
    testimony of, 79–81
Children's Bureau, 3, 4
Children's Justice Act, 4
Christian Scientists, 12
Chronicity of corporal punishment, 58, 59*f*
Clergy, 70–71
Closed-circuit television testimony, 80
Cognitive development and corporal punishment, 60–61, 61*f*
Commonwealth v. Willis, 80–81
Competency of child witnesses, 79–80
Confrontation clause, 80–81
Connolly, Mary Ellen, 2–3
Contributing factors to abuse, 47–48
Convention on the Rights of the Child, 5–6, 7
COPA. *See* Child Online Protection Act
Corporal punishment, 1–2, 9, 57–61, 57*t*, 58*f*, 58*t*, 59*f*
Council on Scientific Affairs, 95
Court-appointed special advocates, 77
Court cases. *See also* Lawsuits
    American Civil Liberties Union et al. v. Janet Reno, Attorney General of the United States, 87
    Carlson v. Humenansky, 97
    colonial period, 2
    Commonwealth v. Willis, 80–81
    Coy v. Iowa, 81
    Fells Acres Case, 88
    Hearndon v. Graham, 98
    Joel Hungerford v. Susan L. Jones, 97–98
    Landeros v. Flood, 23
    Margaret Kelly Michaels Case, 89
    Maryland v. Craig, 81
    McMartin Preschool Case, 88
    Ohio v. Roberts, 81–82
    Pritzlaff v. Archdiocese of Milwaukee, 98
    In re Gault, 77
    Rodriquez v. City of Wenatchee, 85–86
    Rutherford v. Strand et al., 98–99
    State v. Lomprey, 80
    State v. Milbradt, 83